TERRY JONES'
MEDIEVAL LIVES

TERRY JONES'

Medieval Lives

Terry Jones and Alan Ereira

BOOKS

This book is published to accompany the television series
Terry Jones' Medieval Lives produced by Oxford Film and Television
for BBC Television and first broadcast on BBC2 in 2004.
Executive producers: Nicolas Kent and Vanessa Phillips
Series producer: Paul Bradshaw

First published in 2004. Copyright © Fegg Features and
Sunstone Films 2004
The moral rights of the authors have been asserted.

ISBN 0 563 48793 3

Published by BBC Books, BBC Worldwide Ltd, Woodlands,
80 Wood Lane, London W12 0TT

Commissioning editor: Sally Potter
Project editor: Helena Caldon
Copy editor: Tessa Clarke
Art director and designer: Linda Blakemore
Picture researcher: Sarah Hopper
Production controller: Christopher Tinker

Set in Berling and Frutiger
Printed in Great Britain by Butler & Tanner Ltd, Frome
Colour separations by Radstock Reproductions Ltd., Midsomer Norton

For more information about this and other BBC books,
please visit our website on www.bbcshop.com

Contents

Introduction

TERRY'S DAD USED THE WORD 'medieval' as a term of abuse: 'That plumbing is positively medieval,' he'd say. It was a word that people used about anything that didn't work very well or that was barbaric. Even today's newspapers talk about 'cruelty that is truly medieval'.

In this book we're not trying to prove that there was no such thing as cruelty in the Middle Ages or that we've lost out on some beautiful experience by introducing flushing lavatories. But we would like to re-adjust the spectacles through which we view the medieval world. And the first thing you might notice, when you try on these new spectacles of ours, is that the 'medieval world' itself starts to vanish – or at least becomes remarkably blurred. Not a very good start for a new pair of specs, you might think…

MIDDLE AGES? WHAT MIDDLE AGES?

'MEDIEVAL' MEANS BELONGING TO THE MIDDLE AGES. Of course, nobody then thought of the period as the Middle Ages. For them – as for everyone who has ever lived – they were living in the modern world.

The idea that there was a 'middle time' that separated that modern world from antiquity first appears in a letter from a Renaissance bishop in 1469. Giovanni Andrea, like many of his contemporaries, was so besotted with the splendours of ancient Greece and Rome that he thought the classical world was the only basis for civilization. He took pride in the fact that his own world was returning to its values, and was therefore at pains to distinguish it from the *media tempesta* (middle time) – that bleak interlude between then and 'now' when the world was deep in dirt and ignorance.

Of course, we could tell him that he was himself living in the Middle Ages, poor deluded chap.

The phrase 'middle ages' first turned up in English in the seventeenth century, and right from the start it carried with it a judgement – it was never just a chronological expression – and that judgement is the same today as it was in the seventeenth century: from the fourth century AD (or was it the fifth? or sixth?) until the Renaissance, Europe was sunk in feudal superstitious ignorance that needs to be consigned to the dustbin of history. Medieval people, we are invited to suppose, lived out their lives in a kind of fairy tale, unaware of science or real learning, under the tyrannical rule of feudal overlords.

Nowadays we tend to divide this epoch into the 'Dark Ages', which in England apparently ended in 1066, and the 'Middle Ages', which lasted until the crown landed on the head of a Henry Tudor in 1485. But even though this is today enshrined in school and university syllabuses, we should beware of thinking of it as a 'fact'. It isn't a fact at all. It's simply a convenient division – an invention of historians.

Of course, historical 'periods' can be useful. Historians argue about the significance and reality of decisive moments, turning points in history, but it seems absurd to deny that there are real instances of change, when nothing will be the same again, and which force us to think of the past in 'periods'. The Battle of Hastings in 1066 was such a moment in the history of England.

There is an entire academic industry devoted to demonstrating that feudalism existed in England before 1066, that William I changed few of the laws of England, that warfare was not so very different before and after the invasion, that in fact England was little changed by the Norman

Below: The start of a new period of history: King Harold's death as pictured in the Bayeux tapestry.

Conquest. But we all know in our bones that something fundamental did change when Harold fell.

At least half, and perhaps three-quarters, of the male aristocracy of England perished between 1066 and 1070. Their families were dispossessed, and many of their widows and daughters fled to nunneries to avoid being forced into marriage with William's followers. London burned, and many other towns were partly demolished. The agricultural economy was laid waste over huge areas, and in the North repression left nothing but famine, reducing people to cannibalism.

This was a moment of irrevocable change; the Conquest would not be undone. England was permanently removed from the Scandinavian orbit and bound to France. There were some who tried to reverse this. Waltheof, Earl of Northumbria, was executed in 1076 for supporting Danish plots to drive William out. He failed; the clock would not be turned back.

Waltheof's skald (bard), Thorkill, wrote a lament in Old Norse:

> William crossed the cold channel and
> reddened the bright swords and now
> he has betrayed noble Earl Waltheof
> It is true that killing in England will be a
> long time ending

The end of our 'period' is more debatable. There is no comparable moment of change 400 or 500 years later. The defeat of Richard III and the victory of Henry Tudor at Bosworth on 22 August 1485 certainly put an end to the long struggle between the houses of York and Lancaster for the throne of England, and established a new dynasty which was able to rule with reinforced authority. But it hardly compares with 1066, when the entire land suffered wholesale subjection to new men with new ways and a different language.

However, there was one moment when everything changed irreversibly. It came in 1536, with Henry VIII's suppression of the religious houses – the monasteries. In 1066, William I had given over a quarter of the land in England to the Church. His conquest bound the country not only to France but also to Rome.

By the time of the Dissolution there were about 550 religious houses in England, and the monks in them were referred to as 'the pope's army'.

The whole of Europe was changing rapidly, and the break-up of the one universal Church was the most powerful symbol of that change.

In England, the Dissolution of the Monasteries was its visible and dramatic product. The whole religious infrastructure was transformed; the Church of England that emerged would produce a very different society from that produced by the Church of Rome.

Western Europe was already well on the way to developing distinct national states, and the break with Rome confirmed that process in England. On a political level, in a country that had been conquered by William under a papal banner, Rome was now stripped of any authority. In terms of language, in a country where Latin had been the language of learning and French the language of power, the vernacular had taken over. The divergence of English law and custom from that of the Continent, which had been developing steadily over centuries, was now finalized by the elimination of the Pope's jurisdiction from canon law. For a few years, England retained a tiny foothold on the continent of Europe at Calais, but the English Channel had become a much broader sea than in the past, and 'abroad' a far more foreign place than it had been before.

A long era had truly come to an end.

WHO WERE MEDIEVAL PEOPLE?

HAVING ESTABLISHED, FOR THE SAKE OF CONVENIENCE, that our 'Middle Ages' (which never existed as an entity) was the period from 1066 to 1536, we have to recognize that we are talking about 470 years.

This is about as long as the time between the end of the Middle Ages and the present day.

Obviously, in such a long period things change. People in the mid-eleventh century inhabited a very different world from that of the early sixteenth, and did not live out lives that were always the same against an unchanging backdrop. So the very idea of telling stories of 'medieval lives' needs to be taken with a pinch of salt.

But, given the right amount of salt, we should find that we can strip away the mythology of medievalism and enter a world in which people's lives seem remarkably familiar – a world where decisions were made about social and political issues that still impact profoundly on us today. Stripping away the mythology will also allow us to glimpse how much we have lost by dumping centuries of art, argument, thought, literature and discovery into that catch-all 'medieval' dustbin. Some wonderful things have been truly lost, and we would be better off recovering them.

Of all the changes between 1066 and 1536 perhaps the least

Left: In the eleventh century, workers on the land were shown as desperately poor, with shoes a rather rare luxury. This world vanished within 200 years.

significant was the size of population. There were about two million people in England in 1066 and about three million in 1535. There had been four million to five million in Roman Britain, and about 1300 the population rose to some six million, but famine, disease (including the Black Death) and the changing patterns of families' working lives halved this by 1450, and recovery was slow.

But who the two or three million people of our period were, and where and how they lived, changed very greatly. Snapshots of the kingdom at each of those two dates, 1066 and 1536, show two utterly different worlds.

In the middle of the eleventh century barely 10 per cent of the population lived in towns. A community qualified as a 'town' in *Domesday Book* if it had more than 2,000 inhabitants, and there were only 18 such communities. Even London was tiny – perhaps no bigger than present-day Sittingbourne. England was an entirely agricultural country, and its bishops were based in villages.

It was also a society in which wealth was concentrated in the hands of even fewer people than it is today. Analysis of the *Domesday* survey reveals that about 10 per cent of the island's inhabitants were slaves – people who were bought and sold and who could not own property. The labouring classes above them (cottars, bordars, villeins), who made up 75 per cent of the population, were unfree, obliged to perform service on their lords' lands. Five per cent of this society owned everything, landwise.

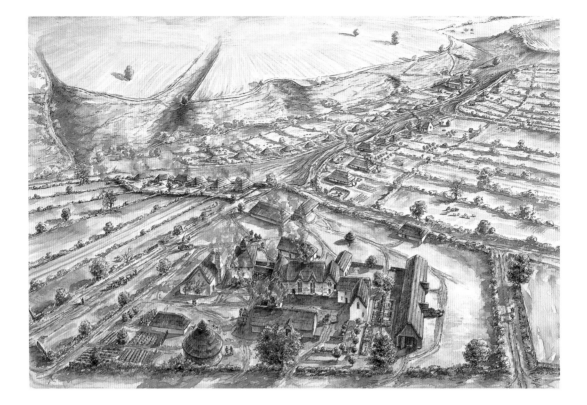

Above: Medieval England was largely organised around 'manors' – estates with a village of peasants set amongst large fields. Originally the villagers were obliged to labour on the lord's land, but by the fifteenth century compulsory labour had virtually disappeared.

The Norman invasion made the divisions in English society even more pronounced than they had been.

There was virtually no literacy outside the Church, and such books as were produced were laboriously hand-copied in monasteries. The ruling class had neither language nor culture in common with those below them. The country lived under a form of martial law, in which whole communities were held responsible if a member of the occupying power was killed.

By the early sixteenth century, however, this was all ancient history. Slavery was long gone, villeinage had, for practical purposes, disappeared and the land was worked by free farmers who paid rent. Towns were now significant urban centres, with their own charters and independent oligarchic democracies. The towns were already old, and many people saw the corporations that ran them as ossified defenders of ancient privileges, blocking industrial initiative.

For there were, indeed, new industrial developments that were already making England prosperous, but they were to be found in the countryside or in unofficial, unincorporated towns.

London had become a major city, and its population was dominated by artisans, tradesmen and educated professionals involved with the court and the law. About 60 per cent of its citizens could read, and there was a ready market for printed books.

England was a very legalistic society, ready to go to court at the drop of a hat. Even the poor could use the law against the rich. Proceedings were in English, and trial by jury was well established.

Our story is not about a long period in which nothing much changed, but about how the England of 1066 turned into that of the early sixteenth century, a story of lives lived in a world that was in a constant state of change.

Above: The Tower of London was originally built by William the Conqueror as a fortress near the burned ruins of London. It was later to become a royal palace in a city that was the core of the kingdom.

HOW THE RENAISSANCE CREATED 'THE MIDDLE AGES'

WELL INTO THE SIXTEENTH CENTURY English architects were still cheerfully refining and developing what was then the modern style of architecture – the soaring, light and airy Gothic that had been all the rage for the last three or four centuries. But modernity was, paradoxically, somewhat out of date. On the Continent, fashion had turned the clock back to imitate the antique styles of ancient Greece and Rome. The Renaissance was not a new, fresh start – it was backward-looking and conservative.

In the end it proved irresistible, even in the somewhat marginalized kingdom of England. In rejecting the recent in favour of the antique, the Renaissance constructed a mental bridge that reached back to the Roman Empire, without having to paddle in the swamp that lay between. That swamp became the Middle Ages:

> The Renaissance invented the Middle Ages in order to define itself; the Enlightenment perpetuated them in order to admire itself; and the Romantics revived them in order to escape from themselves. In their widest ramifications 'the Middle Ages' thus constitute one of the most prevalent cultural myths of the modern world.*

The Renaissance, it should be said, is a term almost as meaningless as 'medieval', though it does have the merit of being used by people who

*Brian Stock, *Listening for the text.*

actually lived at the time. The word was coined by the fourteenth-century Italian poet Petrarch, who condemned those who lived between the fall of Rome and his own time as the inhabitants of a Dark Age: 'Although they had nothing of their own to hand down to those who were to come after, they robbed posterity of its ancestral heritage.' By the time England caught up with the Renaissance, in the mid-sixteenth century, it was essentially over. Historians have proposed that the Italian Renaissance came to the end of its run on 6 May 1527, when Spanish troops looted Rome.

But the idea of a middle age of darkness and ignorance had been launched on the world, and it did not go away. According to Jacob Burckhardt's celebrated book, *The Civilization of the Renaissance in Italy*, published in 1860, medieval people were not even individual human beings, but existed only as members of some corporate group. One section is entitled 'The Development of the Individual'. The English writer John Addington Symonds, whose huge work *Renaissance in Italy* was published later in the century, thought the history of the modern world was a history of freedom, and that achieving this freedom had required a sudden leap forward out of the darkness and bondage of the Middle Ages into the glorious light of the Renaissance.

The Romantics of the nineteenth century began to be intrigued by what they saw as the mysterious glow and gloom of the Middle Ages and, dressed in interesting flowing robes and mocked-up suits of armour, went exploring there with candles. They came back with tales and paintings of a magical, fairy-tale world of knights in shining armour and wan damsels in distress, of bold outlaws and Bad Kings, of alchemists in league with the devil and saintly holy men, of downtrodden peasants and cunning minstrels.

In this fantasy land there was no sense of historical change; the medieval world was essentially timeless. The lack of individual identity which Burckhardt had claimed as a mark of medievalism meant it was convenient and helpful to understand this place in terms of stereotypes. And those stereotypes have become standardized and generalized to the point where everyone now 'knows' what it was like to live in medieval England. An unholy alliance of nineteenth-century novelists and painters with twentieth-century movie-makers has created a period of history that never existed.

This book sets out to examine and deconstruct some of those stereotypes, and replace them with real people living in a changing world. The reality of those 400-odd years is far more interesting, surprising, moving and disturbing than the stereotype landscape.

The strange 'maps' of the world – the so-called *mappae mundi* – that thirteenth-century map-makers created, carry images of a world populated by creatures with their heads in their chests or big feet over their heads – but this does not mean the map-makers actually lived in such a world. Nineteenth-century imaginers of medieval England often took the material of the past too literally and ended up constructing their own fantasies.

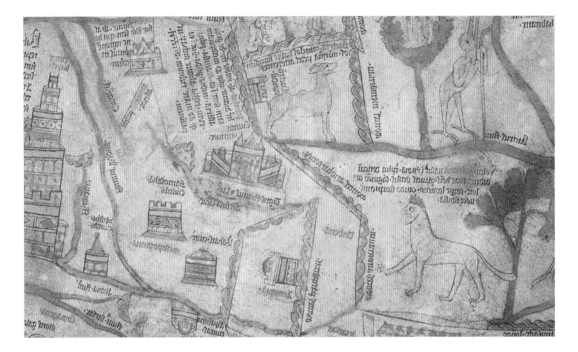

In a quite comical recent book, *The Lord's First Night*, Alain Boureau investigated the truth of the old story that a feudal lord had the right to sleep with the bride of a vassal on her wedding night. From *The Marriage of Figaro* to Mel Gibson's *Braveheart*, this has been the ultimate symbol of feudal barbarism. Of course, it is a complete fantasy – like the chastity belts knights are supposed to have locked on to their wives when they went on crusade.

But this *droit de seigneur* was certainly mentioned in medieval sources. It was described as an ancient custom, in the fourteenth century when supporters of the king raised it as a spectre to rally public opinion against local lords.

Which just goes to show, you should not believe everything you read in books.

Above: Part of the Mappa Mundi in Hereford Cathedral. This section shows a landscape of the mind which was never intended as a literal geography of the world.

CHAPTER ONE

Peasant

BEING A PEASANT during the Middle Ages must qualify as one of the worst jobs in history – but then we're only guessing because the peasants didn't leave much record of their lives. Except once, in the summer of 1381, when they left an indelible mark on the history of England.

It was quite astonishing. From out of nowhere, it seemed, tens of thousands of 'peasants' converged on London. Two large armed bodies of 'commoners and persons of the lowest grade from Kent and Essex'* burst through the gates of the City of London and wreaked havoc. They demolished the home of John of Gaunt and some buildings around the priory of the Hospital of St John. The next day, the rebels in London burst into the fortress-palace of the Tower. They dragged out the prior of the hospital, who was the Royal Treasurer, along with the Archbishop of Canterbury, the Chancellor and a couple of other notables and beheaded them on Tower Hill.

It was the first and last large-scale popular uprising in English history.

By the end of that day there had been quite a massacre. In one place about forty decapitated bodies were lying in a heap, 'and hardly was there a street in the City in which there were not bodies lying of those who had been slain'. The Archbishop's head was displayed on a pike on London Bridge, with his mitre nailed to his skull.

This was, of course, the so-called 'Peasants' Revolt'. The poet-chronicler Jean Froissart, writing shortly afterwards for a readership in the courts of northern France and the Low Countries, felt he needed to explain who the English peasantry were, and what they were complaining about:

*Sir Michael de la Pole, 1383 Rot. Parl., III 150.

It is customary in England, as in several other countries, for the nobility to have great power over the common people, who they keep in bondage. That is to say, they have a duty to plough their lord's lands, to harvest his grain and bring it in, to thresh and winnow it. They also have to harvest his hay and cut his wood and bring it in. They are obliged to perform all these duties for their lords, and there are more of them in England than in other countries. That is how they serve the prelates and nobles. These services are more oppressive in the counties of Kent, Essex, Sussex and Bedford, than anywhere else in the kingdom.

Disaffected people in these districts became restless, saying they were too severely oppressed; that at the beginning of the world there were no slaves, and that no one ought to be treated like one unless he had committed treason against his lord, as Lucifer had done against God: but they were not like that, for they were neither angels nor spirits, but men like their lords, who treated them as beasts. They would no longer put up with this. They had determined to be free, and if they did any work for their lords, they wanted to be paid for it.

The Chronicles of Froissart, Bk. II, ch.73.

Froissart had no sympathy with the insurrection, and did not think peasants had anything to complain about. In fact, he said their lives had become too easy – the trouble was 'all because of the ease and riches of the common people'. Nonetheless, his description helps to reinforce the stereotype of peasant life as being nasty, brutish and short.

Left: John Ball, the radical priest, is shown instructing Wat Tyler and the rebels, seated on a skinny, blinkered nag. These rebels are not depicted as impoverished farm-hands but as well-armoured infantry bearing the banners of England and the King.

A 'village' was where the lord of the manor kept his villeins – men who were bound either to the land itself or to his personal service, and who lived with their wives and children in wretched cottage hovels. They worked partly for themselves but for up to three days a week for their lord (and gave him a share of their produce) and also had to give a tenth of their crop – a tithe – to the Church.

Illiterate, uncouth, little more than an animal, the medieval peasant cuts a wretched figure in our imagination. Froissart's belief that it was dangerous to allow this savage, servile underclass too much scope for troublemaking makes a grotesque kind of sense.

But much of what used to be assumed about 'peasants' is completely untrue. So untrue, in fact, that even the title 'Peasants' Revolt' is now no longer used by professional historians, who have lost confidence in Froissart's description. Froissart, it turns out, was not a very reliable social commentator.

ORDER IN CHAOS

THE RISING WAS NOT THE MINDLESS INSURRECTION of brutalized semi-slaves. It was highly organized and carefully prepared. For a start, many areas of the country rose virtually simultaneously, which indicates that peasants had the capacity for organization on a much larger scale than the purely local. Then there is the interesting chronicle report that, in order to maintain coastal defences against the French, the rebels in Kent decreed that: 'none who dwelt near the sea in any place for the space of twelve leagues, should come out with them, but should remain to defend the coasts of the sea from public enemies…'

Moreover, the rebels' selection of targets in London demonstrates that the violence there was deliberate and specific. The first target, John of Gaunt, had thwarted the Commons' impeachments of unpopular members of the court, and was suspected of trying to make himself king. The first demands made by the Kentish rebels did not even mention serfdom or villeinage. They demanded allegiance to the king and the Commons; that there should be no king named John (i.e., John of Gaunt); that there should be no tax but the traditional levy of one-fifteenth of movable wealth; and that everyone should be ready to revolt when called upon.

On 14 June the rebels met Richard II at Mile End just outside the city of London. There they presented demands which included the handing over of 'traitors'; the end of serfdom; the right to hire themselves out at fair wages; and the right to rent land at a cheap rate. Peasant issues had become part of the matter, but they were not there to begin with.

By the third day the agenda had developed further, and was now revolutionary. To the end of serfdom their leader, Wat Tyler, now added the abolition of outlawry; the repeal of all laws except the 'law of Winchester' (traditional common law); the complete abolition of nobility in Church and state but for one king and one archbishop; and the confiscation and division of Church land.

The targets of the rebels' destruction were places where records were stored: abbeys, priories, lawyers' houses and the like. Thomas Walsingham, whose chronicle contains much malice and invention, describes what happened in a way that brings to mind the 'Year Zero' of the Khmer Rouge in Cambodia, and which must have contained at least a kernel of truth:

> They strove to burn all old records; and they butchered anyone who might know or be able to commit to memory the contents of old or new documents. It was dangerous enough to be known as a clerk, but especially dangerous if an ink-pot should be found at one's elbow: such men scarcely or ever escaped from the hands of the rebels.
>
> *Historia Anglicana*

But this was not a general attack on literacy. It was specifically legal records that were destroyed and others, in many places, were left intact. Some, at least, of the rebels could read.

So if peasants were not illiterate members of a dirty, uncouth, barbarous, rural 'lumpen proletariat', who were they?

AT HOME WITH THE PEASANT

THE WORD 'PEASANT' was not used in English in medieval times. It comes from the French *paysan*, which simply means a country man or woman. At the time, men who worked on the land were either free or were in some degree of serfdom as cottagers, smallholders or villeins. It was the last

Above: This image of the final moments of the revolt is usually described as showing the mayor of London killing the rebel leader Wat Tyler. The 'peasants' seen behind him are expensively armoured with helmets.

group, villeins, that Froissart was describing – men who were not free to leave their land and who owed labour duties to their lords. Probably 30 per cent of men in England were villeins in 1381.

It is often said that peasants lived in primitive one-room 'hovels', but in all the excavations of medieval villages there seems to be little sign of these horrible dwellings. According to the historian Christopher Dyer, 'Most villages that have been excavated seem to consist mainly of substantial houses'. In fact, according to Dyer, 'We should not be looking for tiny buildings, but for structures of standard size, but distinguished from the houses of the better-off by the quality and quantity of the materials used, or the standard of carpentry.'

But even if the lowest semi-slave lived in a substantial house, presumably he and his miserable extended family were crammed in there in a half-starved, overcrowded huddle – grandparents, uncles, aunts, nieces and nephews jumbled promiscuously together?

Well, maybe not.

Where we do have evidence, it tends to show that peasants lived in nuclear families like our own, and that they liked their privacy. From as early as the twelfth century there were upper rooms in quite small rural buildings, and certainly this is how many people were living by the early fourteenth century. This suggests that some houses, at any rate, had private rooms and their occupants did not have to live their lives under the whole family's gaze. The same inference – that peasants liked their privacy – can be drawn from archaeological evidence that, in the thirteenth century at least, houses were surrounded by ditches (and presumably also hedges and fences) and had locked doors, and that goods were kept in locked chests.

What kind of peasants were these? What did they have that was worth protecting? Excavations show pewter tableware, glazed pots, dice, cards, chessmen, footballs, musical instruments and 'ninemen's morris' boards in these hovels. And people seem to have eaten rather better than one might suppose. The evidence is that they didn't simply live on bread and cheese, but ate pork, lamb and beef, fruit and vegetables, and that even in inland villages they ate fish (archaeologists have found fish bones at the deserted village of Wharram Percy in Yorkshire).

Something seems to be not quite right about the traditional picture of peasant life.

The excavations at Wharram Percy are full of surprises. It looks like a neat, planned village, and archaeologists expected to find traces of earlier villages going back to early Anglo-Saxon times. Those traces are missing. Even though Wharram Percy is listed in *Domesday Book*, the village itself

seems to have come into being around the end of the twelfth century. The farmers in the area had previously lived in scattered farms and hamlets.

It now seems as though there were very few, if any, villages in that area of England before the eleventh century. While it is impossible to show a connection between this curious fact and the Norman Conquest, it does

Below: It was thought that the victims of the Black Death created England's deserted villages, but many, like Wharram Percy, actually survived.

look as though the creation of villages was linked to the manorial system. In other words – villages may have been built for the local lord's villeins.

THE PEASANT'S STATUS

AT THE TIME OF THE NORMAN CONQUEST many in the rural population were slaves in the full meaning of the word (and the *Domesday Book* shows that this still applied to about 10 per cent of people in 1086). This was not a satisfactory economic arrangement for the Norman overlords whom the king had installed as landholders. These lords of the manor were military men, expected to provide military service to the king as the price for their landholdings. They wanted the English to work their land, but did not want the responsibility of feeding and caring for them – which is, of course, one of the drawbacks of having slaves. So it seems they preferred to group working families in 'vills' (villages) and treat them as tenants, who had to support themselves from small parcels of land worked when they were not doing labour service for their lord. This labour service was their rent.

These people were villeins. Villeinage had begun to develop before 1066, but the Normans promoted it mightily and slavery disappeared in a couple of generations. Froissart was probably right in saying that the system was more widespread in England than in the rest of western Europe.

Many manorial lords held several manors and spent much of their time away fighting. They needed the manor to look after itself – or rather, they needed their villeins to organize its care for them. This was done through the manor court, which determined how fields were to be farmed and (since villeins held strips of land in large open fields) the days for planting and harvesting, the boundaries of each person's land and the dates on which animals were allowed to graze in different fields. Although the court was presided over by the lord's steward, its officials were villeins elected by the village, and its decisions were made by a jury of villagers. There was the reeve, who acted as a general overseer, the hayward, who watched over the crops and

Opposite: Peasants perform their duties for the month of March in the shadow of Chateau de Lusignan, France. From the Duc de Berri's Très Riches Heures.

brought offenders to court, and so on. The steward's job was to look after his lord's interests (payments and work that was due to him) not to tell the court how to manage its business.

In fact, the manor court had the power to fine the lord, and would do so. The records of one in Laxton in Nottinghamshire show it fined the lord for leaving soil on the common land. The peasants of Albury in Hertfordshire went so far as to petition parliament in 1321 over oppression by their lord, Sir John Patemore, who had imprisoned them and seized their cattle.

Some villages came close to being totally self-governing political entities run by the peasants for the peasants. Villeins resisted authority by quietly ignoring regulations, and manipulated the system by exploiting their influence as officials and bending laws in their own favour. Take the village of Gotham in Nottinghamshire, afforded legendary status by the exploits of its inhabitants.

In about 1200 King John proposed building a hunting lodge near the city of Nottingham. The residents of Gotham realized the implications of this – he would pass through the village on the way to his lodge, making it a king's highway and thus making them liable to new taxes.

So what did they do? The entire village pretended to be mad. It is said that the villagers built a fence around a cuckoo bush to prevent the cuckoo escaping, tried to drown an eel, set about pulling the moon out of a pond with a rake and rolled cheeses down a hill to make them round. Since madness was considered contagious the idea of a whole village of lunatics was perfectly feasible, and apparently the ploy worked.

Villeins were not mindless and helpless, but actually ran the country. The barons who were their masters had to respect their traditions and ways of doing things, and it was normal for the lord of the manor to demonstrate this respect by laying on feasts for them twice a year – wet and dry boon. Does anyone's landlord now treat them to a slap-up dinner twice a year?

At Wharram Percy the lord accommodated the peasants in neat rows of houses beside the church, and the land was recast into regularly planned fields. A manor house belonging to either the Percy or the Chamberlain family (both had some power over the village) was built in splendid style in the twelfth century, but this was soon abandoned and demolished, and its site turned over to peasant houses.

At Cosmeston in Wales there is further evidence of peasants enjoying a reasonable standard of living. Most families lived in two-room houses surrounded by a fence or ditch for privacy. Excavation of the home of the reeve – the villein who acted as general overseer for the manor court – revealed oil lamps and glazed French pottery, and the discovery of a particular kind of jug shows that, far from living in dirt and squalor, he washed his hands between courses when eating. His house had a wardrobe, at least one chair and a timber floor. There was a tablecloth and candle-holders.

The reeve slept on a raised bed with a surprisingly comfortable wooden pillow, and the discovery of a casket key indicates he had possessions that were worth locking up. A herb – fleabane – kept his bed free of insects and a bowl of honey was used as an insect trap. There was an outdoor privy and excrement was collected regularly to be used, with animal manure, as fertilizer.

Below: Cash played little part in early medieval feudalism but that soon gave way to a trading economy. Everything then acquired a cash value – animals, crops and labour.

Coins found on the site are evidence that money was circulating, and so this was not entirely a subsistence economy. In fact, from the thirteenth century labour service began to be replaced by cash rents, indicating that villeins had surplus crops for sale. And when they had paid their rents they had money left over to spend at stalls in the village run by merchants.

They also had money to spend at the tavern, which was in an ordinary house. Ale was essential to life as many villages lacked clean water and it was drunk from leather mugs lined with pitch. Brewing was often viewed as an appropriate activity for widows, who found it hard to farm land. But some villeins had more high-faluting tastes. The excavations at Cosmeston have revealed the remains of wine jugs from France – peasants were drinking im-ported French wine.

This all seems so fundamentally at odds with our picture of the life of a medieval peasant that some explanation is needed – which involves recognizing that the Middle Ages was not a static and unchanging period, but a time of change and development.

IN THE ELEVENTH CENTURY peasant farmers lived pretty close to subsistence level. The year's work began in October, ploughing and harrowing what had been the fallow field with wheat and rye. The aim was to have done this by All Saints' Day, 1 November. A reasonably substantial peasant farmer with 30 acres scattered over three village fields would have ten acres in his fallow field. An acre was in theory the amount of land that could be ploughed in a day – typically, four lands (strips), each of which was covered with five long furrowlengths (furlongs), turning the plough at the end of each furrow. A strip was therefore a quarter-acre.

The farmer would need to prepare these in five weeks, covering 84 miles with the plough and the same again with the harrow. And with one day a week given over to God, and up to three days to the lord of the manor, he had 15 days to do it in. This sounds fine, except that in practice it was not uncommon to cover only half an acre in a day (problems with the plough, problems with the animals drawing it, soil that was sodden with rain or ground that was frozen too hard to be worked).

At Candlemas, 2 February, ploughing would resume. This time, last year's rye-and-wheat field would be ploughed for oats, barley, peas and beans, and the third field ploughed for fallow. The work was supposed to be finished by Easter – ideally by 25 March, but it could go on until the end of April. A long, hard frost could be a serious problem.

Below: Eleventh-century farming was close to subsistence level, and contemporary illustrations show workers skimpily dressed, often barefoot. Much of the work, especially scything and winnowing, was very hard on the back.

In the eleventh century it is likely that the best yield to be hoped for, on good land, was eight bushels of corn per acre. The net harvest, after losses during harvesting and to animals, and after the farmer had handed over his tithe to the Church and produce to his lord, was half that or less – and two bushels would have to be kept back as seed corn. Overall, the farmer would have enough to feed a family of five and there would be a small surplus, but only so long as nothing went wrong with the ploughing, ripening and harvesting of the crops. And so long as no marauding armies came along.

But things did go horribly wrong at times, and there were marauding armies. The *Anglo-Saxon Chronicle* for the end of the eleventh century is a list of things going awry:

AD 1077

This year was the dry summer; and wild fire came upon many shires, and burned many towns; and also many cities were ruined thereby.

AD 1082

… and this year also was a great famine.

AD 1086

And the same year there was a very heavy season, and a swinkful and sorrowful year in England, in murrain of cattle, and corn and fruits were at a stand, and so much untowardness in the weather, as a man may not easily think; so tremendous was the thunder and lightning, that it killed many men; and it continually grew worse and worse with men.

AD 1087

In the one and twentieth year after William began to govern and direct England, as God granted him, was a very heavy and pestilent season in this land. Such a sickness came on men, that full nigh every other man was in the worst disorder, that is, in the diarrhoea; and that so dreadfully, that many men died in the disorder. Afterwards came, through the badness of the weather as before mentioned, so great a famine over all England, that many hundreds of men died a miserable death through hunger. Alas! how wretched and how rueful a time was there! When the poor wretches lay full nigh driven to death prematurely, and afterwards came sharp hunger, and dispatched them withal! Who will not be penetrated with grief at such a season? or who is so hardhearted as not to weep at such misfortune? Yet such things happen for folk's sins, that they will not love God and righteousness.

AD 1098

Before Michaelmas the heaven was of such an hue, as if it were burning, nearly all the night. This was a very troublesome year through manifold impositions; and from the abundant rains, that ceased not all the year, nearly all the tilth in the marshlands perished.

29
Peasant

Things would have been even worse without the strip system, which at least meant that a peasant's lands were scattered and he did not have to put all his eggs in one basket. There was also a system of food-sharing in bad times. This was one beneficial result of tithes – the great tithe-barns of the Church could become charity food stores in times of need. It looks as though there was virtually no chance of starvation for a peasant farming more than 20 acres.* Unless, of course, there was widespread famine.

At the start of a famine people would eat bad bread, often made with rye that had developed a fungus (ergot) that produced a burning sensation in the body and LSD-type hallucinations. Then came starvation.

Starvation kills a healthy human in six to ten weeks. To begin with, a person can lose up to 10 per cent of their body weight without losing much strength or energy. At this stage they can still work and do other normal activities. Then they begin to weaken. When they have lost 15 to 20 per cent of their normal body weight they become depressed and apathetic, and can no longer participate in day-to-day life. As a person continues to lose weight the stomach accumulates abnormal amounts of watery fluids, and balloons outwards. Flesh wastes from the face and the eyes also appear to balloon outwards. The flesh increasingly sags away from the bones and permanent dark splotches from glandular disturbances may appear all over the body. Racked by the pain caused by these changes, a starving person becomes more susceptible to diarrhoea, cholera and dysentery.

The victim can see and feel their body withering away, and becomes obsessed with food. Indifference and apathy replace compassion for their starving neighbours, friends and family. Mothers have been known to snatch food from the hands of their children. Cannibalism is not uncommon. Eventually, when a person has lost about 40 per cent of their body mass, death is inevitable.**

THINGS GET BETTER

THE MANORIAL SYSTEM DEVELOPED during a period when England was getting warmer and wetter. This meant many years of good harvests (which we can see today in the evidence of tree rings) interrupted by rain-driven famines, with all the horrors described above. This is the framework within which the medieval peasant saw his life, and the prospects of an afterlife.

But famine became rarer, and the economics of farming improved steadily in the centuries after the Conquest. In the thirteenth century the

*Cliff Bekar, *Income Sharing Amongst Medieval Peasants: Usury Prohibitions and the Non-Market Provision of Insurance*, (Lewis and Clark College, Oregon, USA).
**M.Treitez, *The Great Hunger of 1044: The Progress of a Medieval Famine*, in *Serve it Forth* 11 (June 1999) and 12 (Oct 1999).

rise in temperature was reversed, and the tempests of the previous 200 years declined. Vineyards, an important part of the English economy for two centuries, disappeared completely by 1300 and the growing season shortened, but winters became milder and summers drier. From 1220 to 1315 there was no famine in England. This coincided with improvements in agricultural technology (primarily faster ploughing as horse teams replaced oxen in favourable areas) and the growth of markets and towns. The result was a golden age for the peasant, and a spectacular rise in the population, from 2.5 million to approaching 6 million by 1315. Wasteland was taken into cultivation, marginal land was converted into manorial farms and the standard of living rose.

There was also a significant broadening of people's outlooks. Villein tenancies were inherited by eldest sons so younger brothers had to find livings elsewhere, which meant a considerable movement of people. The inevitable result was that a large number of peasant families had relatives in newly growing towns and so were probably quite well informed about politics and trade. They were also likely to have relatives in other parts of the country, as the pressure to bring more land under the plough meant people were moving to new manors in areas that had never been farmed before. Although peasants did not exactly go visiting much, they made pilgrimages to famous shrines and travelled to markets, and may not have had much reason to see themselves as country bumpkins.

In fact, at this time the lot of a peasant farmer was in some ways comparable with that of a modern worker. Sundays, saint's days and Church holidays like Easter and Christmas meant he had at least as much free time as a modern employee, and the amount of work required to pay rent and taxes was probably pretty similar to that needed now. Of course, provision for old age was a bit of a problem (as it is now for many people), but peasants didn't often live so long. The truly poor probably made up about a third of the population, as they do today (in fact, one of the oddities of

Above: Illustrations show that, by the thirteenth century, the peasant was better dressed and better fed. His plough is also more sophisticated and productive. The Zodiacal crustacean also looks quite prosperous....

English society is that it has always had roughly the same percentage of the population living on the breadline).

By 1315 the countryside was full, busy and making money. Farming was becoming more sophisticated and trade-orientated; well-managed hay meadows produced a good flow of cash, and eight to ten million sheep supplied wool for the export trade alone. There were also more horses than ever before, both for riding and for draught. In the most advanced regions – eastern Norfolk (the most crowded county in England) and eastern Kent – the old system of common fields was already on its way out because it was inefficient. These areas would be particularly prominent in the 'Peasants' Revolt'.

People were not starving. In fact, their diet was pretty healthy. Today, we are urged to stop eating fast foods with all the nutrition of cardboard and to eat five portions of fruit and vegetables a day. This is actually a return to the peasant diet – a diet that was despised by the nobility. They regarded fruit and veg as poor man's food, believing that greens weren't good for you and that fruit gave you dysentery – the bloody flux.

Peasant bread was much healthier than our white, steam-baked, sliced bread: it was brown, like a good wholemeal loaf. Peas and beans were sometimes added, which made it even more nutritious. In the fields people ate a kind of medieval pot noodle, a paste of dried vegetables, beans and bread to which they added ale to turn it into an instant meal. Eel pasties were another favourite, and preserved foods such as bacon, cheese and sausages were special treats.

Even for the poorest, the countryside was a larder teeming with wild life. Rivers were full of fish – there were even plenty of salmon in the Thames – and peasants had elaborate nets and traps to catch songbirds, eels and rabbits.

The countryside was healthier than the towns. When the graveyard at Wharram Percy was excavated archaeologists found 687 peasant skeletons, enough for them to draw some firm conclusions about health and ageing. It is clear that these country dwellers had suffered fewer illnesses than their urban relatives. A lower rate of infection showed in their bones, and fewer cases of anaemia suggested fewer parasites.

It is also clear, surprisingly, that they ate a reasonable amount of seafood. This is further evidence that trade networks penetrated deep into the countryside. And there was very little tooth decay – none in any of the children's skeletons. In fact the medieval diet, with lots of coarse grains and grit in the bread, was much better for human teeth than our own. It meant they were worn down to a flat plane leaving no crevices for food to fester. But fossilized plaque in some skeletons' teeth does suggest that many of the people at Wharram Percy had suffered from chronic bad breath. This was a bit of an issue in medieval times; in Wales a peasant woman could divorce her husband on the grounds of his halitosis.

In both countryside and towns, babies were breastfed until they were 18 months old, which protected both the child (helping its immune system and keeping its diet free of germs) and the mother (it was believed that breastfeeding can act as a natural contraceptive).

One further surprise at Wharram Percy was a skull with a big hole in it, the result of an injury caused by some kind of blunt instrument. This had clearly been operated on: the skin had been folded back, the wound was cleaned up and then the skin was stitched back again. The person had recovered from the

injury. Even the inhabitants of a small village could hope for skilled and effective surgical help.

Of course, the picture was not entirely rosy. Animals were small (smaller than they had been in Roman times) and grains were tall, low-yielding varieties. Pastures were overused and easily degraded. Village life may have been healthier than life in a town, but nevertheless infant mortality was high, childbirth was dangerous, agricultural labourers were old at 40.

But the kind of peasant Froissart described – the servile villein obliged to work his lord's land – was a diminishing class by the start of the fourteenth century. Most of the land newly taken into cultivation was farmed by freemen who paid rent for it, and they seem to have had larger families than serfs. There were now more of them than there were villeins. Villein duties had anyway often been replaced by money rents, so lords of the manor received nearly 90 per cent of their income in cash. The power of customary laws meant that a villein holding 15 to 30 acres for a fixed rent was often comparatively well off, especially as land was scarce, open-market rents were high, prices were rising and wages were low.

VILLAGE AND CHURCH

VILLAGE LIFE WAS CENTRED not just on work and home, but also on the church. Churches had been few and far between in Anglo-Saxon times, but the Church was an important element in Norman domination, and a village without a church became almost inconceivable.

The building was the physical property of the manor, and the lord appointed the priest (who would be a commoner, but not a serf). The core of any church is the chancel with the altar, and this belonged to the lord. The nave and the tower belonged to the people of the parish, who stood in the nave to hear services. Each person was expected to give one-tenth of their earnings to support the Church. This tithe was evenly divided between the parish priest, the church maintenance fund, the poor and the local bishop.

Manor courts were often held in the nave, but the church and churchyard were also places for parties, plays, pageants and games such as football and tile- or stone-throwing. Many parish priests brewed their own ale and drinking was a big part of any festival.

The church was also the centre of education. By the mid-twelfth century literacy was a real, and not impossibly distant, ambition for large

34
Peasant

numbers of people in the countryside. This is shown by the fact that one in ten boys in peasant families advanced to at least the lowest levels of the clergy, which required the ability to read Latin. There were, inevitably, traditionalists who complained that the Church had become a meritocracy, employing ministers 'raised from the dust'. It was, in fact, a sign that the age of the Conquest was over, and that the Church was no longer an implement of Norman power.

A common illusion about the medieval period is that society consisted of rigid feudal orders, and that if you were born a serf you would die a serf. This is not quite true. For ambitious women there was always the possibility of making a good marriage or becoming a rich man's mistress, and there were many ways for men to change their status – living in a town as a guild member for a year and a day, joining the army or Church, or, of course, entering a life of crime. But it was also possible for a poor boy to rise in a secular profession.

The most astonishing example of this is the career of William of Wykeham, the child of a peasant family who took his name from the village where he was born in 1324. He was educated at the local cathedral school at the expense of the lord of the manor (a not uncommon arrangement), who then took him on as his own secretary. The lord, Uvedale, was governor of Winchester Castle and passed the young man on to the bishop of Winchester.

In the small world of English government William was noticed by Edward III, and when he was in his early twenties the king took him into service. He was obviously clever and careful, had an interest in and talent for construction and design, and could be trusted as a manager. In his early thirties he was clerk of the king's works in two manors, and was made surveyor of Windsor Castle. It seems to have been his idea that Edward should express his Arthurian fantasies by rebuilding the castle, and from then on his rise was irresistible.

By 1364 William had been made keeper of the privy seal and was so powerful that, according to Froissart, he 'reigned in England, and without him they did nothing'. He was the ultimate self-made man, and fully understood the significance of education. He founded a free school, to offer 70 boys from poorer, rural backgrounds – peasants – a proper education, and also a university college to which they could go when they were ready. Both have survived to this

Below: William of Wykeham. The son of peasants, he founded Winchester College and New College, Oxford (overleaf), where he is shown surrounded by teachers and pupils.

Peasant

day: Winchester College and New College, Oxford. William's own motto, 'manners makyth man', became the motto of both institutions; 'manners' means not simply politeness, but being a capable and reliable member of society. This was a peasant attitude rather than an aristocratic one.

William of Wykeham would have been unique in any age. However, by the mid-fourteenth century most peasants knew their ABC, could sound out, and therefore recognize, their names and were familiar with the English equivalents of perhaps ten or 20 Latin words. This allowed them to locate and recognize references to their land in court rolls, and to be aware of and talk about the contents of charters.

THE FOURTEENTH-CENTURY CATASTROPHE

The busy, prosperous and successful rural society of the start of the fourteenth century did not last. Within 15 years nature had dealt it a crushing blow:

> In the year of our Lord 1315, apart from the other hardships with which England was afflicted, hunger grew in the land… Meat and eggs began to run out, capons and fowl could hardly be found, animals died of pest, swine could not be fed because of the excessive price of fodder. A quarter of wheat or beans or peas sold for twenty shillings [in 1313 a quarter of wheat sold for five shillings], barley for a mark, oats for ten shillings. A quarter of salt was commonly sold for thirty-five shillings, which in former times was quite unheard of. The land was so oppressed with want that when the king came to St. Albans on the feast of St. Laurence [10 August] it was hardly possible to find bread on sale to supply his immediate household…
> JOHANNES DE TROKELOWE, *Annales*

This dearth had begun in May. Then came heavy summer rains and the corn did not ripen – the start of a series of agricultural disasters. Villages built on dried-out marshlands sank back into the mud and there was not enough food for the greatly swollen populace. The annals are full of misery. Then, when the famines had run their course, the Black Death came.

Having spread across Europe from the east, it arrived at Weymouth in June 1348. In less than a year the whole country was stricken. No-one could have understood what was happening. Once a person was infected large, foul-smelling swellings developed in their groin, neck and armpits. Death followed within two or three days. The disease killed more than a third of the people and by 1350 the population of England was half what it had been in 1315. Villages shrank in size or were simply abandoned.

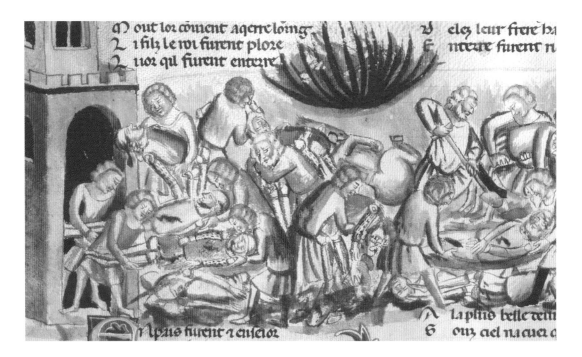

out lor coment aqeire loing.   y eleʒ leur frere ba
ɔ i filʒ le roi furent ploze   ɛ ntoure furent ri
ɔ uoz qil furent entezze

Npzus furent z euseoz   S onʒ ael na euei c

A la pitus belle telli

Above: Nobody knows how many people died in the Black Death. It must have seemed as though all humanity would perish.

The land was covered in images of death. Church walls were painted with depictions of the 'Three Living and the Three Dead' and scenes of the 'Dance of Death'.

The effect of the Black Death was immediately catastrophic for everyone; curiously, those peasants who survived it found their lives immeasurably improved. Labour became scarce and more valuable than abundant land. Landless people were able to take over abandoned holdings, and those who could handle more land simply took it. Wages roughly doubled, while the fall in the population led to something like a halving of the price of wheat.

Villeinage seemed seriously out of date. The whole basis of economic power in England had shifted. The Statute of Labourers in 1351 complained that existing laws were ineffective:

… servants having no regard to the said ordinance, but to their ease and singular covetise, do withdraw themselves to serve great men and other, unless they have livery and wages to the double or treble of that they were wont to take… to the great damage of the great men, and impoverishing of all the said commonalty.

As the country recovered in the decades following the Black Death landowners tried to restore the old systems, rediscovering old laws of

compulsory service that had been forgotten in the good times when England was increasingly moving to a money economy.

It was this growing pressure to turn back the clock that eventually produced the so-called Peasants' Revolt – an uprising of people who were well used to running their own affairs, in manorial courts and militias and in minor public office, and who had stopped believing in the entire structure of feudal authority.

'When Adam delved and Eve span/Who was then the Gentleman?' demanded John Ball, one of the leaders of the rebellion. A question to which, after the insurrection had been put down, there came the firm reply: 'Villeins ye are, and villeins ye shall remain.'

But, of course, they did not.

Although Wharram Percy, like many deserted medieval villages, was believed to have lost its population at the time of the Black Death, excavations have shown this was not the case. It remained inhabited until the fifteenth century, and it was human beings, not bacteria, that determined its fate.

The old feudal consensus had broken down, and the lords realized that if the peasants were now free from any obligation to them, they were equally free from any obligations to care for the peasants. Thus it was that the peasants came face to face with their greatest natural enemy – sheep.

Labour had become expensive and your average lord could now make more money out of sheep than he could out of his peasants. There was more wool on sheep, for a start, and you could also eat them – which is possible with peasants but socially taboo – so the lords started to throw the expensive, troublesome and uneatable peasants off their land and replace them with sheep.

The few remaining villeins, at Wharram Percy and in much of the rest of the country, were made redundant. They were doubtless given encouraging talks about the fact that it was time to move on, that they should view this challenge as an exciting opportunity, and that a gentle-man from the Cistercians would be coming round to see them individually to discuss openings in the lead mines.

Being a peasant in the middle ages wasn't necessarily a terrible life, but it deteriorated when the lords fenced the land off for sheep. It got even worse in the Industrial Revolution, and nowadays small farmers are still going to the wall.

The life of the peasant depends on the sort of society he lives in – and compared with a lot of people's lives today, there were times when the medieval peasant had it pretty good.

CHAPTER TWO

42
Minstrel

T HE STORY OF NORMAN ENGLAND began with a song.

At about nine o'clock on the morning of Saturday 14 October 1066, the minstrel Taillefer rode out on his horse and began to juggle with his sword. As he juggled, he sang the *Song of Roland*.

He was at the foot of Senlac ridge, a few miles from Hastings. Above him on the ridge, stretching for nearly three-quarters of a mile and seven lines deep, was the entire army of Harold, King of England, in battle order. A solid wall of shields was punctuated only by bristling spears and great double-headed battleaxes.

Taillefer was the enemy. This was a gig to be remembered.

The minstrel was a Norman, part of Duke William of Normandy's invading force. The rest of that force was behind him, a little over 100 yards from the Anglo-Saxons. The archers were in front, then the infantry, and at the back were the knights on their small stallions.

All through the summer Harold had been expecting the Normans to invade but by mid-September he had figured it was too late in the season and stood down his coastal defences. Then his kingdom was attacked in Yorkshire by Harald Hardrada, King of Norway, and he had marched north to deal with the threat.

That was when the Normans made their crossing. They had landed at Pevensey on 28 September and since then they had been consolidating their hold on the area around Hastings. They had not expected to be challenged for quite a while yet, and were busy foraging and looting. When the Anglo-Saxon army arrived late the previous afternoon William was taken by surprise. Harold was supposed to be fully tied up in the North and perhaps even defeated. Instead, he had crushed Hardrada a full three days before William invaded, and he then made an astonishingly swift march south, first to London and then onwards to the Norman invasion site.

Harold's arrival was most alarming for the Normans. They were not going to have as easy a time as they had supposed. William decided he had better not leave his troops with any time to think about what was happening, and spent the night gathering up his foraging parties and preparing them for battle. In the early dawn they began the six-mile march to meet the Anglo-Saxons.

When the Normans arrived at Senlac they were presented with a discouraging sight. They were geared up to face an army like their own, with archers in front, then the infantry, and perhaps cavalry behind. Instead they saw a long wall of wooden shields that would be impervious to their arrows. Even worse, there were no Anglo-Saxon archers to shoot

back at them – Normans did not carry many arrows and relied on picking up their enemy's spent ones after the first barrage.

Their infantry would have to attack with the undamaged enemy raining down deadly missiles from above as they struggled up the slope. Then the knights would also have to launch themselves uphill, having to push their horses' flesh against a solid and heavily spiked wall of shields.

It would be a suicide assault.

It appears that the Norman resolve to fight was somewhat uncertain. The Anglo-Saxons would not have helped matters by chanting their prebattle war cry: '*Ut! Ut!*' (Out! Out!). Simple, and intimidating when shouted by 7,000 or 8,000 men armed with spears and axes.

It was at this uncertain point that William's minstrel Taillefer asked for permission to give a little performance.*

According to one account, he rode forward and juggled with his sword. A minstrel was a 'jongleur', a jester, a general entertainer, but if juggling was all Taillefer did it would have been very odd. Another chronicle, presumably based on an account by someone nearer the performance, describes him singing the *Song of Roland*.

The version we have runs to 291 verses, which is a little long for the event. Since it is clear from internal references that it dates from somewhat later than 1066, we can assume that Taillefer was working from an earlier and probably shorter version; and that even then, under the circumstances, he probably went for the edited highlights. The song he sang told a famous story, of battle against impossible odds and heroic death that would never be forgotten.

And then he attacked the Anglo-Saxon line, all by himself. And he was killed.

There have been other battles, even in recent years, when soldiers who were required to attack but were frightened to advance have watched a volunteer from their own ranks go forward to certain death. The result always seems to be the same. The death creates a moral certainty; the survival of the men watching seems not to matter to them any more. Now they will advance with absolute resolution, irrespective of the odds. They do this not to exact revenge or because they feel hatred for the enemy – they advance because they are totally bonded to the man they saw die. In this moment they do not have homes or even lives to return to. This moment is all there is, and the spinning world revolves around what they must do.

This is why the battlefield can be a place of music, of song, of poetry. Taillefer's death-song shaped the history of England, Europe and the whole world.

*Guido, bishop of Amiens, *Carmen de bello Hastingensi*, v. 931–44 (in Mon. Hist. Brit., 1848); Henry of Huntingdon, *Historia Anglorum* (in Rer. Brit. med. aevi script., p. 763, ed. Arnold, London, 1879); Wace, *Roman de Rou*, 3rd part, v. 8035–62, ed. Andresen (Heilbronn, 1879).

The Normans charged. The initial attack was indeed suicidal, but their determination to succeed was now unbreakable. The first assault was followed by another, and then another. The battle continued all day long until eventually, as it began to grow dark, the English defence crumbled, dissolved and disappeared. A new history of England had begun.

The Norman survivors did not see this wonderful tale as being all that heroic. The Bayeux tapestry, a strip-cartoon account of the high points of the conquest of England, leaves Taillefer out. The hint of cowardice, the

Above: This sophisticated court used minstrelry as background music, and evidently paid it no attention.

leadership of a low-born entertainer – these do not seem to have been themes that attracted Odo, bishop of Bayeux, the man who commissioned the tapestry.

THE PUBLIC RELATIONS MINSTREL

AN ELEVENTH-CENTURY JONGLEUR was pretty low down in the social order. Taillefer was a 'jongleur des gestes', a man who entertained the mighty with the heroic epics that fired their blood. The emphasis was entirely on military virtues; women barely figure in the epics of the period. These poems were a validation of the military ethos, placing the listeners inside the world of heroic action and, in effect, inviting them to see their own warfare as participation in a cosmic drama of masculine sacrifice and loyalty.

The role of minstrels naturally developed further as the concept of chivalry became more elaborated; eventually they were expected to act as heralds, turning acts of bravery and prowess during battles and tournaments into songs – *chansons de geste* – that served as celebrations and scorecards. They became PR men and were paid by the hero whose bravery they celebrated. One of the first examples is the specially commissioned life in verse of William Marshal, 'the flower of chivalry' – paid for by his son in 1219, the year of William's death.

The teller of this biographical *chanson de geste* was probably William's

squire. In this rough-and-ready military culture little distinction was made between those servants who could sing or recite poetry and those who could cook or do other chores. Jongleurs were expected to make themselves useful in all sorts of ways. They had instruments and loud voices? Fine, let them act as night watchmen, sounding the alarm in the case of attack or fire.

In 1306, a minstrel called Richard (the Prince of Wales's watchman), raised the alarm at Windsor Castle when a fire started. Thanks to him, the castle was saved. Whether he used it as an opportunity to practise his own art, as a kind of singing telegram ('Windsor Castle's burning down/burning down/ burning down/Windsor Castle's burning down/My fair lady!') is not recorded.

The jongleur who could blow a trumpet, play a fife or bang a drum had obvious uses in the cacophony of the battlefield – to rally the troops or cheer them on, and also to give signals.

The Taillefers of the eleventh century were the guardians and promoters of a culture based on simple piety and violent death, and they were treated exactly as such a culture demands. It cannot have been very rewarding to make a living by reciting poetry to philistines.

Yet out of this strange beginning emerged a literary culture that, by the end of the Middle Ages, was to be one of the greatest achievements of civilization. In most cultures literature is the refined interest of a very restricted group of people. The classical period had produced great epics, histories and the marvellous poetry of an educated and wealthy elite, but its popular culture was profoundly different – it was based around the enjoyment of violent death in the amphitheatre and horse-racing in the hippodrome. Oriental civilizations produced magnificent religious epics, histories, and the subtle poetry and drama of highly sophisticated court elites, while their popular culture tended to exist separately and far more traditionally, based around religious and community rituals. Medieval Europe, most surprisingly, developed forms of story-telling that reached right across the whole of society, with the wit and energy to appeal to an illiterate or semi-literate audience and, at the same time, the subtlety and complexity to satisfy the aesthetes of aristocratic and royal courts.

This was to be intimately bound up with the development of regional (ultimately national) languages which gave an entire society within a language-territory a shared culture. It was, ultimately, the singers and story-tellers, the poets and minstrels, who shaped the history of Europe.

THE BASIC ENTERTAINER

THIS IS HARDLY WHAT ANYONE looking at eleventh- and early twelfth-century minstrels would have expected. A lot of the output of those attached to lords and kings, and wearing their livery, consisted of jokes about farting and copulation, and drinking songs. They were turning into general entertainers rather than carriers of fame and memory. Wandering minstrels were rustic showmen, juggling, doing magic, tumbling and moving from door to door trying to scratch a living. The best seem to have been employed mainly to provide background music at feasts, ceremonies and religious rituals. The status of minstrels was low; the language of literacy was Latin but their performances were almost entirely vernacular,

Right: The power of song in Wales. The Earl of Chester was rescued from a siege here at Rhuddlan Castle, by a relief force of minstrels.

and they probably did not look like the cutting edge of European civilization.

The direction they were apparently heading in was well illustrated in 1212, when Randulf, Earl of Chester, was besieged by the Welsh in his castle of Rhuddlan in Flintshire. He sent an appeal for help to Roger de Lacy, justiciar and constable of Chester, affectionately known in the local dungeons as 'Roger of Hell'.

Roger, casting around for the most effective, vicious and altogether intimidating relief force he could find, realized that Chester was full of jongleurs who had come for the annual fair. He gathered them up and marched them off under his son-in-law Dutton. The Welsh, seeing this fearsome body of determined musicians, singers and prestidigitators bearing down on them ready to launch into an immediate performance of their terrifying arts, fled.

Who but Roger of Hell would have been so ruthless? The event gave rise to the old English oath, now sadly forgotten but well worth reviving if someone would like to make a start: 'Roger, and by all the fiddlers of Chester!'

This rag-tag army were wandering minstrels, not bound to a lord and wearing his livery. A minstrel without a livery was a bit like a band without a record contract. Livery indicated that a minstrel had both status and a regular income, and made it easier for him to be accepted in the right castles and earn a decent reward. But he still needed a full range of entertainment skills.

One thirteenth-century poem defines a true minstrel as one who can 'speak and rhyme well, be witty, know the story of Troy, balance apples on the point of knives, juggle, jump through hoops, play the citole, mandora, harp, fiddle, and psaltery'. He is further advised, for good measure, to learn the arts of imitating birds, putting performing asses and dogs through their paces and operating marionettes.

A certain robustness was needed to survive in an environment where good manners was often just a question of not picking your nose in public. A medieval guide to etiquette warns: don't scratch yourself or look for fleas in your breeches or on your chest; don't snap your fingers; don't comb your hair, clean your nails or take your shoes off in the presence of lords and ladies. Messengers arriving at a house removed their weapons, gloves and caps before entering – though they were permitted to keep their caps on if they were bald. The guide also recommends not urinating in the hall – unless you happen to be the head of the household. Which minstrels were not.

The guide also goes into the details about the polite ways to belch, fart and – interestingly enough – defecate.

And the entertainment demanded by early medieval monarchs was reassuringly downmarket. For example, Henry II's favourite minstrel was Roland Le Pettour. The king rewarded him with 30 acres of land for his masterwork, described as 'a leap, a whistle and a fart'. Roland's great musical talent, it seems, was that he could fart tunes. The land was solemnly passed down from father to son for many generations, on the condition that the incumbent turn up at court each Christmas Day to perform the leap, the whistle and the fart!

Another act that was apparently popular with English royalty was a version of putting your head in a lion's mouth, although this one involved a minstrel who spread honey on his member and then brought in a performing bear. What happened next isn't actually explained, but whatever it was probably doesn't figure in *Winnie-the-Pooh*.

Not everyone approved. John of Salisbury, bishop of Chartres, a historian and elegant Latin stylist of the twelfth century, thought jongleurs were quite simply appalling:

> Even they whose exposures are so indecent they make a cynic blush are not debarred from distinguished houses… they are not even turned out when with more hellish tumult they defile the air and more shamelessly disclose that which in shame they had concealed. Does he appear a man of wisdom who has eye or ear for such as these?
> *Policraticus*

Below: Minstrels were all-round knockabout entertainers.

THERE WERE, OF COURSE, many different kinds of minstrels and entertainers, some of whom the Church had no problem with – after all, there were said to be minstrels in heaven. Other performers, though, who encouraged dancing and ribaldry, were plainly servants of the devil. And some minstrels evidently had career paths that led to higher things, the most famous of these being one Rahere.

According to his own account,* Rahere was a low-born character who managed to infiltrate himself into the court of Henry I on the basis of his entertainment value. While it is not clear what this means, and it has been suggested that he may have held a clerical position, the language he uses suggests that he performed as a jongleur or jester. He evidently made a significant sum of money – given the rewards available some years later for a leap, a whistle and a fart, it is likely that minstrelsy was the best way for a poor boy to do this. But there was obviously more to him than that; a 'Rahere' is listed at the time as a canon of St Paul's Cathedral.

For some reason he made a penance-pilgrimage to Rome where he fell seriously ill, and vowed that if he recovered he would build a hospital for the poor. On his return journey he had a delirious vision of hell, followed by one of St Bartholomew who instructed him to build a church in the London suburb of Smooth Field (Smithfield), where there were horse and cattle markets.

Henry I gave Rahere a licence to build a church and hospital on land to the east of the market; most of it was marsh but there was a firmer piece of rising ground used for public executions, and Rahere had the gallows moved so that he could construct a large priory and, nearby, a hospital. A charter of 1147 defines the purpose of St Bartholomew's Hospital as to provide shelter and care for the poor, the sick, the homeless and orphans.

The site was consecrated by the end of 1129 and Rahere became the first prior. Crowds of pilgrims, the sick and people who had been cured in the hospital gathered at the church on St Bartholomew's feast day, and in 1133 Rahere was given a royal charter which licensed a three-day St Bartholomew's Fair, one curious feature of which was that no outlaw or criminal could be arrested while attending it. The hospital and fair became enduring features of London life, and the

Opposite:
St Bartholomew's Church in London. The most enduring monument left by any minstrel.

*Norman Moore, ed. The Book of the Foundation of St. Bartholomew's Church in London, Early English Text Society, no.163 (1923).

choir of the priory is one of the few medieval structures still standing in London. Rahere himself, like Dick Whittington, became a mythologized figure of poor-boy-made-good.

EDWARD II'S MINSTRELS

THE FORTUNES OF ENGLISH MINSTRELS probably reached their zenith during the reign of Edward II, who was a minstrel fanatic. His father was away a lot and the nurse who brought him up was a minstrel, which may explain why he was so fond of them. So fond, in fact, that the treasury rolls showing the expenditure for his coronation list 154 musicians. They also show that on the anniversary of the death of his lover, Piers Gaveston, Edward cheered himself up by travelling to France and being entertained by Bernard the Fool and 54 naked dancers.

Edward seems to have been in the habit of throwing money at anyone who made him laugh – and it evidently didn't take much to make him laugh. Jack of St Albans was paid 50 shillings because 'he danced before the king on a table and made him laugh very greatly'. And he awarded the princely sum of 20 shillings to one of his cooks 'because he rode before the King… and often fell from his horse, at which the King laughed very greatly'.

The barons tried to restrict Edward's extravagant entertainment budget by creating exact job descriptions for every member of the household. This meant an end to multitasking minstrels – now they had to be either jugglers or flute players or whatever, and their numbers were to be strictly limited: 'There shall be trumpeters and 2 other minstrels, and sometimes more and sometimes less, who shall play before the king and it shall please him.'

The barons were not the only people who were trying to limit the number of minstrels. The minstrels themselves were trying to protect their profession and to make it more exclusive. Fraternities or guilds of musicians seem to have been formed in London at least as early as 1350. One of their main objectives was the exclusion of 'foreign' musicians (those who were not Londoners). Another was to stop amateurs from performing in taverns, inns and at weddings. The route to minstrelsy was now through apprenticeship, and the guilds in London, York, Beverley and Canterbury were careful to restrict the number of trainees.

If this seems to be an industry under threat attempting to protect itself, that is about right. The English music and story-telling business was

Opposite: Nothing's new. This German relief shows some fifteenth-century minstrels apparently break-dancing. They are actually performing a fashionable dance from Moorish Spain.

taking a new turn, evidenced by the appearance in the fourteenth century of a new vernacular literature in the form of romantic poetry. The poems were mostly translations of French romances.

ROMANCING THE EPIC

IN FRANCE (AND TO SOME EXTENT ITALY AND GERMANY) a change had been taking place in the content of *chansons de geste* since the middle of the twelfth century. Like the earlier ones, they were still usually stories of conflict between Christians and Saracens; but magical and romantic themes had begun to take over, with evil knights, the rescue of ladies and the frequent appearance of magic rings, belts and swords. A heroic tradition is converted into a romantic one. There is an emphasis on describing Islam as idolatrous, and Muslims as superstitious, treacherous and polygamous; the Saracen world is as exotic as it is dangerous, and Muslim women are presented as lascivious and seductive, irresistibly attracted to Christian knights and, after willing conversion, faithful only to them. Some historians of the literature have suggested that a little wishful thinking might have been involved, but this seems mean-minded. All adventure stories involve wishful thinking; the interesting question is the nature of the wish.

One of the most significant examples of the new mood in European poetry is *Le Roman d'Eneas*, a French version of Virgil's *Aeneid* which appeared anonymously in about 1160. The emphasis is on story elements that were new to Virgil as well as to French poetry – the feelings of two women, Dido and Lavinia, who are in love with Aeneas. A new literary principle had appeared: the principle of overpowering love.

This, of course, indicates that the whole world of performance must have changed. The audience and the location for the entertainment are different. This is not material for the battlefield or for a hall of warriors. And it assumes a new kind of performer.

This new performer had first appeared in southern France in the twelfth century. He was called a troubadour.

Opposite: A troubadour entertains in the famous song collection of Alfonso the Learned of Spain: Las Cantigas.

INVENTING TROUBADOURS

THE PIONEER OF THE NEW STYLE OF POETRY was not a professional musician but an aristocrat – the gloriously randy Duke William IX of Aquitaine,

whose court was in Poitiers. According to his thirteenth-century Provençal biographer:

> The Count of Poitiers was one of the most courtly men in the world and one of the greatest deceivers of women. He was a fine knight at arms, liberal in his attentions to ladies, and an accomplished composer and singer of songs. For a long time he roved the world, bent on the deception of ladies.

55
Minstrel

According to the chronicler William of Malmesbury, after a disastrous crusade of his own devising in 1101, Duke William plunged most enthusiastically into a life of sexual entertainment and frivolous versifying to amuse his companions. He was obviously strongly influenced by his travels; half his surviving songs draw on a particular form of Arab mystical poetry (the *zajel*) for their detailed metrical structure and conventional expressions.

The word 'troubadour' meant an author or composer who discovered something new – literally the 'finder' of something that had not been known before. Duke William was playing with novelty, and demonstrating that poetry and song could be about absolutely anything – or about nothing at all.

I made this verse on sweet F.A.
There is no person to portray
No talk of love or youth at play –
Nothing, of course.
Composed while sleeping yesterday
Sat on my horse

Above: A carving of a minstrel at Beverley Minster, Yorkshire.

Opposite: Troubadours' songs were collated in volumes that included notional portraits and biographies of the composers, in an effort to give them higher status than mere jongleurs.

Duke William was without doubt a true original. He was excommunicated twice. On the first occasion, in 1114, when the bishop of Poitiers imposed the penalty for some unknown offence, he held the bishop at sword point in the cathedral and demanded absolution. He didn't get it, which says something for the bishop's courage and possibly explains why the duke's crusade hadn't achieved anything. The second excommunication was caused by William's affair with the Viscountess of Chatellerault, alarmingly known as Dangerosa. It was said he kidnapped this mother of three and installed her in a tower in his palace at Poitiers. William of Malmesbury says he even had her portrait painted on his shield, so 'I could bear her into battle as she had borne me into bed'. The duke's wife was not happy at all about this.

William also fantasized about establishing a convent of prostitutes, and his verse includes a great deal of crude sexual joking, with women

portrayed as fine horses to be mounted, or as captives, and he jokingly records his seduction by two ladies whose only concern was to avoid disclosure.

But he also wrote some verses that conveyed a much more reverent attitude to women, which would become the basis of what is called 'courtly love'. In these poems his lady is a married woman, and is as aloof as she is desirable. There is a frequent theme that the lover must be patient and, as he waits for the lady's favours, behave with courtesy to all about him. For the courtly lover, the lady alone has the power to kill or cure; in her hands alone lies his salvation.

The language of Duke William's compositions was the southern French vernacular, Occitan. This was itself a radical move, as up to this time the language of all intellectual life had been Latin. But it was no more revolutionary than the idea of a lover addressing his love song to a married woman. This was conventionally liable to bring the death penalty and was regarded as the equivalent of casting a spell on her.

This courtly romanticism flourished under William's son, and then his granddaughter, the redoubtable Eleanor of Aquitaine. She established her own court in Poitiers, which was dominated by the idea of courtly love and, supposedly at least, run by its rules. The court culture there was in the vernacular tongue, and the old, heroic warrior entertainments were deeply out of date.

Shortly before Christmas 1182 the Limousin troubadour Bertran de Born spent time at Henry II's court at Argentan in Normandy, and complained about the boorishness of the old warrior culture: 'A court where no one laughs or jokes is never complete; a court

57
Minstrel

without gifts is just a paddock-full of barons. The boredom and vulgarity of Argentan nearly killed me.'

Troubadours were often great lords themselves, but less boorish than those of Argentan. They performed their own songs and employed jongleurs or minstrels as their accompanists. Aristocratic troubadours even took part in singing competitions.

Not that these men weren't warriors. Eleanor's sons Richard I and King John were both tough and violent. But Richard 'the Lionheart', whose idea of a satisfying life involved the use of extreme force on a face-to-face, or even a nose-to-nose basis, was also a man who had been raised in a troubadour culture. He wrote and performed elegant songs, both at court and while on campaign. Two of his poems have survived, one with the music.

BLONDEL

IT WAS BECAUSE OF RICHARD'S POETIC INCLINATIONS that the story of his rescue by his minstrel, Blondel, had such wide currency. In 1192 Richard was captured by Leopold of Austria while returning from the Third Crusade. (He was alone and in disguise – typical of Richard, no other English king would have created such an adventure.) He simply vanished, and it was said that Blondel set out to find him. The minstrel wandered from castle to castle, and outside each he sang part of a song they had composed together. At the castle of Dürnstein he heard Richard answer his song by completing it. The king, having been found, could now be ransomed.

This is a good poetic tale in itself, but probably apocryphal. Blondel de Nesle was certainly a well-known troubadour, the composer of many love songs. But he was not Richard's minstrel, a supporter of the English; he was actually from northern France and wrote in the Picardy dialect. The tale is probably a minstrel's invention – the minstrel in question being the unknown author of *Récits d'un ménestrel de Reims*, which appeared in about 1260. Presumably he wanted to convey a clear moral: 'Look after your minstrel and he'll look after you.'

The career of Blondel de Nesle is an illustration of the way in which the troubadour influence had spread north to the Loire and beyond, out of the Langue-d'oc. (Dante distinguished three cultural regions which were defined by their word for 'yes': *si* in the south, *oc* in the middle and *oïl* in the north.)

Although the romanticization of song and poetry spread into northern France, where the poets were called '*trouvères*', troubadour poetry was uniquely linked to the culture of Provence, shaped by the experiences of Provençal crusaders in the Middle East. It was within this framework that the world of courtly love flourished, chivalry became concerned with courtesy and the adoration of noblewomen, and a new kind of literature arose: the poetic, epic romances of heroes like Arthur and his knights.

CATHARS

AT THE SAME TIME, Provençal religious beliefs were changing significantly. Hostility to the worldliness and greed of the Church was widespread throughout Europe, but in Provence the belief that it was a fraudulent and pompous organization that had misunderstood Christianity mutated into a new form: Catharism. The Cathars believed the world was seized in a combat between two divinities, God and the devil, and that the material world was the territory of evil and the devil. They understood the Bible not as a historical document but as an allegory, and saw Jesus not as a man but as an angel.

They maintained that humans could free themselves from the evil world by being good. The *perfecti*, 'pure ones', were idealistic, pacifist vegetarians. Many members of the Languedoc nobility supported and were sympathetic to the Cathars.

There was an obvious contradiction between the earthy enthusiasm of Duke William's poetry and the flesh-denying asceticism of the Cathars. To some extent this was moderated as Catharism came to dominate Provençal courts. Troubadour music and poetry became more high-flown, rhetorical and allegorical. Just as some of the music of the 1960s was the voice of protest and hippy idealism, some of the troubadours of the thirteenth century were the voice of Cathar protest. Even the use of their own language rather than Latin had an anti-Rome flavour to it.

Pope Innocent III was deeply hostile to the movement. Recognizing that its appeal was largely a reaction against the venality and corruption of his Church (a criticism with which he thoroughly agreed), he tried to win people back by sending poor preaching friars into the region, including a group led by St Dominic in 1205. They failed to attract Cathars back to the fold.

In 1208, after the murder of a papal legate, Innocent III changed tack and invited the chivalry of Europe to stop killing Saracens and start killing Cathars – a worthy deed for which they would be granted absolution from sin. This holy war, the first crusade deliberately launched against Christian 'heretics', lasted until 1229 and decimated the Languedoc. It was called the Albigensian Crusade as the Cathars were identified with the town of Albi and known by the northern French as Albigensians.

It was ruthlessly savage. Arnold Aimery, the papal legate at the siege of Béziers, ordered his men: 'Show mercy neither to order, nor to age, nor to sex… Cathar or Catholic, Kill them all… God will know his own.' The attackers were Anglo-French Normans eager to seize property in the Dordogne (nice farmhouse, needs some repairs…) This was how Simon de Montfort was granted control of the area encompassing Carcassonne, Albi and Béziers.

The troubadours had to flee or be killed. They sought refuge in northern Italy, the Iberian Peninsula and the north, producing new musical movements across Europe. In fact, the only real survivor of the slaughter was the troubadour sensibility; an outflow of poetic refugees had an impact on the rest of Europe comparable to the flight of intellectuals from Nazi Germany. The comparison is not far-fetched. The Albigensian Crusade was truly genocidal in intent, and it has been estimated that a million people were slaughtered.

TRIUMPH OF THE VERNACULAR

ONE EXAMPLE OF THE TROUBADOUR INFLUENCE is in the work of Wolfram von Eschenbach, a Bavarian who is remembered as the most brilliant of Germany's narrative poets and who wrote the epic *Parzival*, which was clearly based on Chrétien de Troyes' Arthurian romance, *Perceval*. Wolfram said he used extra material given him at the time of the Albigensian Crusade by one Kyot of Provence; apparently Kyot had taken refuge in Spain, like many Provençal troubadours, before going to Germany.

The legacy of the troubadours far outlasted their own shattered culture. The impact on writers in other lands was profound, even when they had no sympathy for the ideology of Catharism. The most important and influential of these admirers was the Italian Dante Alighieri, who at the very beginning of the fourteenth century wrote a Latin essay, 'De Vulgari Eloquentia' (On Vernacular Language), in which he extolled spoken language (as opposed to Latin) as a suitable vehicle for literature.

He identified as exemplars three great troubadours, one of whom, Arnaut Daniel, he quoted in Occitan and immortalized in his *Divine Comedy*.

Arnaut's poetry is quite astonishing. He writes with an unforced lightness of touch, constructing rhyme-schemes and scansion that are beautifully calculated and precise. The more you recite his verses the more complexity is revealed beneath a surface that is entirely natural and open, one human being speaking to another. It feels as though the language has been borne along with the poem. This makes it quite untranslatable; it is impossible to mimic the rhyme, scansion and spirit while translating the meaning into another tongue. The joy of the poetry and the language that expresses it are inseparable.

No vuelh de Roma l'emperi	*I don't want the Empire of Rome*
ni qu'om m'en fassa postoli	*or for someone to make me the Pope*
qu'en lieis non aia revert	*if I can't find a place by her*
per cui m'art lo cors e'm rima;	*by whom my heart is burned and scorched*
e si'l maltrait no'm restaura	*and if she does not cure this injury*
ab un baizar anz d'annueu,	*with a kiss within a year*
mi auci e si enferna.	*I die and to hell with her*

A great deal of effort went into making troubadour verse seem respectable, and collections of poems were produced with biographies of the poets attached to the verses attributed to them. (Usually no-one was quite sure who had written what, and the biographies were to some extent derived from the content of whatever poems were attributed to the troubadours by the collator.)

The new emphasis on the validity and importance of vernacular language began to have an impact on the courts and even the politics of western Europe. It became important for monarchs to stake out their intellectual territory as clearly as they did the geographical boundaries of their power. So to this end they started employing intellectuals as court poets and writers.

These new poets were decidedly sniffy about the old minstrels. In France, Eustache Deschamps said, 'The artificial music of the minstrels could be learnt by *'le plus rude homme du monde'* (the most uncouth man in the world).' Deschamps was a gentleman-usher to Charles V of France in the 1370s, and rose and fell as a courtier while producing a quantity of poetry which could hardly have been learnt by the most couth and studious man in the world – some 82,000 verses – virtually a courtly poetic diary.

The danger faced by a court poet was not the risk faced by Taillefer, of death on a battlefield, or by a crude jongleur, of dying of penury and cold in a ditch, but the danger of his verse being seen as subversive or dangerous. Deschamps could not resist satirizing those he despised, including members of the nobility, the government and the Church, and financiers, lawyers and even women.

His parody of a pert young lady demanding attention seems, at a distance, entertaining and nicely ironic:

I would say that in my view
I have good looks, a sweet face too
And my mouth red like a rose.
Tell me if I am fair

My smile is sweet, my eyes like dew
A lovely nose, hair blonde right through,
Nice chin, my white throat shows
Am I, am I, am I fair? ...

Both courteous and kind, that's who
If strong and bold and handsome, too
Will win this prize so rare.
Tell me if I am fair…

Now discuss it between you
Think of what I've told you true
So ends my little song.
Am I, am I, am I fair?

Of course, such a poem might be satirizing some silly little girl. But it might equally well be read as an allegory in which the fair young girl is a satirical image of a nobleman fluttering his eyelashes at potential co-

conspirators. Or such a nobleman, sensitized to the new delicacy of vernacular poetry, might interpret it that way.

Deschamps ended up losing all his positions and his income.

THE VERNACULAR IN ENGLAND

THE NEW, COURTLY VERNACULAR came rather later to England than to the rest of Europe. This was because, until the mid-fourteenth century, England's aristocracy had its own vernacular, which was different from that of the common people. This tongue, Norman French, was a survival of the Conquest. Although it became increasingly anglicized from the early thirteenth century, the linguistic division between nobility and commoners remained a real divide until about 1360. It was not until 1362, when the Statute of Pleading was passed, that English became the language of the law courts. But then the old Anglo-Norman French seems to have faded away quite rapidly.

The English court in 1350 had been happy to listen to vernacular poetry but it did not regard any particular regional language as its own. In that year Edward III decided to deal once and for all with the piratical depredations of a well-connected Spanish freebooter, Don Carlos de la Cerda, who had been busy loading treasure, supplies and loot at Sluis in Flanders to be shipped back to the Basque coast. Edward obviously felt that the very survival of his kingdom depended on asserting control over the English Channel, and decided on a do-or-die challenge to Don Carlos.

He assembled his fleet at Winchelsea, with himself on one flagship, the *Thomas*, and the Black Prince on another. The entire royal lineage was there, even the king's younger son, the ten-year-old John of Gaunt. The royal ladies were lodged in a convent, from which they would be able to watch the battle.

Waiting for the encounter, Edward prepared himself and his troops by watching his minstrels perform a German dance, and listening to a knight, Sir John Chandos, singing in French with his minstrels.* They were entering as full participants into the world of heroic epic battle, but this King did not see himself as particularly English.

The battle was indeed heroic. The *Thomas* went to the bottom, as did the Black Prince's ship, but the heroes survived and the Spanish lost 14 of their 40 ships. This was, in fact, a more dramatic and bloody victory than the better-known struggle of 1588 against the Spanish Armada. But the

*Froissart describes the moment. He does not say that Sir John sang in French, but when Chandos' herald composed a poem-chronicle life of the Black Prince, that was in French, so it is unlikely that he would sing in English.

63
Minstrel

poem that recorded what had happened was not in German or French. It was in strikingly powerful English:

I shall not hold back from telling, and hope to succeed in the task,
Of men who were brave with weapons and admirable in armour
That now are driven to the grave, and dead despite all their deeds
They sail on the sea bed, fishes to feed
Many fishes they feed, for all their great vaunting
They came at the waning of the moon…*

A new literature was emerging in England, in which the English language was being used in innovative ways, and which bridged the gap between the court and the general population in the most extraordinary way. William Langland's poem *Piers Plowman*, a huge allegorical work on the Christian concept of a good life, which first appeared around 1360, was copied and recopied endlessly and was evidently well known by all classes of people – lines from it were used as slogans and signals in the so-called Peasants' Revolt of 1381. Poetry was alive and dangerous.

Something similar was happening in Wales, where at the beginning of the fifteenth century there was a decree that said: '… no rimers, minstrels or vagabonds, be maintained in Wales whom by their divinations, lies and exhortations are partly cause for insurrection and rebellion now in Wales.'

But the Welsh bardic 'rimers' were reaching back into old heroic tradition, finding subversive nationalistic matter in the Welsh versions of Arthurian legends, and using them as sustenance for the national rebellion led by Owen Glendower. In England, the dangerous poets were new men creating a new literature in their own tongue. The old minstrels looked shabby and outdated. The situation was rather like that of the mid-twentieth century, when the old vaudeville comedians – with their distinctive repertoire of hand-me-down material culled from many years of touring music halls – found themselves displaced by the university-educated satirists of the television age who wrote their own fresh material every week.

A DANGEROUS GAME

TOWARDS THE END OF THE FOURTEENTH CENTURY Richard II clearly saw literature as territory to be occupied by the crown as firmly as any physical territory and, having inherited a court poet from his grandfather, gave him

*How king Edward & his menye met with the Spaniardes in the see, The Poems of Laurence Minot 1333–1352. Originally published in The Poems of Laurence Minot 1333–1352, edited by Richard H. Osberg, trans A. Ereira, (M.I. Kalamazoo: Western Michigan University for TEAMS, 1997).

every assistance and encouragement. His name was Geoffrey Chaucer, and he was destined to become one of the major figures in English literature – second only to Shakespeare.

Richard's court, like that of Charles V in France, tolerated a relaxed easy-going intellectual atmosphere in which satire and lampoons were allowed to flourish. Chaucer took advantage of this to satirize the way the Church had become corrupted and commercialized. For example, he told the tale of a friar who was taken down to hell by an angel and happily observed that he couldn't see any friars there. He assumed this meant they were all in heaven. Oh no, said the angel, there are plenty of friars down here; and he accosts Satan.

> 'Hold up thy tail thou Satanas' said he
> 'Show forth thine arse and let the friar see
> Where is the nest of friars in this place!'
> And ere that half a furlong way of space
> Right so as bees come swarming from the hive,
> Out of the devil's arse began to drive
> Twenty thousand friars in a route.
> And throughout hell they swarmed all about
> And came again as fast as they may gone
> And in his arse they crept in every John!
> *The Summoner's Prologue*

To offer satire at court is a dangerous game, especially when one year's patron is the next year's outcast. Richard II was violently overthrown. His usurper, who became Henry IV, was helped to the throne by Thomas Arundel, an archbishop of Canterbury who had been exiled by Richard, and who was determined to stamp out any criticism of the Church, especially criticisms in English, which any Tom, Dick or Harriet could read and understand. Within a year, Arundel began burning 'heretics' at the stake, and even banned the use of English to discuss

Below: Geoffrey Chaucer, as one of the Canterbury pilgrims.

religion. Chaucer's writing, filled as it is with criticism of the Church in the vernacular, was exactly the sort of thing that was being stamped out.

Which may be the explanation for one of the unnoticed mysteries of history. Chaucer, the father of English literature, disappeared without trace at about the same time that Arundel was trying to limit the use of English in literature.

Chaucer was probably the most famous commoner in the kingdom, yet there is no record of his death, he did not leave a will and we do not even know when he died. All we have is an illegible inscription on a tomb, erected a century and a half after he disappeared, which does not mark the site of his burial and as far as we know never even contained his remains. He undoubtedly vanished quite mysteriously. It may be that he was deliberately removed.

Opposite: Geoffrey Chaucer recites his poem Troilus and Criseyde *to Richard II and his court. They seem to be swooning over this story of sex and the human condition.*

DECLINE OF THE MINSTREL

THERE WAS NO POSSIBILITY of undoing the changes that had begun. Traditional minstrels, the old jongleurs, were out of fashion. They went downmarket and became itinerant entertainers performing at fairs and on street corners. Unemployed, they were outside the control of rich patrons and could pretend to belong to whomever they wanted – even the king.

It got so bad that Henry VI instigated an investigation board to clamp down on them. Any minstrel convicted of falsely claiming to have royal patronage would be fined and forced to pray for the king's soul.

The luckier minstrels were hired as civil servants by towns, to bolster citizens' self-importance in civic ceremonies. In the fourteenth century towns had given short-term contracts to minstrels in the service of aristocrats when they needed a performance on a feast day or for an armed muster, but by the fifteenth it seemed the supply was drying up. For example, York Corporation had a trio – the 'city waits' – on retainer from the time of Henry VI. They were provided with uniforms each Christmas and performed at Easter, Corpus Christi, Christmas and on a couple of saint's days.

There were still court musicians, but few of them were minstrels in the old sense of being general entertainers. And in courts where sovereigns increasingly wrote poetry and performed their own songs, musicians were accepted into very polite company. This was obviously the case with a young dancer and harpsichord player, Mark Smeaton, minstrel to Henry VIII and his queen, Anne Boleyn. One spring day in 1536 he was invited

to the home of Thomas Cromwell, Henry's chief minister. There, almost certainly under torture and with a promise of immunity, he 'made revelations' about the queen, confessing to being her lover. It can be deduced from the general incredulity at the confession ('How could she stoop so low?') that Smeaton did not come from a noble family.

He named several other men, including Anne's brother George, Sir Henry Norris, Sir William Brereton, Sir Francis Weston and Sir Thomas Wyatt. Wyatt, a poet and songwriter whose work is as fresh today as it was 500 years ago, had told Henry before the marriage that he had been Anne's lover.

> Blame not my Lute !
> Farewell! unknown; for though thou break
> My strings in spite with great disdain,
> Yet have I found out for thy sake,
> Strings for to string my Lute again:
> And if, perchance, this sely rhyme
> Do make thee blush, at any time,
> Blame not my Lute !

The men named were arrested, providing the pretext that allowed Henry to dispose of Anne Boleyn and replace her with Jane Seymour. Wyatt was released; it may be that Henry had a soft spot for songwriters. He was one himself, and wrote a new arrangement and lyrics for an old tune, which he called 'Greensleeves'.

> Alas, my love, you do me wrong,
> To cast me off discourteously.
> For I have loved you well and long,
> Delighting in your company.

Any affection Henry might have felt for fellow-performers did not extend to Smeaton, who was tried for treason on 12 May 1536. He was not allowed to defend himself. He was hanged, cut down while still alive, his stomach was cut open and his intestines were pulled out in front of his still-conscious eyes. Then his body was butchered.

The revels were ended, the Middle Ages had given way to the ruthless cruelty of Renaissance power.

And what was left of the minstrels? Quite a lot; they had vanished as a class, but mutated into something far broader. The literature, poetry and

drama of England now embraced and entertained the whole nation; and could weave together the most sublime and powerful emotions and delicate language, with the lowest comedy, to create a single, extraordinary experience. This was made evident later in the century, when Shakespeare's work appeared. His colleagues in the high-minded enterprise of presenting high tragedy and sophisticated comedy included Will Kemp, a fellow-shareholder in the Globe Theatre – clown, dancer, singer, instrumentalist and a man who fully appreciated the audience appeal of a leap, a whistle and a fart.

Left: Will Kemp, a clown in William Shakespeare's company of players, represents the jongleur tradition of entertainers. As artists they were full participants in a new age of sophisticated dramatic performance.

And the queen under whose rule they flourished, the daughter of Anne Boleyn, was said (very quietly) to bear more than a passing resemblance to Mark Smeaton.

CHAPTER THREE

Outlaw

Above: Young men training to be knights. There was a very short distance between socially sanctioned violence and violent crime in medieval England.

THE OUTLAWS OF MEDIEVAL ENGLAND are still the stuff of legend. Heroes who bestrode the greenwood, fearlessly wearing only tights and little short tunics that hardly covered their bottoms – the figure of the medieval outlaw has come to represent freedom and justice for the common man.

Outlaws inhabit a kind of border territory in our medieval myth, crossing back and forth between the pantomime vision of a jolly and well-ordered medieval kingdom and the dark image of horribly violent and barbaric lawlessness. Taking a cool look at reality not only reveals the truth and falsehood in both these images, but also clarifies a central theme of this whole book; the way in which medieval lives in England became different from those in the rest of Europe, as a distinct national society emerged.

Perhaps the most surprising example of that distinctiveness is that in England, uniquely in Europe, bold robber outlaws were necessary for the effective functioning of the kingdom.

This will all be explained as we investigate whether bandits like Robin Hood really existed, whether the forest was truly a place of freedom and escape, and, of course, the key question, did outlaws never wear trousers?

There certainly were plenty of outlaws in the Middle Ages, in fact, more than one might imagine. By the end of the period, historians tell us, practically everyone got outlawed at some stage of their lives. It had become a minor inconvenience – a bit like having your credit card stopped.

It is true that there were some other outlaws whose violence blighted society, but even there things are often not quite what one might expect.

Take the drama that engulfed the little village of Teigh, in Rutland, one afternoon in 1340.

A REAL-LIFE OUTLAW GANG

A GANG OF ARMED MEN broke into the church, and the rector, whose place of worship it had been for twenty years, was dragged outside into the street and beheaded. The twist, however, is that the gang of armed men who slew the man of God weren't the outlaws. It was the rector who was the outlaw. His name was Richard Folville and he was one of six brothers who made up the notorious Folville Gang.

A generation after their deaths, the Folvilles were celebrated as the kind of outlaws who righted wrongs. One chronicle tells how they: 'took the law in to their own hands' and rode out to right injustice with the force of arms. 'Folville's Laws' became a synonym for 'justified robbery'. They killed

Right: Robin Hood is probably the only man in European history to have a civic statue erected celebrating his identity as a criminal.

a widely-hated judge in the court of the Exchequer, and kidnapped a justice of the King's Bench whom a contemporary poem indicted as corrupt.

So were the Folvilles the real-life Robin Hoods? It would be exciting to report that they were, but they weren't.

The Folvilles were the younger sons of minor aristocracy, who drifted into a life of crime to support themselves in the style to which they were accustomed. They weren't robbing from the rich to give to the poor, they were simply robbing, raping, beating, kidnapping and killing as a livelihood.

And yet they were still held in some esteem in later years. They were acquitted on charges of murder when brought to trial and the justice of the peace who rid the world of Richard Folville, the rector, was forced to do penance – touring the local parishes and being beaten at each church.

It seems that people in the Middle Ages may have had an ambivalent attitude not simply to the Folvilles but to outlaws in general and to the very question of bold robbers. Maybe that's how one of our most popular legends came about.

THE REAL ROBIN HOOD?

IF THERE EVER WAS A REAL ROBIN HOOD, he's surprisingly hard to pin down. There is confusion over where he lived (Nottinghamshire? Yorkshire?), when he lived (the twelfth century, in the age of Bad King John and Good King Richard? the fourteenth century?) and even *whether* he lived (the occasional record referring to a criminal called Robin Hode or Hood may be the origin of the story or the perpetuation of a legend).

But the medieval landscape would clearly be incomplete without him. Robin Hood somehow represents a fundamental image of English identity. Partly, of course, this is the bizarre English pantomime-identity of innocent transvestite jollity, but he also carries a message of political morality. A victim of injustice and of a corrupt, self-seeking sheriff, hiding out in the forest with his company of rogues, he is a symbol of natural justice, admired by the poor and hated by the fat cats of medieval England.

PRIDE IN ROBBERS

THE STRANGE FACT IS THAT THE ENGLISH always have been, and still are, proud of their outlaw robbers – not just fictional ones, but real robbers like

the Folvilles. They regarded them as unique. Outlaws in other countries may have had codes of honour among themselves, but they were not regarded as stout bold fellows as they clearly were in England. There was felt to be the world of difference between an honourable robber and the mugger who makes a sneak attack. In much medieval writing about outlaws there is a presumption that their activities are honourable if robbery is performed boldly, face to face. In fact, it seems to be treated much like trial by ordeal: if God were not on the robber's side he would be defeated by his victim.

This admiration for outlaws could be found in the Middle Ages even among those whose job it was to hang them. In 1470 Sir John Fortescue, who had been chief justice of the King's Bench from 1442 to 1461, was educating the Lancastrian Prince Edward, son of Henry VI, who he expected would replace the Yorkist Edward IV as king. The prince, his mother Queen Margaret and Fortescue were in exile in Flanders at the time, and Fortescue wanted the prince to understand that the English were a more courageous people than the French. He knew this, he explained, because they made such bold outlaws:

… Frenchmen are seldom hanged for robbery, for they have no heart to do such a terrible act. There are therefore more men hanged for robbery and manslaughter in England in a year than are hanged in France in seven years for such crimes… If [an Englishman] is poor and sees another man having riches which may be taken from him by might, he will not spare to do so, unless that poor man should be very law-abiding.

Could it be true that the medieval outlaw was fundamental to the development of a unique English identity? If so, the story is very different from that of the Robin Hood of pantomime. We imagine the outlaw as essentially non-violent and honourable; this is what makes him deserve our sympathy and affection. But just take a closer look at the actual medieval Robin Hood.

ROBIN HOOD'S BRUTALITY

ROBIN AND HIS MEN are depicted as being from the yeoman class, and as a band of ruthless killers. But this does not affect their status as the heroes of these medieval tales. Robin Hood's virtue apparently lies less in his sense of social justice than in his devotion to the Virgin and his hostility to sheriffs and monks.

The oldest of the stories, 'Robin Hood and the Monk', is believed to date from around the time of the Folvilles. Right at the start, Robin is determined to take the risk of praying at a shrine. On the way there he gambles with, and tries to swindle, Little John, whom he then strikes. They fight and John abandons him. Robin is then spotted by a monk whom he has robbed. The monk raises a hue and cry and the sheriff of Nottingham and his men try to catch Robin:

> But Robin took out a two-handed sword,
> That hanged down by his knee;
> There as the sheriff and his men stood thickest
> Towards them went he.
>
> Thrice he ran right through them,
> In truth I to you say,
> And wounded many a mother's son,
> And twelve he slew that day.

Robin Hood is eventually captured. Little John and another outlaw, Much, then come across the monk travelling with his page, and discover what has happened. Without a second thought, John kills the monk and:

Above: A sixteenth-century image of Robin Hood: a criminal for all ages.

> Much did the same to the little page,
> For fear that he would tell.

Little John and Much have killed a man who has acted lawfully throughout; and they have also murdered a child witness. This is not supposed to show them in a bad light. On the contrary, it shows the excellence of their loyalty to Robin. A gangster who casually kills a child witness is, to a modern reader, an irredeemable monster and a very long way from the pantomime version.

ANGLO-SAXON OUTLAWS

OUTLAWRY WAS AN IMPORTANT PART of Anglo-Saxon law, but its meaning was changed by the Norman Conquest.

Our concept of the 'outlaw' is shaped by our very strong notions of personal liberty. We see feudal society with its strict definitions of status,

where people were legally attached to the land and work was compulsory, as oppressive. The Robin-Hood-type outlaw appeals to us as someone who lives free of that oppression. But in the world of the eleventh century, 'freedom' was the very opposite of what we take it to mean today. Everyone was bonded into a place in society; every man and woman belonged, quite literally, to someone else. This was the basis of their existence. Outlaws were people who had abandoned this bond to live as, in effect, wild creatures.

At the time of the Norman Conquest, England was a very highly structured society. Everyone had to be bound to a lord and to their own family. A 'lordless man' was a suspect, if not dangerous, person; if he did not have a lord who would take responsibility for him, his family had to find him one; if they failed he could be dealt with as a rogue and vagabond. Law was understood to be traditional, the property of the population. Royal declarations of law were not intended as new legislation, but as restatements by kings of the laws of their predecessors, and the legal process was entirely at a local level. Courts were held in shires (counties) and hundreds (a division of a shire).

There was no distinction between civil and criminal law. All legal processes came down to one person making an accusation against another and demanding retribution. Criminal law, in which the state detects the offence, takes the accused to court and demands and imposes punishment, simply did not exist in early medieval society. Every householder had his own 'peace', and a breach of this (a theft or act of violence) was followed by an appeal to the local court, demanding cash payment in recompense.

The accused was required either to produce a set number of people, 'oath-helpers', who would swear his innocence on oath or to pay the cash price associated with the offence. The value of a man's oath depended on his social status. This weighting also determined the number of oaths an accused man needed to clear himself in court and the size of the payment, if one was made in recompense for his offence. Every life had a cash value (the *wergild*, or 'man price'). An aristocrat's (thegn's) life, and his oath, were worth six times that of a common man (1,200 shillings as against 200).

Anglo-Saxon law codes read like modern insurance policies. For example, the list of compensation payments set out in the laws of Ethelbert, King of Kent from 560 to 616, include:

If an ear be struck off, twelve shillings.
If the other ear hear not, twenty-five shillings.
If an ear be pierced, three shillings.

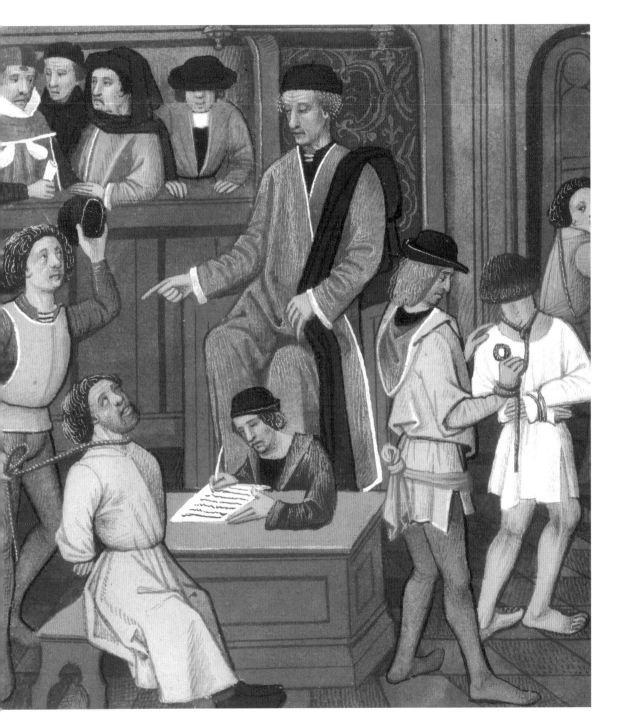

If an ear be mutilated, six shillings.

If an eye be (struck) out, fifty shillings.

If the mouth or an eye be injured, twelve shillings.

If the nose be pierced, nine shillings.

If the nose be otherwise mutilated, for each six shillings.

Let him who breaks the chin-bone pay for it with twenty shillings.

For each of the four front teeth, six shillings; for the tooth which stands next to them four shillings; for that which stands next to that, three shillings; and then afterwards, for each a shilling.

And so the list went on, painstakingly costing fingers and toes, nails and skin, bruises and bones. This, naturally, gave everyone a great interest in the law. If the offender refused to pay up the victim was entitled to conduct a private war, with the support of his hundred (local district).

Oath-taking was a religious ritual – one mistake in the recitation of the formula, and the oath was discarded. If the accused could not find enough oath-takers, but maintained their innocence, they were tried by ordeal. If God brought them safely through the trial of hot iron or hot water, or immersion in cold water, they were judged innocent.

Outlaws were men and women who had decided to hide rather than face trial. (Actually, women could not be outlawed but became 'waifs', which was much the same.) Such a person was part of no community and so was regarded with deep fear. Outlaws had no oath value and therefore no price could be attached to their lives. They could be killed with impunity. It was an offence to feed, shelter or communicate with them.

It would take real desperation for a man or woman to choose to live outside society, to voluntarily forfeit all their goods, to become a 'wolf's head' who could be legally slain by anyone. It would be an unlikely step unless they were without hope of finding oath-helpers and were terrified of the ordeal – in other words, were already virtually excluded from society.

But in 1066 this elaborate structure suffered a shattering blow when William the Conqueror and his Normans took over England.

CONQUEST

IN 1066 ENGLAND BECAME AN OCCUPIED COUNTRY, whose new masters knew nothing about the land they held or the people they ruled, and who did not even speak the language. And Normans kept turning up dead, murdered, in fields, woods and lanes. Although William decreed that the shire- and

hundred-courts should carry on working, the legal system depended, obviously, on the victims of crime or their relatives naming the criminals. It depended, in fact, on a close-knit community. The Normans were not part of that community. They needed to force it to hand over any culprits.

William demanded an oath of fealty from every freeman, and that each man (unless he was part of the household of a lord) should be enrolled in a 'tithing', a group of ten people who were obliged to produce him in court if necessary. Proceedings were held at the court of the local lord. This system was administered by the sheriff (shire reeve), and if an accused failed to turn up when summoned the tithing was fined. The penalty for outlawry was now exacted on the community from which the outlaw had fled, reinforcing the sense of living under an alien occupation.

When a Norman was killed William imposed a fine on the district where the body had been found, unless the killer was promptly produced by the community. The system was changed from one of community law enforcement into one of collective punishment, similar to the regime imposed in France by the Nazis during their occupation in the early 1940s.

Below: Trial by battle: the combatants have come with their biers, ready to prove their arguments by sheer violence.

The Norman system was totally based on violence; it had come to England as a result of violence and it required all landholders to pay for their land by doing military service. Oath-taking survived, but the Normans found it unsatisfactory and insisted that in cases between themselves they were entitled to trial by battle. A victim of violence, appealing to the local lord for justice against the wrongdoer, could (if denouncer and denounced were both of noble blood) be required to fight the person they named.

This was supposedly a fighting man's equivalent of trial by ordeal; God would, in theory, ensure that in a fair fight victory went to the

Right: Hanging, drawing and quartering became an English punishment at the end of the fourteenth century.

righteous. In reality, of course, it was a recognition and direct enforcement of the fact that for the Normans might was right.

An Englishman accused by a Frenchman was not allowed to defend himself with oath-takers, but instead had to choose between battle and ordeal. And if the roles were reversed an English accuser faced a similar problem. So if you were an elderly freeman whose son had been murdered by a big, young, vigorous Norman you could go to a lord's court, name the killer and find that he demanded the right to do battle with you. Oh, good.

The inevitable result was the deep reluctance of victims to accuse the perpetrators of crimes. In fact, in the twelfth century half of all appeals against murderers in local courts were brought by women, who could not be made to do battle. The law had become something to be avoided, to the extent that, at least in private appeals involving murder, almost one in five was ignored by the defendant. After being summoned four times and failing to appear he was declared to be an outlaw.

After the conquest William, the new owner of all land in England, also replaced the system of cash compensation with one of fines and confiscations to himself, along with corporal punishment.

People were reluctant to denounce aggressors to the sheriff not only because they might have to face a battle challenge, but because the accused might pass an ordeal and be declared innocent, in which case the plaintiff would be heavily fined for false accusation. Claims over land were also normally settled through trial by battle, and that, too, was an uninviting prospect.

The bulk of the population had much less interest in using the law. And outlawry – escaping the clutches of the law – changed its moral category. Instead of simply being fugitives from decent society, outlaws were now rebels, even guerrillas, hiding from a legal system that lacked moral authority.

According to Matthew Paris, writing nearly 200 years after the Norman Conquest and the traumatic events that followed it:

> The English nobility and gentry were driven out from their possessions. Ashamed to beg, ignorant of how to dig, they and their sons and brothers took refuge in the woods. They robbed and they raided rapaciously, but only when they were lacking in game and other victuals.*

In other words, noble outlawry had come into being. In the chaos of the early twelfth century, after the Conqueror's death, many of the hundred-courts ceased functioning altogether.

*G. Spraggs, *Outlaws & Highwaymen* (Pimlico 200)1, p.24.

THE JURY

Above: The Norman forest was a place where deer had more rights than humans.

BY THE TIME HENRY II CAME TO THE THRONE in 1154 the system of law enforcement had collapsed and he needed to establish a new one. The originality, in fact the sheer brilliance, of what he did almost beggars belief. He invented new forms of law, new forms of court and new forms of legal process from the ground up, creating a legal culture in England that was totally distinct from any other.

Offences committed on highways or during feasts and fairs had been treated as injuries to the King himself, breaches of 'the King's Peace'. This was now extended to all acts of theft and violence; they were now 'crimes' and prosecution no longer depended on victims appealing to their local court for recompense. Crimes were dealt with by the royal court, and this meant that the royal court (or at any rate its judges) would from now on turn up on people's doorsteps and hold trials.

Obviously, Henry had to force people to report criminals rather than relying on victims to do so. In the Assize of Clarendon (1166) he demanded that 12 men in each hundred, and four in each vill (village), swear before the king's sheriff or a justice of the peace, upon oath, whether or not there was anyone charged as a criminal in their district. Anyone they named would be arrested and held in gaol (another novelty) until the king's own travelling judges – the 'justices of the general eyre' – arrived.

This reporting panel was called a jury but it was not a jury as we know it, there to hear evidence of events of which they knew nothing. It was there because its members already knew what had happened, and they were described at the time as witnesses. In fact, for an independent witness to give evidence to them was itself a criminal offence, called 'maintenance'. The jury was intimately connected with royal justice; it had no place in local customary courts. When the king's judges arrived they might ask all manner of questions of the jurors, such as what local customs existed, who the landowners were, whether X had thrown Y off his land and so on and so forth.

When the jury nominated someone for trial there was no weighing of evidence for and against him. Nor was trial by battle an option in the royal courts. If there was plain evidence against the accused (such as possession of stolen goods) or 'if he bear an ill name and have a notoriously bad reputation' he would be held to be guilty, otherwise he would be tried by ordeal ('the judgement of water'). A confession, once made, could not be retracted.

The ordeal of water involved being trussed up and thrown into it. If the accused floated, the water was rejecting him on account of his guilt. If he sank, he was hauled out legally innocent, but:

> … if they have a very bad reputation and are publicly and scandalously decried on the testimony of many lawful men, shall forswear the king's lands, to the effect that within eight days they shall cross the sea unless the wind detain them; and with the first wind which they have thereafter they shall cross the sea, and they shall never return to England unless by the grace of the lord king; and there let them be outlaws, and if they return let them be taken as outlaws.

Right: This picture from the Spanish codex Sophilegium *shows a form of continental justice, the presentation of the accused before a tribunal. The English system, of present-ment and trial by jury, meant more involvement for the community in executing justice.*

The ordeal was soon seen as a rather pointless formality; people did not trust it and anyone who was accused was usually damned whether he passed or failed. In 1215 it was dropped (the church forbade priests to take part, putting an end to the notion that God was judging the case) and a second or 'petty' jury took over to judge the facts in criminal trials. Its members still did not hear evidence; their job was to know what had happened and report accordingly. The penalty for most crimes was hanging.

Since the petty jury had no authority through customary law the accused could refuse to be tried by it; and as the trial jury might well include members of the panel who had named him as a criminal in the first place, this might be quite sensible. He was then held in gaol *'peine et dur'* (which it certainly was) until he agreed to be tried. In the fifteenth century this was felt to be inadequate, so even more severe pressure was applied:

The prisoner shall sit on the cold, bare floor, dressed only in the thinnest of shirts, and pressed with as great a weight of iron as his wretched body can bear. His food shall be a little rotten bread, and his drink cloudy and stinking water. The day on which he eats he shall not drink, and the day on which he has drunk he shall not taste bread. Only superhuman strength survives this punishment beyond the fifth or sixth day.*

*H. Rothwel, ed., *English Historical Documents 1189–1327,* (New York: Oxford University Press, 1975) III, pp. 566–7.

Some people were pressed to death in this way. The advantage of this was that as the accused had not yet been convicted his property still passed on to his next of kin. The crown seized the property and land of a convicted felon.

JUDGEMENT

BY THE MID-THIRTEENTH CENTURY the travelling judges of the general eyre were so overwhelmed with work that they only visited each county every seven years. If an accused person could not find guarantors for his court appearance (the equivalent of bail), he could be held in gaol for a very long time which could prove to be a death sentence in itself.

The problem was eased by establishing a more regular circuit of judges: the assize court, which tried cases twice a year. The function of the royal court had changed. It was no longer an extraordinary tribunal, a court for great men, for great causes, for matters that concerned the king; it had become an ordinary tribunal for the whole realm.

England now had an extraordinary and unique legal structure, entirely invented by an ingenious and desperate monarchy. Its most remarkable feature was the amount of power, however messily administered, it placed in the hands of the local community. English law was quite unlike that on the Continent. There, law was run from above and was based on Church law (canon law) and Roman law. In England, it was totally dependent on a popular understanding of law, and the job of the courts was to enforce 'common law'. The juries who laid accusations and tried cases were made up of people who supposedly knew what had happened. This meant they consisted very largely of people who were legally in various degrees of servitude. This would have a very striking effect on the development of the law. It meant that the ordinary Englishman, even though he was a villein or even a serf, was familiar with the law and the courts, not as a victim but as a participant in the legal process.

Below: Hanging became the likely fate of the man who could not buy his way out of a conviction or demonstrate his literacy and claim church protection. Faced with this prospect, outlawry was a rational choice.

It also meant that people might not be convicted, even in the face of the plainest evidence, if a jury believed a hanging would be unjust. One jury claimed that 'when playing ball the ball had hit an unseen barbers hand so that he cut his customer's throat'. Another declared, apparently with a straight face, that 'the deceased walked backwards into the path of an arrow'.

BOROUGH COURTS

EACH TOWN HAD ITS OWN LAWS AND BOROUGH COURTS, so there too the 'common people' became used to using the processes of the law and developing their own notions of legal fairness. These courts usually dealt with offences such as trespass, property disputes, assault, petty theft and debt – minor matters that the royal courts at first preferred to avoid, if they could.

However, the fourteenth century saw an increase in litigiousness as avenues opened up for people to complain about any perceived wrong, and as the royal courts opened themselves up to appeals of even minor cases from lower courts. The jurisdiction of the boroughs, based on customary law, was thus undermined.

The borough courts, though, were busy with much more specific matters. Certainly, from the time of the Black Death between 1348 and 1349 and the Statute of Labourers in 1351, which attempted to control wages, local authorities regulated the price of all bread and ale that was sold. The courts used the law to enforce these regulations, and imposed their own systems of punishment (town courts could not outlaw criminals), which ranged from mutilation to forcing offending traders in bad goods to eat their produce in public, or have their bad drink poured over them. As with rural juries, maintaining the law was a matter of shame and reputation.

Haggling over basic commodities was illegal, and in most food markets any bargaining was punishable by a fine and holding an auction was seen as a criminal act, held in secret. The 'law of supply and demand', that insists on higher prices at times when goods are in short supply, was regarded as anathema and therefore not allowed to operate in these medieval markets.

It can be argued that the true end of the Middle Ages came in the seventeenth century, when prices were allowed to rise in times of dearth, and the laws of supply and demand took over.

OUTLAWED BY GOSSIP

THE GREAT ACHIEVEMENT OF THE REVOLUTION in English law was that it did not dilute the effectiveness of law as an instrument of royal power, but allied it to the morality and gossip of local communities. This had the paradoxical effect of driving quite a lot of people into outlawry while making outlaws into symbols of righteous disaffection.

> This rhyme was made in the wood, under a laurel tree.
> There sing blackbird and nightingale, and the hawk ranges.
> It was written on parchment to be better remembered,
> And thrown into the highway so that someone should find it.*

This is from a poem of about 1306 which purports to have been written by an outlaw. It gives a fairly clear insight into what might make some men become outlaws.

According to this outlaw poet, living in medieval England was like living in a neighbourhood-watch police state. Getting on badly with the neighbours was likely to end in indictment, with those neighbours forming the jury:

> Ill-disposed people, from whom God keep his pity,
> out of their lying mouths have indicted me
> of wicked robberies and other crimes,
> so that I do not dare to visit my friends…
>
> If these wicked jurors refuse to mend their ways
> so that I may go riding to my country,
> if I can capture them, I'll make their heads fly off.
> I'll not give a penny for all their threatening words.

Even your own servants could denounce you:

> Sir, if I wish to punish my serving-boy
> with a thump or two, to mend his ways,
> he will lay information and have me detained,
> and before I leave jail I must pay a large ransom.

The gossip of the poet's neighbours and servants handed power to the local officer of the crown, a man whose main

*Translated by G. Spraggs from 'Trailbaston', ed. I.S.T Aspin in *Anglo-Norman Political Songs* (Oxford, Blackwell for the Anglo-Norman Text Society, 1953), pp. 67–78.

duties had nothing to do with law enforcement but who would naturally seek to make what he could out of his position:

Forty shillings they take for my ransom,
and the sheriff turns up for his bribe
for not putting me in a deep dungeon.
Now, lords, consider, is this fair?

In the mid-thirteenth century many poor people refused to attend their trials and were therefore labelled 'outlaws'. The wealthy could handle the legal system by paying bribes – it was said they were hanged by the purse, as a poor man would be hanged by the neck. The literate had their own way of escape by pleading 'benefit of clergy' – anyone who could read a line of scripture in Latin was taken to be in holy orders, and was therefore entitled to be turned over to an ecclesiastical court where the severest sentences were usually degradation and the imposition of penances. But a poor man who knew no Latin, and was disliked by his neighbours, needed to hide from a system that would kill him for sure. And then he would hide as a robber:

I have not the goods to arrange a ransom,
but if I were in their bailiwick, I'd be given over to death [I would die in prison]

Whoever began this business
will never amend in his life.
I tell you the truth, there is too much sin in it,
because for fear of prison many will turn robber.

Some will become robbers who never used to be,
who dare not lead a peaceful life for fear of jail;
they lack what it takes to keep them alive each day.
Whoever began this business embarked on a great task.

SANCTUARY

ONE ALTERNATIVE WAS TO RUN LIKE HELL for the nearest church and claim sanctuary. Almost any religious building could offer immunity from arrest for 40 days; one or two select establishments (such as Westminster Abbey and Beverley Minster) could even offer perpetual sanctuary.

The whole system of sanctuary may seem extraordinary to us. Why on earth should the Church be prepared to harbour thieves and murderers and protect them from the law? Actually the same thought struck a lot of people at the time.

In 1402 the Commons complained that the sanctuary associated with the London church and college of St Martins le Grand, just north of St Paul's near Aldersgate, was being abused by 'murderers, traitors and disturbers of the King's peace' who 'hide out by day and at night go forth to commit their murders, treasons, larcenies, robberies and felonies'.* And a century later a Venetian traveller, visiting England in the time of Henry VII, recorded his amazement that so many villains were permitted to conduct organized criminal activities under the shelter of the Church.**

The idea of sanctuary dates back to ancient times, and was vigorously defended by Saxon kings. It may be that in the days of vendetta, when law was a matter to be settled by individual families, the church could offer a cooling-off period during which some accommodation could be arrived at. However, as the law developed such considerations began to appear outdated.

But for much of the Middle Ages, sanctuary was a hotly disputed subject. In some places the area of sanctuary around a given religious building was enormous – the boundaries being clearly marked by special 'sanctuary posts'. For instance, around both Hexham Abbey and Beverley Minster, crosses were erected in a radius of one mile to indicate the area of sanctuary.

To qualify for a permanent position as a Sanctuaryman in Beverley, the accused had to make a full confession of his crime, which was then duly recorded in a register that was kept in the Minster and which still exists. The Beverley records show that the most common perpetrators of crimes of violence were butchers, while the most frequent debtors were builders. *Plus ça change…*

Most sanctuaries, however, could only offer a short-term solution to the average criminal's woes. If he refused to leave at the end of the forty days, he was as good as dead. Any layman who even communicated with him after the forty days were up would be hanged. When he finally emerged, he would be immediately seized and executed on the spot, unless he swore on the Gospels to 'abjure the realm'. In which case he would be issued with a crude sackcloth garment, without a belt, and a wooden cross to carry and he would have to make for the nearest port. There he would have to take the first ship out of England, and for every

*Rot. Parl. III 504.
**A Relation of the Island of England about the year 1500 (Camden Soc., 1847) pp. 34–5.

day he failed to find a passage, he would have to wade into the sea up to his knees.

It's probably the only time that paddling has been used as a form of punishment.

If the criminal could not leave within forty days due to bad weather, then, in theory, they could seek new sanctuary in another local church and start the whole business all over again. However, there is no record of this ever happening. The majority of them just threw away their wooden crosses on a lonely stretch of road and melted away into the woods to take up a new identity or join the many bands of outlaws that plagued the country.

THE GREENWOOD REFUGE

THE OUTLAW POET contrasts the 'false dealing' and 'bad law' from which he is fleeing with the fairness of nature:

> For this reason I shall stay in the woods, in the pleasant shade;
> there is no false dealing there, nor any bad law,
> in the wood of Belregard, where flies the jay,
> and the nightingale sings daily without ceasing.

'Robin Hood and the Monk' begins with a strikingly similar evocation of the woodland idyll:

> In summer, when the woods do shine,
> And leaves be large and long,
> It is full merry in fair forest
> To hear the birdies song,
> To see the deer draw to the dale,
> And leave the hills so high,
> And shelter in the leaves so green,
> Under the green wood tree.

The notion of the 'greenwood' as an Arcadian idyll runs through the outlaw legends. Today we associate it with forests, but 'forest' was a technical term in the Middle Ages and stood for something that was far from idyllic. It is not at all obvious why the 'green wood' should have been described as a place of sanctuary from the law.

Opposite: The forest was just an area of land and trees were not essential. The greenwood was a symbolic landscape, representing freedom from oppression, the very opposite of a forest.

93
Outlaw

ONE OF WILLIAM'S FIRST ACTS as conqueror of England was to create 'The New Forest'. This didn't mean he planted a lot of nice trees so people could enjoy a picnic in the shade. What he was doing was ear-marking a vast tract of land as his own personal hunting-ground. This is what the Norman word 'forest' meant. Whether there were trees or not wasn't really the point. The 'forest' was wherever 'Forest Law' applied, and 'Forest Law' was not something anyone wanted to live under.

Towns and villages could be, and were, destroyed, and every animal and tree became royal property. The forest was administered by royal

officials with draconian powers, who replaced the community as denouncers before the court.

The *Anglo-Saxon Chronicle* says of William:

> He made many deer-parks, and he established laws therewith; so that whosoever slew a hart, or a hind, should be deprived of his eyesight. As he forbade men to kill the harts, so also the boars; and he loved the tall deer as if he were their father. Likewise he decreed respecting the hares that they should go free. His rich men bemoaned it, and the poor men shuddered at it.

The poor men shuddered at it because they were now under a set of laws that had nothing to do with common law, under which William destroyed their towns, villages and churches.

Hunting was an activity reserved by law for the nobility. It was, of course, their main occupation apart from warfare. Nevertheless, no king needed all the designated land for hunting; there was simply too much of it. It formed an alternative kingdom, from which he drew revenues and profits directly. Every monarch from William I to Edward I was denounced at one time or another for extending the royal forest and the abuse of the power associated with the law. This became a perpetual grievance, with kings forced to back off between bouts of afforestation of open country.

Forest law was deeply resented as a form of tyranny, and records show that entire peasant communities living in royal forests were often brought to trial for concealing offenders, protecting them, and refusing to help catch them or take part in investigations. The greenwood of the poems appears to represent a notional, pre-Norman land where officers of the Church and the king were, in effect, foreigners at the mercy of the English, who lived by their own ancient codes. It is a nostalgic fiction, which serves as a standing reproach to those in power. The outlaw poet again:

> You who are indicted, I advise you, come to me,
> to the green wood of Belregard, where there is no entanglement,
> just wild animals and pleasant shade;
> for the common law is too unreliable.

This nostalgia did not mean that outlaws were non-violent. The earliest Robin Hood poetry is very comfortable with violence, and the outlaw poet is hardly a pacifist (he says, 'I was never a killer, of my own will, at least'). But compared with the evil of the corrupt world of public administration, symbolized by the sheriff, the outlaw was a model of propriety.

Opposite: Hunting was reserved for nobility. A medieval illustration of Ovid's description of hare coursing.

SHERIFFS

Above: Breamore Church in the New Forest, a Saxon church serving a community that suddenly found itself incorporated into a Royal forest.

THE REAL SHERIFFS OF NOTTINGHAM lived up to the one immortalized in the Robin Hood tales pretty well. Philip Mark, sheriff from 1209 to 1224, was celebrated for robbery, false arrest, unjustly throwing people off their property and persistent attacks on local landed interests, both secular and ecclesiastical. Henry de Faucemberg, sheriff from November 1318 to November 1319, and again between 1323 and 1325, was so in debt that he owed over £285 to the king and had to face charges of extortion. John de Oxenford, sheriff from 1334 to 1339, was accused in 1341 of 'illegal purveyance, abusing his authority in regard to the county gaol and its prisoners, as well as various extortions'. He didn't show up in court and was himself outlawed.

Another sheriff, Sir Robert Ingram, was an ally of the Coterel gang, notorious fourteenth-century bandits who terrorized Derbyshire and Nottinghamshire, including Sherwood Forest, from 1328 to 1332. These were no common criminals. They were 'gentlemen' like the Folvilles, probably the younger sons of landed gentry, who, when they were not committing crimes such as robbery, extortion and murder, often for money, were serving in Edward III's wars in Scotland and France while holding public office as bailiffs and even Members of Parliament. The Coterels created their own framework of social roles, with lieutenants, recruits, organization, division of labour, maintainers and laws; one of their lieutenants, Roger de Sauvage, referred to the gang as 'la compagnie sauvage'. James Coterel was accused in one indictment of recruiting 20 members in the Peak District and Sherwood Forest.

NOBLE OUTLAWS

THE COTEREL GANG INDICATES THE EXISTENCE of a different kind of outlaw. There were many robber gangs that consisted largely of men of good birth who had no way of making a living except during wars. This was, to some extent, the consequence of a system of inheritance that passed everything to the eldest son. Outlaws were therefore often linked directly into the governing class. One of the accomplices in the Folvilles' kidnapping of Richard de Willoughby was Sir Robert de Vere, constable of Rockingham Castle in Northamptonshire. The castle was a base for armed gangs who came and went after dark. No-one bringing provisions to it was allowed to enter, to prevent them knowing who was there.

Some of these outlaws threatened to use violence to right the evils of bad government, under the banner of some kind of alternative rule. A letter from one gang leader has survived from the time of Edward III. Addressed to Richard de Snaweshill, parson of the church at Huntington in Yorkshire, and written in French in 1336, it commands in the name of 'Lionel, King of the Rout of Raveners' that he remove a priest from his office in the vicarage of Burton Agnes (evidently a relative of de Snaweshill) and then replace him with the man chosen for the job by the abbot of St Mary's:

> And if you do not do this, we make our avow, first to God and then to the King of England and to our own crown that... we shall hunt you down, even if we have to come to Coney Street in York to do it... Given at our Castle of the North Wind, in the Green Tower, in the first year of our reign.*

*M. Keen, *The Outlaws of Medieval Legend*, Routledge, p. 200.

There are plenty of examples of robbers coming from noble and semi-noble families. It appears that the career of outlaw was perhaps seen as a legitimate one for a well-born, high-spirited younger son – or a cast-off serving man of ambition. Ballads about outlaws imply it was not fair that death on the gallows should be the reward for intrepid and sometimes prankish feats – especially if the victims were mere usurers, monks or tax-gatherers.

This may be linked to another unique feature of England in the Middle Ages: the fact that knighthood was not hereditary. Primogeniture had become established over much of western Europe in the eleventh and twelfth centuries, and from the thirteenth century knights had to offer 'proofs of nobility' – show they were the elder sons of knights. This meant there was a universal younger son problem, but only in England could those younger sons earn a knighthood.

Moreover, only in England was knighthood a potential career for all comers – only there could a servant or the son of a tradesman win the spurs of military command.

This was possible because the feudal levy only produced a militia who served for a limited number of days a year and did not have to travel overseas. But England was an island kingdom fighting long campaigns overseas. This is why landowners were allowed to pay a tax rather than serve. Their service was not very useful. It made more sense to create knights from the ranks of landless men who needed pay. So England, more than anywhere else, offered wartime careers of status to landless men.

But what was to happen to these knights, esquires and hopefuls between wars? They had no land to go to. A life of bold robbery became, in practice, a necessity for men who had no living of their own, and who had failed to make much out of the last war but were hopeful of doing so from the next.

At least until the mid-fifteenth century (and the end of the Hundred Years War), outlaw robbers were, in fact, a national resource and kings depended on them. This explains some of the ideas behind the outlaw ballads, including the fact that Robin Hood stories often end 'happily' with him being released from outlawry by the king. This is not particularly fanciful. Many outlaws were pardoned, usually in return for fighting in the army or helping the king in some other way. These acts of amnesty were necessary to stop the number of outlaws increasing endlessly. And the men involved were important recruits to the army and administration. England needed its bold outlaws. It needed them so much that they could buy their pardons, and be recruited into respectability.

Not all of them remained respectable. In 1335, the outlaw gangster Nicholas Coterel was made the queen's bailiff for the High Peak District of Derbyshire. Within two years he was accused of interfering with tax collection and 'having been guilty of many other oppressions by the pretext of his office', but that is hardly surprising. Similarly, when two outlawed associates of the Coterels, Sir William de Chetulton and Sir John de Legh, were pardoned and then commissioned, together with James Stafford, a well-known gang leader, to capture two other robbers it was only a matter of months before they were in a Nottingham gaol accused of attempted rape. Both of them subsequently served their king in his Scottish wars: in 1336 they were instructed to recruit archers in Cheshire and lead them north into Berwickshire.

It was the same story with the surviving Folville brothers. After 16 years of criminal activity they were all pardoned. One of them, Eustace, was even knighted for his 'good services' to the king. But in the course of only six years he received no less than three more pardons – two of them because he had fought against the king's enemies – for crimes that included murder, rape and armed robbery.

England depended on its bold outlaws. And its admiration of these men would echo throughout its history, with the forest ultimately transferred to colonial frontiers where Billy the Kid, Ned Kelly and a hundred other lawless men would inherit this strange tradition.

CHAPTER FOUR

THE MEDIEVAL MONK is an emblem of un-worldliness. Shut away in his cloister, he dedicated himself to a life of prayer, hard work, poverty, self-denial and silence. He cut himself off from the temptations of the ordinary world in order to give himself to God. The life of a medieval monk was literally 'out of this world'. The story of the monastic life should be uneventful from beginning to end. But of course it isn't. Monks couldn't totally cut themselves off from the material world, even when they wanted to.

And there were times when they didn't want to. On the morning of Sunday 18 October 1327, for example, the monks in the abbey of Bury St Edmunds ended their prayers, filed out through the abbey's crenellated gate and proceeded to the parish church. This was full of men, women and children. The monks threw off their habits – revealing that some of them wore armour under their robes – and burst into the church. They seized a number of citizens by force and dragged them back to the abbey as prisoners.

Above and opposite: Images of the unworldly monk – harvesting wheat and felling a tree from Gregory the Great's Moralia in Job. *Produced for the Abbey of Citeaux in 1111, this illuminated text portrays an ideal of monastic life.*

Sometime later the townsfolk assembled at the abbey to demand the prisoners' release. The monks replied with a hail of missiles, killing a large number of people. Later in the day the town bells summoned a larger party of armed men including aldermen, burgesses, a parson and 28 chaplains, who all took a solemn oath to live or die together. They then set fire to the gates and stormed the abbey.

Obviously no-one in Bury St Edmunds associated these monks with the contemplative life. Monks were the constant target of satire and lampoon in fourteenth-century England. To appreciate what had gone so badly wrong at Bury, we must understand what had happened to the monastic ideal.

THE START OF MONASTICISM

THE IDEA OF LIVING IN A COMMUNITY cut off from your fellow men in order to worship God didn't really get going in the West until around AD 500, when a Roman nobleman by the name of Benedict got fed up with life in the big city. Rome was far too full of people enjoying good food, drink and sex for his taste. So he took a servant and settled in the countryside where, unfortunately, his reputation for being able miraculously to mend broken pottery started to attract the crowds.

So he sought out a reasonably inaccessible cave halfway up a cliff face, with no modern conveniences and no plumbing. A monk from one of the nearby religious establishments came every day to lower a basket of food down to him. And Benedict made sure there was no oyster sauce or deep-fried wontons in his daily picnic – indeed, he didn't want anything he could actually enjoy. As far as Benedict was concerned, God placed us in this world to give us the opportunity to refrain from enjoying our brief time here, in order to concentrate on thanking him for placing us in this world.

It was a philosophy that seems to have appealed to a surprising number of people, and news of Benedict's sanctity spread throughout the region. He ended up founding his own monastery. There he wrote his famous Rule (or set of regulations) which became the foundation stone of the monastic movement in the Middle Ages.

As far as he was concerned, he was founding a community where men worked and prayed 'for the service of the Lord', and he didn't want it to be too strict. The Rule states: 'We hope to introduce nothing harsh or burdensome.' However, Benedict was a Roman patriarch, and he put a great emphasis on obedience. And not just any old obedience – it had to be instantaneous, unquestioning and done with a good grace.

And don't think you could get away with just putting a good face on it:

> For if the disciple obeys with an ill will and murmurs, not necessarily with his lips but simply in his heart, then even though he fulfil the command yet his work will not be acceptable to God, who sees that his heart is murmuring. And, far from gaining a reward for such work as this, he will incur the punishment due to murmurers…

As well as disliking 'murmuring' Benedict wasn't a fan of laughter: 'As for coarse jests, and idle words, or words that move to laughter, these we condemn everywhere with a perpetual ban.' He also laid down that monks should not speak except when given permission to do so by their superior. And to avoid what he called 'the vice of private ownership', they should own nothing, have no private possessions, and beds were to be examined frequently by the abbot to make sure they hadn't hidden anything.

Otherwise, Benedict's Rule gives detailed instructions for the monastic community – the number, order and choice of psalms and the hours of offices, the correction and punishment of monks, the way they are to sleep, what and how much they should eat (no meat unless they were very ill) and even what sort of person the cellarer should be. If a monk went on a journey he was forbidden to relate what he might have seen or heard outside the monastery, which Benedict saw as a hermetically sealed, self-contained unit.

The main ways in which the Rule can be said to avoid anything 'harsh or burdensome' is that, unlike some regimes, it did not prescribe a starvation diet or demand sleep deprivation. It also allowed monks to wear clothes appropriate to the climate – though no mention is made of underpants, an important omission, as we shall see later.

For the next half millennium, Benedict's Rule was disseminated throughout the monasteries of western Europe – first under the aegis of Pope Gregory the Great and then under Charlemagne. By the eleventh century his form of monasticism had a virtual monopoly of religious houses, but whether he would have approved of the way his Rule was being interpreted is quite another matter, as a would-be monk by the name of Herluin found out.

HERLUIN BECOMES A MONK

HERLUIN WAS A NORMAN WARRIOR who, at the age of 40, decided he was getting too old for the business and became a conscientious objector. Besides, he had been told that he would go to hell if he killed people. He determined to trade in his sword for a prayer book and become a monk, and in 1031 he walked into a monastery to see what it was like. As his biographer, Gilbert Crispin, records, he got quite a surprise.

After offering a prayer he approached the door of the cloister with great reverence and nervousness, as if it were the gate of Paradise: he was very eager to find out what was the way of life of the monks, and what were their customs. He saw that they were all far from observing the serious way of life which the monkish life demands; he was distressed, now completely uncertain what kind of life he should choose. At this point the warden of the monastery saw him entering and, thinking him to be a thief, hit him as hard as he could on the neck and dragged him out of the door by his hair…
Vita Herluini

Herluin had gone to the trouble of teaching himself to read and write, and was not to be put off so easily. He tried again:

Next Christmas he went for the same purpose to another, better-known monastery. As the brethren went out in festive procession on this solemn day, Herluin saw the monks smile at the lay folk all around with unbecoming familiarity, delighting in showing off their lavish ornamentation, and as they got to the door, quarrelling noisily as to who should go first. One monk punched his fellow who was jostling to get in, and then laid him flat on his back on the ground. Such, as we have said, were still the barbaric manners which were common throughout Normandy.

Vita Herluini

Herluin ended up building his own small monastery. The local bishop ordained him as a monk and made him abbot, so his monastic career was obviously off to an excellent start. He lived as he thought a monk ought, eating one light meal a day, wearing old, black woollen robes and combining hard physical work with regular prayer according to the monastic rules laid down by St Benedict. He soon attracted an enthusiastic little community, and had to build a bigger monastery at the village of Le Bec-Hellouin, southwest of Rouen in Normandy, to accommodate it.

It may seem surprising that an ex-warrior like Herluin should take the strict observance of Benedict's precepts so seriously. But, strange though it may seem, the activities of monks – cloistered and cut off from the world though they may have been – were regarded as an essential back-up to the Norman military machine.

SAVING THE SOULS OF FIGHTING MEN

THE PROBLEM GOES BACK to that inconvenient Commandment: 'Thou shalt not kill.' In the eleventh century this was taken to mean what it said: Thou shalt not kill. And just because you were having a war was no excuse. This was a bit awkward if you happened to be a fighting man, professionally

Left: Knights depended on monks to pray for their souls and also to redeem them from the divine penalties incurred by their acts of violence.

engaged in the business of breaking that commandment in particular (amongst many others).

Like most people, however, warriors had every confidence in the power of prayer. They were also convinced that the purer and simpler a person's life was, the more likely God was to listen favourably to them. Since monks were supposed to live the purest and simplest of lives their prayers were seen as a hotline to God, and they provided an essential service for the Norman armies – saving warriors' souls once the fighting was over.

The soul of a tenth- or eleventh-century fighting man would not be easy to save. It required the strenuous effort of a significant number of monks to pray him out of damnation. Homicide in a public war, even at the command of a legitimate ruler, required doing penance for 40 days and abstention from church. William the Conqueror, with overall responsibility for some 10,000 deaths, needed (if anyone were ever to do the arithmetic, which they did not) about 1,100 years of serious religious effort. He would not have finished yet – not until 2162.

After the Battle of Hastings each Norman soldier was told to do 120 days' penance for every man he had killed, which would have created even greater problems. But of course the Church was ever willing to subcontract the work, at a price. If William's penance was split between a couple of hundred monks, his soul could be cleansed in less than six years. He founded an abbey at the site of the battle. He founded another at Barking in Essex; and another at Selby in Yorkshire (he had to kill a lot of people in Yorkshire). And he and his wife and sons, perhaps feeling insecure, gave a great deal more money and land to a great many other churches and abbeys.

In fact, by the time William died, 26 per cent of all the land in England belonged to the Church.

THE MONASTIC CATCH-22

IT BECAME THE CUSTOM for rich people and fighting men like the Norman soldiers, whose ways of life put their souls in such great jeopardy, to pay monks to do the praying they were too busy to do for themselves. This had one profound effect: prayer became a commodity. It gained a commercial value and this was eventually to prove the undoing of the whole system.

The essential thing about monks was their religious way of life – the fact that they lived lives of poverty, simplicity and devotion. The snag was

*Left: The church's
success in winning
substantial gifts from
lay patrons was a
direct result of the
compelling way it
explained what
would happen to
them after death.*

that the poorer, simpler and more devout a particular institution was, the
keener the rich and violent were to shower money and land on it to
assuage their consciences.

    Thus the poorer, simpler and more devout a monastery was in its
beginnings, the more likely it was to get rich and powerful quickly. And
once it became rich and powerful it was no longer, by definition, poor and
was therefore less likely to remain simple and devout.

THERE WAS ALSO A BUILT-IN TENDENCY for the monastic movement to accumulate power. Even when the rulers of monasteries were ostensibly confronting the worldliness of their institutions, they simply couldn't help becoming powers in their own right…

When Herluin was building his monastery at Bec, for example, a rather celebrated Italian scholar, by the name of Lanfranc, turned up. Lanfranc had initially come to Normandy because he had heard that there was a dearth of learning in the region and thought he would be able to 'gain wealth and honour' there. He then decided to move into the area of religion. Perhaps still in pursuit of wealth and honour, he decided to seek out the poorest and most despised monastery he could find – which happened to be the ex-soldier's humble establishment at Bec.

Herluin, as someone with plenty of fighting experience but no book learning, welcomed the famous scholar with open arms, and gave him special treatment in the monastery. This bred envy amongst the other monks, and Lanfranc soon announced that he was off to become a hermit. Herluin dissuaded him by offering him the post of prior.

Lanfranc now started rebuilding the monastery's abbey in a more substantial manner, and became less interested in hermitic ways and rather more interested in his developing friendship with William, Duke of Normandy – the future William the Conqueror.

Lanfranc seems to have helped to persuade the pope to back the duke's invasion of England, and after the Conquest William repaid him by installing him as archbishop of Canterbury. The 70-year-old Lanfranc was the spiritual edge of the Conqueror's sword. He imposed Norman abbots, bishops and forms of worship on Anglo-Saxon churches and abbeys. His aim was to obliterate the distinct Anglo-Saxon religious tradition, and he removed all but two of England's saints from the English Church's calendar.

This meant their shrines were no longer in operation. English saints were replaced by foreign ones who took over places of worship just as foreign secular lords had taken over land. The shrine of St Cuthbert at Durham, for example, was eliminated in 1072 (his remains having been evacuated by fleeing monks in 1066) and replaced with a Benedictine priory staffed by reliable monks, and a new Norman castle. The new Norman bishop of Durham was Walcher of Lorraine, who paid William £400 to be made Earl of Bamborough. He lived in the castle as prince-bishop, with the right to raise an army and levy taxes, and was protected

Opposite: For the prince-bishops of Durham, the castle came first and the cathedral somewhat later. As a result, the Anglo-Saxon monks who had lived there became refugees.

by a gang of thugs. The bishop and his cronies were killed in a popular uprising in 1080.

All the while Lanfranc, an Italian archbishop in the service of a Norman warlord, wrote letters about 'we English' and 'our island'. It was presumably in the role of proprietor that he stripped the English Church of its valuables, sending its great works of art and books to France, Normandy and Rome, and melting down its gold and silver.

Of course, all this was done in the name of 'reform'. Lanfranc was able to accuse the English Church of being as sloppy in its ways as Herluin had found the Church in Normandy to be. There were only about a thousand monks in all England, and men in holy orders were even allowed to marry. That, of course, was stopped quite abruptly. The archbishop imposed more discipline on his monks, and encouraged the Norman victors to pay for new abbeys – which were far more glamorous than Anglo-Saxon ones.

The reality was that the Church was synonymous with power, and Lanfranc set an example of prelate power that would retain its force for centuries. Even William bowed to it. He conceded that the Church should be able to hold its own courts for its own people, and that monks and priests would not be subject to royal jurisdiction.

It was an act of power, not piety, for Lanfranc to appoint the totally illiterate Herfast as bishop of East Anglia. The man was a standing joke in Normandy, but a useful thug in England. An even more useful thug was Tousain, the man Lanfranc installed as abbot of Glastonbury. The monks there sang Gregorian chants that had been introduced by St Augustine when he evangelized the southern English, but Tousain told them to use new ones approved by Rome. He stationed archers inside the abbey to ensure obedience. When the monks began to sing their beautiful old chant, and it swelled to echo from the vaulted ceiling, the archers shot 21 of them.

But, although Lanfranc was clearly a man deeply interested in power, he always accepted the overlordship of Duke William – now King of England. He never challenged the king's right to appoint archbishops.

There was another monastic movement, however, that was not prepared to submit to any lay power.

THE CLUNIACS AND POWER

Opposite: The jaws of Hell – best avoided.

IN 940, DUKE WILLIAM OF AQUITAINE decided that by paying for monks to do their monkish thing in his old hunting lodge at Cluny in Burgundy he would buy himself a place in heaven. The duke noted with engaging candour: 'Although I myself am unable to despise all things, nevertheless by receiving despisers of this world, whom I believe to be righteous, I may receive the reward of the righteous.'

The problem was, as Duke William saw it, that even when proper godly men had been selected they needed to be protected from violent men like himself while they were quietly praying for his soul. He decided

that the best solution was a hearty curse on anyone who messed with the monks. They should know they would go to hell: 'Let him incur the wrath of almighty God; and let God remove him from the land of the living and wipe out his name from the book of life… let him incur everlasting damnation.'

Well, that was a start. But, on reflection, a bit more deterrence might be needed. There should also be some immediately obvious punishment: 'In case it seems to human eyes that he is passing through the present world with impunity, let him actually experience in his own body the torments of future damnation… his members putrefying and swarming with vermin…'

Yes, that's better. But perhaps still not quite enough to keep these poor helpless monks safe. How about calling on the pope to inflict some additional punishment: 'And let him, unless he come to his senses, have the key-keeper of the whole hierarchy of the Church as an enemy and one who will refuse him entrance to the blessed paradise.'

Oh, sod it. When you come down to it, there's probably no substitute for earthly power: 'But as far as the worldly law is concerned, he shall be required, the judicial power compelling him to pay a hundred pounds of gold to those he has harmed; and his attempted attack, being frustrated, shall have no effect at all.'

There, that should do the trick.

William of Aquitaine had made his abbey at Cluny completely independent of any landowner, thus ensuring that no feudal overlord was in a position to install their own chap as abbot. This had been a very deliberate move, and was the reason for all these protective curses. When the abbots of Cluny later began setting up other 'Cluniac' houses they decided to scrap the Benedictine rule that provided for the independence of each abbot. Instead, abbots of Cluny exercised absolute authority over all the houses, whose regimes were subject to inspection by the mother monastery.

Of course, the abbots claimed this centralization was simply in order to control standards of monastic piety, but it also created a convenient power base for anyone interested in wielding power… and what happened next was inevitable. When a Cluniac monk called Hildebrand became pope in 1073, it became an article of faith that Cluny's independence from secular power should apply to the whole Church. This was not, of course, a two-way street. The Church, in the Pope's view, for its part should be able to tell Lords, Kings and Emperors how to behave.

Lanfranc's successor, Anselm (who had also been one of Herluin's monks at Bec), flatly refused to be invested as archbishop of Canterbury by anyone except the pope, and then refused to accept bishops and abbots nominated by Henry I.

Eventually an agreement was signed between the king and the pope, according to which Henry and all other secular overlords lost the power to appoint bishops and abbots. The English Church was now a department of the universal or Roman Church, which was no longer just an expression or an idea but a real working organization with its own law, courts and rights over property. It was also growing: the number of monks in England rose from about 1,000 in 1066 to 13,000 by 1215. The church was assertive, confident and persuasive. It would be hard to distinguish how much of this growth came from idealism and commitment, and how much from the opportunities the Church offered for career advancement and an alternative life from farming and fighting.

The new power of the Church inevitably went together with increased splendour, wealth and political authority. Monks were now part of a visibly powerful apparatus that was very much in the world. Which, of course, was the exact opposite of what Lanfranc's original reform was meant to achieve.

MONKS WITHOUT UNDERPANTS

EVEN AT THE END OF THE ELEVENTH CENTURY the already increasing worldliness of the Cluniacs and other orders had begun to leave a niche in the market for another 'back to basics' form of monasticism.

In 1098 a 70-year-old monk, Robert of Molesme, founded an abbey at Citeaux in Burgundy, a few kilometres east of the great wine-producing village of Nuits-Saint-Georges. The Cistercian order which he established was intended to be a form of Benedictinism that was stricter and more primitive than anything then existing. A few years later the abbey was invaded by a fanatical 22-year-old called Bernard, and 30 of his relatives (many of whom were soldiers, some married), who effectively took over.

Bernard believed in fasting, sleep deprivation and a life of physical suffering. The abbot (then an Englishman) put up with it for two years and then, in 1115, dispatched Bernard to set up a monastery in the most desolate spot he could. Bernard came close to perishing but Clairvaux, the abbey he founded in Champagne, became the most influential in Europe.

Bernard was very scathing about the Cluniacs. He didn't like their

architecture: 'The immense height of their churches, their immoderate length, their superfluous breadth, costly polishings and strange designs that, while they attract the eye of the worshipper, hinder his attention.' And he didn't like their leader, Peter the Venerable: 'He commends gluttonous feasting; he damns frugality; voluntary poverty he calls misery; fasts, vigils, silence, and manual work he calls madness.'

And he didn't like their diet:

Course after course is brought in. Only meat is lacking and to compensate for this two huge servings of fish are given. You might have thought that the first was sufficient, but even the recollection of it vanishes once you have set to on the second. The cooks prepare everything with such skill and cunning that the four or five dishes already consumed are no hindrance to what is to follow and the appetite is not checked by satiety… The selection of dishes is so exciting that the stomach does not realize that it is being over-taxed.

Right: A fifteenth-century illustration showing a procession of Cistercian monks. The simple modesty of their abbey may look rather grand to cynical eyes.

The Cistercians' strict discipline emphasized fasts and vigils, manual labour and a vegetarian diet. Bernard himself was so austere that his excessive fasting created a dreadful stomach condition, with the result that he smelt so bad that people often could not bear to be in his company; there was even a special place where he could be sick during monastic services.

Unlike other monks, Cistercians wore plain, undyed wool – for which reason they were known as the 'White Monks'. The return to heroic monasticism meant that they ate only the coarsest wheat bread, and were ordered to avoid coloured glass in their chapel, and gold and silver on the altar.

And they were not allowed to wear underpants. St Benedict had not mentioned them in his list of permitted clothing for monks, so the Cistercians would have no truck with the evil things – much to the amusement of a number of their contemporaries. Some called it 'bare-bottomed piety' and Walter Map, the twelfth-century author, wit and foe of the Cistercians, suggested they shunned underpants 'to preserve coolness in that part of the body, lest sudden heats provoke unchastity'.

The Cistercians also insisted on a plain liturgy – which allowed more time for things like manual labour. Aelred, the abbot of Rievaulx in Yorkshire, mocked the Cluniac monks for deliberately making their services attractive and inviting a lay audience to attend them:

> To what purpose, I ask you, is the terrible snorting of bellows, more like the clap of thunder than the sweetness of a voice? Why that swelling and swooping of the voice? … Sometimes you see a man with his mouth open as if he were breathing his last breath, not singing but threatening silence, as it were, by ridiculous interpretation of the melody into snatches. Now he imitates the agony of the dying or the swooning of persons in pain. In the meantime his whole body is violently agitated by histrionic gesticulations – contorted lips, rolling eyes, hunching shoulders – and drumming fingers keep in time with every single note. And this ridiculous dissipation is called religious observance… Meanwhile ordinary folk stand there awe-struck, stupefied, marvelling at the din of bellows, the humming of chimes and the harmony of pipes. But they regard the saucy gestures of the singers and the alluring variation and dropping of the voices with considerable jeering and snickering, until you would think they had come, not into an oratory, but to a theatre, not to pray but to gawk…
> Aelred, *Mirror of Charity**

McMONASTICISM

CURIOUSLY FOR A MOVEMENT that was formed specifically to get back to the basics of the Benedictine vision, the Cistercians soon did away with that awkward principle of St Benedict's regarding the independence of each

---

* Aelred, *Mirror of Charity*, bk. II, ch. 23, trans. E. Connor, cited by Julie Kerr in 'An Essay on Cistercian Liturgy in Yorkshire' in the University of Sheffield's Cistercians in Yorkshire project.

abbey. The Cistercian order became the most centrally controlled of all the monastic orders.

Conformity was the name of the game. Under Bernard's eagle eye Cistercians all wore the same clothes, ate the same food, read the same books and lived in architecturally identical buildings. It was said that a blind monk from Scotland could easily find his way around a Cistercian monastery in Scandinavia. There was also an 'annual general meeting' which every Cistercian abbot was obliged to attend.

This was less a movement than a successful franchise – a sort of McMonasticism. In their first 11 years, the founders of McDonald's saw their chain expand to over 100 restaurants. By the time Bernard died in 1153, the Cistercian order had founded 343 abbeys in western Europe. As Conrad of Eberbarch put it: 'Like a great lake whose waters pour out through a thousand streams, gathering impetus from their rapids, the new monks went forth from Citeaux to people the West.'

Bernard himself envisaged the order as an army. He saw his monks as 'soldiers of Christ', the spiritual equivalent of Crusaders. Bernard of Clair-vaux was himself the most effective pro-crusade preacher of his generation.

In 1131 he wrote to Henry II of England:

In your land there is an outpost of my Lord and your Lord, an outpost he has preferred to die for than to lose. I have proposed to occupy it and am sending men from my army who will, if it is not displeasing to you, claim it, recover it and restore it with a strong hand.

THE CISTERCIANS IN ENGLAND

IN 1132, TWELVE MONKS FROM CLAIRVAUX arrived in a desolate part of Yorkshire – 'thick-set with thorns, fit rather to be the lair of wild beasts than the home of men'. To begin with the monks had to live in wooden huts and suffered terrible hardship. But whether or not they were motivated by the desire to practise heroic monasticism, they were actually part of a deliberately structured business plan.

The choice of Rievaulx had been carefully made. There had been a reconnaissance party, seeking out somewhere 'far from the concourse of man', in part because this fulfilled the Cistercian quest for the 'desert' but also because the Cistercians were experts at exploiting land, both for sheep farming and for mineral resources such as iron and lead. All this was envisaged right from the outset. The abbey also had to be near water, a plentiful supply of timber and a quarry for stone. Rievaulx was perfect: the

river Rye ran through the valley, and was even diverted in order to create enough space for buildings; stone quarries were just four miles away.

This was the first of many Cistercian houses. Within 20 years there were an astonishing 50 Cistercian abbeys in Britain. The original, small wooden structures at Rievaulx were just phase one of a business plan that looked forward years, and envisaged the transformation of landscape, the acquisition of land, deforestation and the exploitation of mineral resources.

The great critic of the Cistercians, Walter Map, took a cynical view of their entrepreneurship:

It is prescribed to them that they are to dwell in desert places, and desert places they do assuredly either find or make… Because their rule does not allow them to govern parishioners, they proceed to raze villages, they overthrow churches, and turn out parishioners… Those upon whom comes an invasion of Cistercians may be doomed to a lasting exile.

Walter was an itinerant justice, and he always exempted Cistercians from his oath to do justice to all men since, he said, 'It was absurd to do justice to those who are just to none'. This was not a joke; Map's reports of Cistercian atrocities are extraordinary. For example, he says that the monks of Byland once wanted land belonging to a knight who would not give it up to them. One night they entered his house, 'muffled up and armed with swords and spears', and murdered him and his family. A relative, hearing of the deaths, arrived three days later to find that all the buildings and enclosures had disappeared and in their place was a well-ploughed field.*

The Cistercians refused to accept land on normal feudal terms. They insisted they could only accept it as 'fee alms', which meant that instead of having to provide lords and kings with labour or fighting men they had to pray for them.

Pretty soon the Cistercians owned so much land they simply could not throw everyone off it, so they started collecting rents and tithes (Church taxes) from the lay folk around, and before long they were rolling in money. Their abbeys were huge commercial enterprises.

The Cistercians were natural businessmen. At Fountains Abbey in Yorkshire they turned wool production into a major money-spinner, breeding a super-sheep that produced the highest-quality wool in Europe. By the end of the century they were responsible for most of the wool exported from England. Meanwhile, at neighbouring Rievaulx the monks moved into heavy industry, developing mining and iron-smelting technology that put them way ahead of their time.

* Edward Coleman, 'Nasty Habits – Satire and the Medieval Monk', *History Today*, volume 43, issue 6, June 1993, pp. 36–42.

Of course there was a problem with this engagement with the business world. It wasn't what monks were supposed to do. Benedict's Rule instructed them 'to become a stranger to the world's ways'. They were supposed to be busy praying for the souls of the people who had endowed them, and working at modest self-sufficiency, not running blast furnaces or moving into the wool trade.

Above: Fountains Abbey, Yorkshire, with the monks' refectory in the foreground.

119
Monk

120
Monk

Moreover, according to the Rule of St Benedict, monks were supposed to do all their own chores and not employ servants. But the Cistercians had a genius for interpreting the Rule. They simply invented a new class of monks, whom they called 'lay brothers'.

These were usually illiterate peasants who worked as servants. Sometimes they were the very peasants the Cistercians had turned off the land they now occupied. In every respect lay brothers were second-class citizens. They weren't really monks at all – it was a convenient fiction. They weren't allowed to eat with the other – 'choir' – monks, or pray with the choir monks, or even mix with the choir monks. They were there simply to do the menial chores the choir monks ought to have been doing but wanted to avoid. In Fountains Abbey, for example, a wall kept the lay brothers and monks separate.

Opposite: The lay brothers' refectory, Fountains Abbey; a contrast with the grander architecture of other parts of a Cistercian abbey.

TURNING FAITH INTO MONEY

ABBEYS SIMPLY COULD NOT HELP BUT become huge financial machines. Abbeys never married and never died, so that their land never came onto the market, and were outside the medieval merry-go-round of land redistribution through violent death and confiscation of estates. There were occasional exceptions, such as Rievaulx being plundered by the Scots after they defeated Edward II's army in 1322, but such misfortunes were rare.

Given the natural processes that poured money towards abbeys like rain running down gulleys, it took some kind of special genius for an abbot to run into financial trouble, but it happened with impressive frequency. There was a tendency to spend ever more lavishly, to invest ever more grandly, and to finance these noble activities by borrowing money against future income, for example, selling wool from their sheep years in advance at a discount. It was a form of gambling, of course, but with God on their side what could go wrong? Sheep murrain for a start. In the 1280s, Rievaulx was unable to deliver the wool it had pre-sold and was driven into the medieval equivalent of bankruptcy. It was taken into Royal protection, under the supervision of the Bishop of Durham.

With forward contracts concentrating their minds, many abbots became more concerned with the activities of the large numbers of lay brothers than anything else. They became in effect Managing Directors who tended to regard the 'choir monks' as rather a burden on the place, even if they were from more socially acceptable families.

They needed to find ways to improve their cash flow, and that was

the attraction of the pilgrim business. In the 11th century, sinners were instructed that a visit to a particular church, and the bestowal of pious gifts upon it, would mean they would be let off their penance. The number of qualifying churches steadily grew until there were thousands of pilgrimage churches. And the reward changed, in the 13th century, from a remission of penance to a release from God's punishment, whether in this life or in purgatory. In the 14th century pilgrim indulgences were extended even further, negating guilt itself and giving the opportunity of acquiring an indulgence for the souls of those already in purgatory.

What's more, if you decided not to take the pilgrimage you could achieve the same result by paying the Church the money you would have spent if you had gone. The Holy Grail of the tourist trade had been found: 'Don't bother to visit, just send your money!'

The system meant that abbeys, cathedrals and churches were in competition with each other to attract the most pilgrims, and there were several ways of doing this. The first was to offer indulgences and pardons for pilgrims. Some churches ran 'bargains of the month'. The monastery at Shene, in Surrey, for example, offered the following in the fifteenth century:

ITEM: On the Feast of St John the Baptist whoever comes to the monastery and devoutly says a Pater-noster shall have ninety days of pardon…

ITEM: Whoever comes to the said monastery on the Feast of St Paul the Apostle, says one Pater-noster and one Ave Maria, shall have one hundred days of pardon…

ITEM: On the Feast of Mary Magdalene whoever comes to the said monastery shall have one hundred days of pardon granted by Bishop Stafford, Archbishop of Canterbury…

ITEM: On the feast of St Thomas the Apostle and in the Feast of St Michael the Archangel they shall have three years and forty days of pardon…

But the chief way to attract holy tourism was to possess a famous relic. This could be anything from an object belonging to a saint, or touched by them, to a bit of their skeleton. Such an object was regarded as a contact point between earth and heaven that radiated miraculous power. Churches and abbeys did everything possible to get hold of sacred relics for people to visit.

Saints' relics were a sufficiently important source of revenue for Anselm, Lanfranc's successor as archbishop of Canterbury, to reinstate the English saints; they were, after all, far more likely to draw a good crowd.

A new shrine was constructed for Cuthbert at Durham, and his remains were restored there.

At Canterbury, St Thomas Becket's tomb in the cathedral was also to become a major draw – more particularly, the saint's head. You could see where the sword had split his skull in two! Visitors could also marvel at the sight of 'Aaron's rod', 'some of the stone upon which the Lord stood just before He ascended into heaven', 'some of the Lord's table on which the Last Supper was eaten', and even 'some of the very clay out of which God fashioned Adam'. There was also some of the Virgin Mary's knitting – well, weaving to be exact.

THE CHURCH COMMERCIALS

MONASTERIES WERE TRADING OPERATIONS, and communities even founded their own towns to handle the trade. This brings us back to Bury St Edmunds and its war between the monks and the townspeople. The town belonged to the abbey, which had benefited so much from various kings that it also owned the entire county of West Suffolk. The abbots built or expanded the town of Bury St Edmunds, and controlled its commercial life. Every business transaction involved a cut for the monks – whether a tradesman ran a barge on the river, a stall in the market, sold fish or supplied building materials. The abbey administered justice and pocketed the fines it took. It ran the royal mint – being abbot of Bury St Edmunds was literally a licence to print money. The abbey even owned the horse droppings on the street – and of course the monks took their cut.

Whether it was collecting manure or grinding corn, every abbot guarded his monopoly jealously.

Take Adam Samson, for example, who ran Bury with a rod of iron in the later twelfth century. One day he learnt that the dean, Herbert, had built a windmill without permission. Samson 'boiled with fury and could hardly eat or sleep'. He summoned Herbert and told him: 'I thank you as much as if you had cut off both my feet! By the face of God! I will never eat bread until that building is destroyed!'

It was a subtle hint, but Herbert took it and destroyed the mill immediately.*

By 1327 the townspeople had had enough. In January they stormed and plundered the abbey demanding a charter of liberties. When they were cheated of this they attacked again in February, and then again in May. The monks' raid on the parish church, on 18 October, was reprisal for these attacks.

* Jocelin of Brakelond, *Chronicle of the Abbey of St Edmund's*.

Some years later, in 1345, a special commission investigated the abbey for other reasons, and found that the monks lived away from it, dressed like everyone else and were up to anything and everything.

Throughout the monastic movement, austerity proved to be quite incompatible with monastic wealth. One of them had to go. Unfortunately, even acknowledging the financial incompetence of many abbots, it was not going to be the wealth.

THE HYPOCRISY OF MONKS

FORTUNATELY FOR THE CONSCIENCES of the monastic community, monks of all orders proved to have a genius for finding a variety of ways of living within the letter of Benedict's Rule, while leaving it dead on the cloister pavement.

For example, no well-to-do monk wanted to sleep in a cold dormitory with all the other monks, so, since the infirmary was the only place where a fire was allowed, monks with money began to move in there, establishing

individual 'bachelor pads' – each a private room with its own fireplace, and with a bedroom above complete with en-suite lavatory.

Benedict had prohibited 'eating the flesh of four-footed animals', but an exception was made for the sick. So meat was available in the infirmary – or misericord ('compassionate heart') – where dietary regulations were suspended for the infirm or elderly. And guess what? Pretty soon the brothers gave up eating in the refectory and ate in the misericord instead. Monkish logic.

Another snag about eating meals under Benedict's Rule was that the monks were not allowed to talk while dining. But they could sign if they wanted something… like the salt (Benedict actually says they can communicate *sonitu signi* – 'by sound of a sign'). So they compiled an entire sign language. They would also whistle to each other.

Gerald of Wales describes a visit to Christ Church, Canterbury, in the twelfth

Below: The monk's infirmary. The temptation to move into this more comfortable accommodation proved irresistible.

Opposite: Monks in the refectory awaiting their dinner.

century, during which he was appalled at the way the monks behaved during meals. It was, he claimed, 'more appropriate to jesters… all of them gesticulating with fingers, hands and arms, and whistling to one another in lieu of speaking'.

The same signs were used in monasteries all over Europe – a sort of dumb Esperanto. So whatever country a monk found himself eating in he could always convey exactly what he wanted to a fellow monk. Most of the signs were about food – which isn't surprising because in a monastery there was an awful lot of food to talk about…

DINING WITH MONKS

BENEDICT HAD IN MIND a frugal diet for monks. He advised only two cooked dishes at a meal, and one pound of bread per monk per day. However, most monks took this advice with a pinch of salt – and a lot more.

Food was of absorbing interest to medieval monks. For example, one chapter meeting of the monks of Westminster was preoccupied with the question of whether a particular dish should include four herrings or five. At Bury St Edmunds, the thirteenth-century book of rules and customs records an important discussion about how long a pike should be for the Feast of Relics. It was eventually decided that it should be 22 inches long from head to tail.

Below: Wine making and brewing were an important aspect of monastery life.

Every week contained at least one feast day on which the unfortunate monks would have to deal with something like 16 dishes. But even on a normal working day the menu available to them was one that most lay folk could only have dreamt about. The records for Westminster Abbey, for example, show that on a typical day beef, boiled mutton, roast pork and roast mutton were served at dinner in the misericord, while meat fritters and deer entrails were served in the refectory. Later, at supper, there was tongue and mutton – with sauce.

One historian, Barbara Harvey, has calculated that the daily allowance for the monks of Westminster could have been as much as 7,000 calories – over twice the daily requirement of an average man today. Of course, it is not inevitable that they ate all this – what they left would be given to servants or the poor at the monastery door. But monks were habitually made fun of in literature as being fat, and now the archaeological evidence seems to be bearing out the caricature.

Excavation of the medieval hospital and priory of St Mary Spital in London has produced the bones of thousands of monks and their patients. It is clear that the monks were taller than the lay people (suggesting they

were better nourished all their lives) and had much worse teeth (indicating a sweeter diet).

Monks were equally serious about drink. In his Rule, Benedict admits to some misgivings about recommending how much anyone ought to drink, but bearing in mind 'the standards of the weak' he recommends a hemina (half a pint) of wine a day. Mark you – it was only a recommendation, and the monks treated it with caution. Recent studies have shown that alcohol seems to have accounted for something like 19 per cent of monks' energy intake (it provides 5 per cent of ours).

Gluttony was not the only sin monks fell prey to. Records for 1447 note a brothel in Westminster called the 'Maidenshead', which was much frequented by Benedictines. With up to £12 pocket money a year, the monks could afford to go there. And churchmen did not just use brothels; they owned them. The bishop of Winchester was the owner of one of the brothels in Borough High Street in London – the girls were known affectionately as 'Winchester geese'.

RESISTING THE MONKS

IN 1348 THE WHOLE MONASTIC SYSTEM in England came close to collapse when the Black Death killed off something like two-thirds of all people in holy orders. In enclosed monastic communities it spread like the plague – you might say.

Many of the communities never recovered. At the Cistercian abbey of Rievaulx, for instance, a population that had once numbered 400 was reduced to just 18 people by 1381. Only three of them were lay brothers. The situation at Fountains Abbey was similar. Since the Cistercian system depended on these working pseudo-monks it had ceased functioning.

But while their religious communities declined, monasteries lost nothing of their wealth. They retained their lands, their riches, their political power. This may have made little sense previously, but now the

disproportion between such wealth and so few monks became a public scandal. Popular hostility to the 'private religions', as they were called, inevitably grew.

People once more looked back to a 'golden age' in which monks had lived lives of simple poverty and work, but those lives were totally incompatible with the huge properties that the abbots were supposed to run. In fact, something quite extraordinary was happening. The Church itself was the great teacher of morality, insisting that power and privilege were justified only in relation to the responsibilities that went with them. Churchmen had, since the twelfth century at least, emphasised the moral failings of every level of society, with particular emphasis on the failings of churchmen themselves. In the thirteenth century the Church had begun to encourage the use of English for prayer and study by ordinary people. But within 100 years this freedom of expression was being used by the lay population to criticise abuses within the church, and that was a very different kettle of fish.

A mass of materials from the fourteenth century tell this story. It is there in popular ballads, such as the early ones of Robin Hood, which treated monks and abbots with contempt, and depict a powerful contrast between them and wandering friars and preachers, whose Christianity was not practised within a wealthy and politically well-connected institution. It shows in popular religion too, for example in *The Book of Margery Kempe*, where an illiterate bourgeois woman describes her religious experiences, and has no hesitation in dealing directly with her maker, without the Church acting as her intermediary. This is also the core theme of *Piers Plowman*, in which the only 'indulgence' on offer is a paper saying 'Do well, do better, do best', and in which the ploughman himself is identified with Christ and must save the world, including the Church.

The intellectual core of criticism was provided by the foremost academic of his day, John Wyclif. From his base at the University of Oxford, he issued a devastating deconstruction of ecclesiastical corruption and hypocrisy. This powerfully moral attack on the Church erupted in the national uprising of 1381. Modern historians tell us that the causes of the revolt were economic and political, but in 1381 the Church itself had no doubt that the chief instigators were John Wyclif and his followers who had been busy for the last decade stirring up criticism of the ecclesiastical hierarchy for the precise reason that the church now lay at the heart of the economy and of politics. The rebels beheaded the Archbishop of Canterbury and many abbeys came under attack.

At Bury St Edmunds the abbey was once again sacked and looted. The prior was executed and his severed head stuck on a pike in the Great Market. At Norwich the rebels were unfortunate enough to run into a fighting bishop, Henry Despenser, who for most of his ill-spent youth had been one of the pope's military commanders. The bishop happened to be fully armed and armoured. He personally executed the leader of the party.

The uprising was crushed, but the Church's critics were not. Wyclif continued to insist that the clergy ought not to own property, and that the king could legally confiscate any held by the Church. It was an interesting proposition to which many theologians felt they could subscribe. But the men who then ran the Church were not theologians. The most powerful bishops and archbishops were career politicians, with little or no theological training. For them the Church was a political and economic power base. There was no way these proud and wealthy prelates were going to heed a call for a return to biblical simplicity and poverty. They would do whatever they could to hold on to their wealth and power.

THE CHURCH DEFENDS ITSELF WITH FIRE

THEIR TACTIC WAS NOT TO DEFEND the indefensible but to go on the attack. Luckily for them, Wyclif had challenged the official Church position on the Eucharist – the part of the Mass where the bread and wine are blessed and become the body and blood of Christ. Since 1215, the line had been that a miracle takes place, and after the blessing there is no bread and no wine left – they become, despite what our senses tell us, flesh and blood.

However, the Church in England had never pressed this point and people were left to interpret the miracle as they liked. Wyclif proposed that the bread and wine became the body and blood of Christ in a spiritual or symbolic sense. It was a proposition that would have roused little controversy in the past, but after 1381 the worldly bishops, headed by the aristocratic and powerful William Courtenay, archbishop of Canterbury, saw the issue as a block on which to lay the heads of the Church's critics. From 1401 archbishops were able to enjoy the privilege of handing over anyone who suggested that the bread and wine were not literally the body and blood of Christ to be burnt at the stake – a brutally effective way of retaining the status quo.

Nonetheless, opposition to corruption in the Church struggled on. In 1410 there was an attempt to pass a Bill in Parliament to strip the Church and the monasteries of their assets. But Henry IV had been helped to the

throne by the then archbishop of Canterbury, Thomas Arundel, and the Bill was indignantly rejected. In fact, an abject Commons had to beg for it to be struck from the record.

THE END OF THE MONASTERIES

THE UNPOPULARITY OF THE MONASTERIES simmered under the surface. When religious houses were founded as penance for the murder of Richard II, it was very difficult to find anyone to inhabit them. Syon monastery near London, for instance, was occupied by a Swedish order of nuns, who later took over another of the new foundations at Brentford, also near London, which had remained empty since being established.

Nuns had, in fact, replaced monks in people's minds as being value for money. The classic idea of a nunnery had been a place of retreat for well-off ladies with nowhere else to go; but in the decades that followed

Below: Nuns turned out to be a better bet than monks for rich sinners in search of pious intercession through song.

the Black Death the attitude to women in religious life changed rather dramatically.

Nuns evidently chose to live by different standards from those of monks with their rich endowments and glorious buildings. People seem to have been much more conscious of this by the fifteenth century, and also to have become aware that if they were donating funds for anniversaries, for pittances, for regular prayers, for burial, women were more likely to deliver the goods. Wealthy men and women frequently made bequests to 'the poor nuns who will pray for their souls', and increasing numbers of women's religious houses were founded. This suggests that women's prayers were perceived to have more efficacy than men's, and that donors and patrons thought nunneries were doing a better job than monasteries.

Monks and nuns were both finally swept away in the years following 1535, when Henry VIII dissolved the monasteries and redistributed their phenomenal wealth among his cronies. The inquiry by Thomas Cromwell which led up to this produced a spectacular list of abuses and scandals, none of which represented anything new, but which were now being exposed in a world in which reform, rather than abolition, hardly seemed an option any more.

And all we have left are beautiful fairy ruins… that whisper of a life of dedication and piety and simplicity that became corrupted on a magnificent scale.

Perhaps money is the root of all evil.

Of course, there were always sincere and dedicated monks who devoted themselves to a life of prayer and religious contemplation. But looking back through the story of the monasteries it's possible to conclude that once prayer had acquired a monetary value, the game was up. The monasteries – the prayer factories – became commercial enterprises; and subsequently there was just no way they could fulfil their original function.

Monks couldn't really cut themselves off for ever from the wicked world, no matter how hard they tried. They were part of the wicked world and, what's more, a lot of the time they ran it. But they were never allowed to get away with it unscathed. Criticism and condemnation was constant; it was the motor that drove one new monastic movement after another, and ultimately pulled down the entire edifice. The true legacy of the medieval church in England, and all those fat monks, is the powerful sense of social justice that the monastic movement itself taught, that it used to speak out against its own corruption, and that in the end became the weapon that destroyed it.

And that has shaped political debate in England ever since.

CHAPTER FIVE

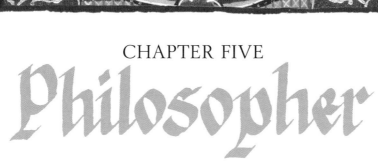

Philosopher

Nature, and Nature's laws lay hid in night.
God said, *Let Newton be!* and all was light.

Alexander Pope's epitaph for Sir Isaac Newton, written in 1730 (three years after the great man's death), seems to tell us all we need to know about medieval science. The natural philosophers of the Middle Ages floundered in ignorance and superstition until Newton changed the study of the world by basing his investigations on experiment and mathematics.

The typical medieval experimental philosopher was, supposedly, a man like the thirteenth-century Franciscan friar Roger Bacon, hunting for the philosopher's stone. Bacon was an alchemist who tried to turn base metals into gold, pursuing delusions, and who was then forbidden by his own order to continue his strange experiments.

Odd, then, that it should be Bacon who said 'Mathematics is the door and the key to the sciences' and wrote an explanation of experimental science for the pope. Odder still that Isaac Newton was also actually an alchemist, and that by far the greater part of his writings was devoted to alchemy and interpreting the Book of Revelation. We choose to ignore the truth about the history of natural philosophy. It doesn't fit into the story of human progress as we like to tell it.

THE ALCHEMISTS AND THE SEARCH FOR GOLD

The roots of science lie in alchemy – the study of how one substance can be changed into another. Alchemists were exploring a world whose nature, in their eyes, derived not from mechanical laws but from the mind of God.

The word 'alchemy' comes from Arabic and Egyptian roots (*al-khimia* refers to the black soil of the Nile); the study was said to have been devised by the god Hermes, creator of the arts and sciences. It was called the Hermetic art and was certainly explored by Greeks in Alexandria in the third century AD. Much of the Eastern Roman Empire, including Egypt, was ultimately conquered by Islam in the seventh century, and Arab inquirers pursued, and elaborated on, the ideas and knowledge that had been developed there. Eventually the secrets of alchemy were passed on to medieval Europe through Arabs in Spain.

Roger Bacon explained that, 'Alchemy is a Science, teaching how to transform any kind of metal into another: and that by a proper medicine, as it appeared by many Philosophers' Books.' And alchemy certainly had the transmutation of base metals into gold at the top of its priorities. Gold was special but that was because it was so very different from any other substance – this was its significance for alchemists. Gold cannot rust. No natural process damages it. Heat it to white-hot and when it cools off it will be the same metal as it was before. It can be hammered to one-thousandth of the thickness of a sheet of newsprint, and drawn into a wire finer than a human hair, and remains quite unchanged. In a mortal world, gold is incorruptible.

To the alchemists it was perfection. The basis of alchemy was the belief that the world contained the possibility of perfectibility, and it was the duty of the inquirer to strive towards that. Once, in the Garden of Eden, everything had been perfect. Then sin had been introduced, men and women were barred from the garden and the world was now corrupt. But everything – animate and inanimate – was slowly striving to restore itself, and the existence of gold, rare as it was, demonstrated that such a restoration to perfection was real and did happen.

And because everything was tending towards a state of perfection, all metals that were still underground must be gradually changing themselves into gold. The alchemists were simply helping a natural process. Giving God a hand.

Before we scoff, we should bear in mind that even in the twentieth century miners have argued that metals grow in the ground. In a sense, they are correct. For example, if you leave scrap iron in a wet place in a worked-out copper mine, and seal the mine, a few years later you will find that copper has grown. It has migrated into the scrap iron from the moisture, copper atoms replacing iron ones.

To the alchemists it seemed to follow that, if metals grow, those that are left in the

Above: The Egyptian god Thoth (who the Greeks knew as Hermes) was the supposed originator of alchemy.

Opposite: A fourteenth-century manuscript illustration of the alchemical substance that heals the world.

Below: An alchemist at work; detail from a sixteenth-century engraving after Peter Brueghel the Elder.

Right: Roger Bacon (Dr Mirabilis) c. 1220–92, English philosopher and scientist.

Opposite: A fourteenth-century French manuscript depicting a philosophy lesson.

ground for the longest time will grow closest to perfection. That explained why there was so little gold in the world – in the fourteenth century all the gold in Europe would have filled a medium-sized room. Most metal, it was deduced, is brought to the surface too soon. The purpose of alchemy, as Bacon wrote, was to provide the solution to this problem:

Alchemy therefore is a science teaching how to make and compound a certain medicine, which is called Elixir, the which when it is cast upon metals or imperfect bodies, does fully perfect them.

This was the basis for the hunt for the philosopher's stone (or elixir). Alchemy required that an inquirer should study all knowledge. Human beings, the heavens and the earth were intimately linked, having been created together in the mind of God.

PHILOSOPHERS LIKE ROGER BACON did not see themselves as challenging biblical orthodoxy. Their credo was 'as above, so below'. In other words, the world itself is part of creation, so studying its secrets can help you to understand the Bible. Bacon argued that scientific study was essential to perceiving the hidden meaning of religious texts – only when you know about the world can you see what is being said. Alchemy was a religious inquiry that happens to look like bad science to our uncomprehending eyes.

For example, Bacon described the vastness of the universe in a way that sounds surprisingly modern:

> Even the smallest of the stars visible to our sight is bigger than the earth; but, compared to the heavens as a whole, the smallest star has no effective magnitude at all… The sun is about 170 times as big as the whole earth, as Ptolemy proves (Almagest 5)… One could walk all the way round the earth in less than three years. So we see that the magnitude of things below is simply incommensurable with that of the heavenly bodies.
> BACON, *Operis Majoris*

Just as we assume that Newton transformed physics by 'introducing' the importance of mathematics, we are taught that Galileo transformed cosmology by inventing the astronomical telescope. But Bacon describes how to use lenses, and his own use of them in an instrument that must have been a telescope. He claimed it could make the most distant object appear near, and that it could make stars appear at will. But every time we think an alchemist is talking modern science, we are mistaken. Bacon goes on…

> … we see that the magnitude of things below is simply incommensurable with that of the heavenly bodies. Nor can their effectiveness be compared, since the effectiveness of things below is caused by that of things above. The combined influence of the sun below the slanting course of the ecliptic, and the aspects of the planets above, is the cause of all that happens here below them on the earth.

Since all things must be connected Bacon, like other philosophers, was also an astrologer. It followed, of course, that he believed his telescope gave him the power to see into the future. We have a different view of the world. Any modern astronomer knows that a telescope is a way of

looking backwards in time, not forwards – since it takes time for light to pass from distant objects to earth, the further away the object, the longer ago the image was created.

Bacon's inquiries were essentially inspired by religion; the pope supported his work and was eager to read what he wrote. He was also doing what we think of as real science, and alarmed his students by breaking white light up into the spectrum of colours: 'The experimenter considers whether among visible things, he can find colours formed and arranged as given in the rainbow.'

When Bacon created a rainbow by passing light through some glass beads he was 500 years ahead of Isaac Newton – especially when he measured the angle of displacement of the beam correctly. He was demonstrating that experiment is a form of knowledge that can clarify the study of the Bible.

THE ALCHEMISTS WERE (ALMOST) RIGHT!

OUR CONTEMPT FOR THE THEORY OF TRANSMUTATION is rooted in the work of the French chemist Antoine Lavoisier in the 1770s. He produced a theory of matter that said metals like iron, lead and gold are chemical elements that are fixed and unchanging. This new 'truth' became the basis of scientific understanding for nearly 200 years, and helps us to forget that the transmutation of one metal into another is now used all the time. It is how a nuclear reactor works. One metal – uranium – turns into others, including plutonium and thorium. We call the process radioactivity, but that's just our word for transmutation.

The alchemists were right in thinking that nature transmutes metals very, very slowly – though somewhat more slowly than they assumed. It takes 4.5 billion years (about the age of the earth) for half a lump of uranium-238 to turn into thorium. Obviously, some trick is needed to speed the process up, which is what nuclear physics is all about.

As for the transmutation of lead into gold – in 1972 it was reported that Soviet physicists at a nuclear research facility near Lake Baikal, in Siberia, found that the lead shielding of an experimental reactor had done exactly that after a time under continuous nuclear bombardment! However, just in case you think this is an experiment worth repeating, please be advised that the gold must have been heavier than lead (which it normally isn't) and intensely radioactive, and that it rapidly 'decayed' back to lead.

Of course, alchemists were not pursuing radioactivity. Their theory was that they were trying to purify matter. So, they reasoned, the first step must be to produce pure substances. They did this by distillation – heating something until it produced a vapour, then collecting the condensation. The processes could be unbelievably complicated: the Islamic alchemist Jabir ibn Hayyan recommended one particular procedure that involved 700 distillations.

In their attempts to purify matter alchemists produced entirely new substances with extraordinary properties. Distilling a combination of saltpetre and alum produced nitric acid – a liquid that would completely dissolve silver. It took longer to learn how to distil alum alone as the condensation destroyed metal vessels. Eventually alchemists began using containers made of glass, which the acid did not eat away. And the liquid produced would dissolve iron and copper. It was sulphuric acid. Then they discovered that distilling salt and alum, and passing the vapour through water, produced something even stronger: hydrochloric acid which, when mixed with nitric acid, would even dissolve gold.

These discoveries literally changed the world, by transforming European technology. Until the alchemists got to work the strongest acid known had been vinegar.

In addition, alchemists actually had reason to suppose they were on to something, because they found that they could make a substance that seemed to be gold. Adding a little gold dust to a flask of mercury and powdered silver resulted in a golden liquid. When this was heated and boiled away it produced (in addition to highly noxious fumes) what looked like a lump of gold – it's called 'butter of gold'. Nowadays, there are tests to show it isn't the real thing, but these weren't available to the old alchemists. So it is possible they thought they were closer to their goal than they were.

Above: Preparation of experiments, a fifteenth-century manuscript illustration.

FRAUDSTERS AND CHEATS

PERHAPS IT'S NOT SURPRISING, in an enterprise involving comparatively large quantities of gold, that some practitioners were in the business of extracting as much of it as they could for themselves. In *The Canterbury Tales*, written in the fourteenth century, Geoffrey Chaucer's alchemist's assistant calls alchemy 'this cursed craft':

This cursed craft – whoever tries it on
Will never make a thing to live upon
For all the cash on it that he forks out
He'll lose; of that I have no doubt.
CHAUCER, *The Canon's Yeoman's Tale,* 830–3

The assistant goes on to tell how a fraudulent alchemist tricks a priest into believing there is a process that turns mercury into silver, and cons £40 (a fortune) out of him for the secret. Of course, it does not work and the priest never sees the alchemist again.

Chaucer was clearly writing with first-hand knowledge of these charlatans. There must have been plenty of them.

One of the earliest was Artephius, who appeared in the twelfth century claiming he was 1,025 years old. So old, he claimed in a book, that he was now ready to reveal the secret of the elixir of life:

I, Artephius, after I became an adept, and had attained to the true and complete wisdom… was sometimes obscure also as others were. But when I had for the space of a thousand years, or thereabouts, which has now passed over my head, since the time I was born to this day… by the use of this wonderful quintessence – when, I say, for so very long a time, I found no man had found out or obtained this hermetic secret, because of the obscurity of the philosophers' words, being moved with a generous mind, and the integrity of a good man, I have determined in these latter days of my life to declare all things truly and sincerely, that you may not want anything for the perfecting of this stone of the philosophers.
The Secret Book of Artephius

Tragically for all would-be immortals, no-one can make head or tail of his instructions. Which is a shame, because by his own account he clearly went to literally fantastic lengths to gain his knowledge. He had not simply 'gone the extra mile' in search of the recipe, but had (he said) descended into hell, where the devil sat on a throne of gold, surrounded by imps and fiends.

Perhaps, though, this is an experience shared by all pioneering investigators in one way or another.

However, a lot of people desperately wanted the alchemists' experiments to work. Henry IV, for example, exhorted learned men to study alchemy in order to pay off England's debts – and he wanted illicit alchemists imprisoned to stop them undermining the currency. In the sixteenth century Elizabeth I sent an envoy to beg the English alchemist Edward Kelly to return from Prague and help her pay for her defence against Spain.

These rulers understood that the existence of frauds did not mean the theory of alchemy was rubbish. If this seems gullible, just consider the extent of fraud in contemporary research. Today's equivalents of the philosopher's stone include the nanocomputer – a full-scale computer too small even to be seen with an ordinary microscope. Dr Hendrik Schon, of Bell Laboratories, published 25 papers in three years on his breakthrough work on this and was considered to be a serious candidate for the Nobel Prize. But in October 2002 16 of the papers were declared to be fraudulent. The journal *Science* withdrew eight they had published and Schon was fired.* In 1999 alone, the US Public Health Service received reports of 'misconduct' (fraudulent publication), in biomedical science alone, from 72 institutions.** But no-one jumps to the conclusion that modern science is worthless.

Medieval critics of research tended to be rather less tolerant of scientific fraud than we are. In 1350, Edward III threw an alchemist by the name of John de Walden into the Tower of London – he had been given 5,000 crowns of the king's gold and 20 pounds of silver 'to work thereon by the art of alchemy for the benefit of the king'. Obviously not very successfully. Hendrik Schon, on the other hand, remains a free man at the time of writing.

In the fourteenth century the Dominicans and Cistercians banned alchemy following a papal bull against alchemical fraud. But the same pope who issued that edict in 1317 gave funds to his physician in 1330 for 'certain secret work'.

THE SECRECY OF THE ALCHEMISTS

MARK YOU, THE ALCHEMISTS WERE A PRETTY SECRETIVE LOT. They operated in a world of elliptical allusions and allegory. And a lot of what they wrote was designed not to elucidate but to confuse. As the 1,025-year-old Artephius put it: 'Is it not an art full of secrets? And believest thou O fool that we plainly teach this secret of secrets, taking our words according to their literal signification?'

*'Breakdown of the Year: Physics Fraud', *Science,* Vol. 298, 20 December 2002, p.2303.
**Office of Research Integrity, Annual Report 2001.

The Hermetic art was never to lose its emphasis on mystery. George Ripley, a fifteenth-century canon of the Augustinian priory of Bridlington in Yorkshire, explained that alchemy was a 'holy science' reserved for the few, and that he wrote in code:

… to discourage the fools, for although we write primarily for the edification of the disciples of the art, we also write for the mystification of those owls and bats which can neither bear the splendour of the sun, nor the light of the moon.

GEORGE RIPLEY, *The Compound of Alchymie conteining Twelve Gates,* 1475

As it happened, Ripley's code involved pictographs and his resulting book, known as the Ripley Scrolls, is among the most attractive of medieval manuscripts. In his text a king clad in red is gold, the queen in white is silver, a salamander is fire, and a dragon being killed by the sun and moon is mercury being combined with gold and silver.

BACON THE BLACK MAGICIAN

THE MYSTERY SURROUNDING ALCHEMY encouraged the suspicion that alchemists were devotees of the black arts. The 1279 edition of the Franciscans' *Constitutiones Generales Antiquae* forbids alchemy along with magic, sorcery and the summoning of demons; and in the late sixteenth century Roger Bacon was portrayed as a figure like Faust, who engaged

in a devilish pact to work magic. A popular drama around 1580 showed him constructing a brass head that could speak, and whose incantation would (had it not been destroyed) have surrounded England with a protective brass wall. But the Church did not generally see natural philosophy as a challenge to Christianity.

Bacon was certainly viewed with considerable anxiety by his Franciscan brotherhood, but that had more to do with his outspoken views on the order itself than with his scientific interests. A ferocious debate was going on in Franciscan theology, with one group, the 'Spirituals', demanding total commitment to a life of poverty and the other justifying a compromise with something more comfortable. Bacon sympathized with the spiritual and, like a number of other Franciscans, was virtually imprisoned by the order. Early in the next century Spirituals would be condemned as heretics and burned. But the Church's attitude to scientific inquiry was complex, and not as condemnatory as has often been assumed.

Bacon was based in Paris, and thirteenth-century Paris was throbbing with new ideas about philosophy and theology. At the heart of the ferment was the study of Aristotle's writings, and the way his ideas were being handled in a Christian context by scholars like Thomas Aquinas. One establishment response was the so-called 'General Condemnation of Philosophy and the Sciences' by the bishop of Paris in 1277. This has traditionally been described as an attack on reason – which is rather misleading. The Church was trying to resist a new dogmatism of rational certainty which seemed to challenge the omnipotence of God and the value of theology. The bishop particularly condemned the propositions that:

> Theological discussions are based on fables.
> Nothing is known better because of knowing theology.
> The only wise men of the world are philosophers.

In fact, the condemnation rejected a number of propositions which, if they had been accepted as orthodoxy, would have dramatically limited scientific debate and made heretics of many theorists. Some of these propositions were:

There was no first man, nor will there be a last: there always was and always will be a generation of man from man. Nothing happens by chance. The first cause [that is, God] could not make several worlds. God could not move the heavens [that is, the sky and therefore the world] with rectilinear motion; and the reason is that a vacuum would remain. God cannot be the cause of a new act [or thing] nor can he produce anything new. God cannot make more (than three) dimensions exist simultaneously.

These propositions would have made Darwin and Newton heretics, and quantum, probability, the theory of continuous creation, ideas of multiple universes and dimensions would all have been heresies. The Bishop insisted that these possibilities must remain open because human reason cannot limit God's omnipotence. By rejecting these propositions the bishop made it an offence to deny the possibility of evolution, quantum probability, Newtonian motion, the multiverse, continuous creation and multiple dimensions!

Opposite: This image of a wolf consuming a king, and then being burned while the king is resurrected, is from Michael Maier's Atalanta Fugiens *(1617). Maier was a physician in the alchemical court of Rudolf II in Prague. The imagery seems to show the effect of one substance on another, followed by a distillation.*

IT DOES LOOK AS THOUGH MODERN PEOPLE are as likely as those of the Middle Ages to hold false certainties. One of the oddest of these is the widespread conviction that medieval people thought the earth was flat. This is a modern mistake – there was no such belief in the Middle Ages. Perhaps 'mistake' is too kind a word. It is a lie that has been elevated into a fact.

The lie was concocted by two writers at around the same time: a French antireligious academic, Antoine-Jean Letronne, in his *On the Cosmographical Ideas of the Church Fathers* (1834), and the American novelist, Washington Irving. Irving was the author of such reliable historical texts as 'The Legend of Sleepy Hollow' and 'Rip Van Winkle'. In 1828 he wrote an equally reliable biography of Christopher Columbus. This includes a scene in which the great navigator, about to set off westwards to the Indies, is confronted by the Church authorities at Salamanca in Spain. They accuse our hero of heresy because he says the world is round. It's a gripping scene and one that has held imaginations in thrall through the ensuing years.

The only snag is that Washington Irving simply made the whole thing up. The Church had never taught that the world was flat. It's nonsense.

But it was a great idea with which to attack the Church, even if it wasn't true. Ledronne was an anti-Christian polemicist and the Darwinists, when they were attacked by the Church authorities for saying that humans were descended from other animals, connected his falsehoods with Irving's fantasy and called religious zealots 'flat earthers'. Irving's nonsense was repeated by a succession of lazy authors* and ended up in a number of well-respected histories of science, and in the *New York Times* editorial that ushered in the first day of the new millennium.

There is no doubt that intelligent people in the Middle Ages knew perfectly well that the earth was a globe. Aquinas, in the thirteenth century, wrote that, 'the astronomer and the natural philosopher both demonstrate the same conclusion, such as that the world is round; yet the astronomer does so through mathematics, while the natural philosopher does so in a way that takes matter into account.'

Roger Bacon, living at the same time as Aquinas, had been taught that Greek mathematicians had measured the earth's circumference. It was obvious that it was round – for how else did things disappear beyond the horizon? As he wrote: 'The… curvature of the earth explains why we can see further from higher elevations.'

*Jeffrey Burton Russell, *Inventing the Flat Earth: Columbus and Modern Historians* (Greenwood Press, 1997).

What is more, medieval scholars were actively considering the possible existence of America. They realized that the people of the world they knew inhabited only one hemisphere, and devoted a lot of discussion to what happened on the other side. Some said it was all water. But some postulated the existence of another land mass, the antipodes, 'on the opposite side of the earth, where the sun rises when it sets to us' (that is, in the far west). And whether or not these 'antipodes' were inhabited was a matter of intense speculation. The fifth-century theologian St Augustine had thought not, on the very rational grounds that all humans must be descended from a common ancestor and such lands, if they existed, were too far away to have been settled.

Columbus had no problem with the Church's geography. He found the antipodes.

MAPPAE MUNDI

Surely, though, the maps of the Middle Ages demonstrate beyond doubt that medieval people had no idea of the shape, size, look, nature, plan, organization or concept of the earth as it really is?

The standard medieval image of the earth – described as a T-O map – was a circular disc divided by bodies of water in the shape of the letter T (see illustration right). The area above the T represents Asia; the lower left quadrant (separated from Asia by the Black Sea) represents Europe and the lower right (separated from Asia by the Red Sea) represents Africa. The upright of the T, separating Europe and Africa, is the Mediterranean, and Jerusalem is in the centre of the map.

Well, it's reassuring to be able to laugh at the ignorance of our forebears, but the trouble is that laughter often betrays our own ignorance. It's unlikely that anybody who looked at such a 'map' in the Middle Ages thought it portrayed a geographical representation of the earth. The T-O map is more like an acronym, an aid to help people remember the significant points of the then-known world: the three continents and the waters in between.

And what of the wonderful and elaborate *mappae mundi* – such as the one in Hereford

cathedral – that show strange and idiotic distortions of the earth? They are so obviously the products of a map-maker with less of a clue than the average primary-school student of today that it's hard to take them seriously. And it's certainly true that if you tried to use one to get from London to Stuttgart you probably wouldn't get as far as Noah's Ark – which usually figures prominently in such maps, along with the Tower of Babel, the dog-headed people converted by Thomas Aquinas, people with heads in their chests and people who protected themselves from the sun by holding their single gigantic foot over their heads like a parasol.

But once again we're mistaking the purpose of the beast. These were not maps. *Mappa* simply means 'cloth' and a *mappa mundi* is not a 'map of the world' but a 'cloth of the world'. The fact that we have derived our word 'map' from these cloths is not the fault of the people of the Middle

Opposite: The Mappa Mundi in the Cathedral at Hereford is more of an encyclopedia than a geographical guide.

Left: Matthew Paris, a thirteenth-century monk at St Albans produced this itinerary map – each section indicates a day's travel or 'journée'.

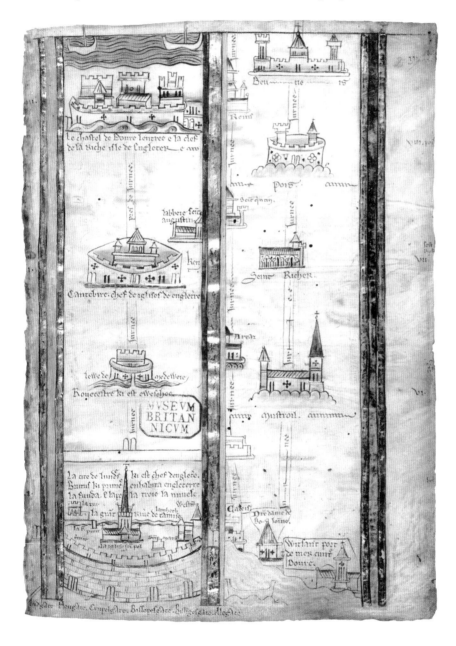

Below: Medieval
illustrators con-
stantly referred to
the spiritual danger
of building high
towers.

Opposite: The
building of
Hunstanton, 1251,
showing medieval
tools and building
techniques.

Ages. If there's any blame to be apportioned it's our fault for forgetting where the word comes from.

And a cloth of the world had an entirely different purpose from an atlas (a seventeenth-century idea). A *mappa mundi* is a depiction of the world as a place of experiences, of human history, of notions and knowledge. It's more like an encyclopedia. It's certainly not – and was never intended to be – a chart to be followed by travellers.

More than likely, a *mappa mundi* would have been a conversation piece in a rich man's house. A fashionable – and expensive – ornament to prompt after-dinner discussion. For journeys people needed not maps but travel itineraries, and that is what they had. The most famous of the English ones was drawn by Matthew Paris, a monk of St Albans, in the thirteenth century. It shows the roads of England, and towns and villages and the time it takes to walk between them. The word 'journey' comes from the walking times on itineraries of this kind; '*journée*' referred to a day's travel.

THE GREATEST EXPERIMENTS OF THE MIDDLE AGES

THE MEDIEVAL CHURCH was by no means opposed to the pursuit of knowledge. On the contrary, it was churchmen who were responsible for many of the discoveries of the age. And the fabulous churches, cath-

edrals and abbeys that were constructed throughout the Middle Ages were the result of technical experimentation on a monumental scale.

The style of religious building that immediately followed the Conquest was essentially connected with fortification: thick stone walls with small windows were surmounted by barrel vaults supported on sturdy pillars.

The architecture of fortification was a natural field for innovation and experiment. By the late thirteenth century Edward I was building castles in a revolutionary new form created by a European master-mason, James of St George. In place of the old design, in which everything helped to defend a

massive core called the Keep, Edward was dominating Wales with castles of concentric rings of wall, each wall protected by covering fire from towers. The gloomy, thick-walled Keep had been, in effect, a prison for the castle's master; Edward's castles were not only stronger but had at their heart an open space where a King or his lieutenant could live in more palatial comfort. But Church architecture had gone off on a totally different tack.

The Church had found a new confidence and it wanted to demonstrate that confidence. In fact, it now wanted to dominate the landscape. Abbots and archbishops became interested in constructing buildings with high towers, that would celebrate rather than defend their power.

We are so familiar with these enduring constructions that it is easy to forget that at the time they were built architects were experimenting at the limits of their technology and beyond – and all too often they learnt what those limits were the hard way: Winchester Cathedral's tower collapsed in 1107, during the building work. At Gloucester Abbey, built in 1100, the southern tower of the west front fell over in 1170.

But these minor drawbacks did not create architectural conservatism. On the contrary, theology said that God is light, and the Church wanted to get away from the dark, introspective architecture of the past and let the light of God shine in on worshippers.

So, when the choir of Canterbury Cathedral burned down in 1174, the monks decided to build something altogether more ambitious in place of the previous heavy, rough-hewn pillars, rounded arches and wooden ceiling. And they allowed a French architect, William of Sens, to talk them into an entirely new architecture – far taller and lighter, finely chiselled and with its pointed arches coming together in graceful vaults, soaring to the glory of God and the Church. Nothing like it had been seen in England before.

In fact, William had conned the monks into it. He won the contract against other bidders by saying he thought they had overestimated the amount of work that needed doing, and then 'for some time concealed what he found necessary to be done, lest the truth should kill them'. It has often been said that medieval cathedrals were built by anonymous communities of dedicated men. The truth is they were built by internationally famous architects like William, who took advantage of ambitious churchmen to put up hugely expensive monuments to their own genius.

The problem of preventing the sides of a building being pushed outwards by the weight of the stone roof was solved by propping them up. At Canterbury the props developed in the course of the work from solid, triangular buttresses into flying buttresses – a new invention that would be the mark of 'Gothic' architecture.

This was a wildly experimental architecture, as was the process of putting it up. William was five years into the project, and about to start installing the great vault, when the scaffolding collapsed and timber, stone and William fell 50 feet. He survived, and tried to carry on directing the work from his bed, but in the end he had to return to France. It was another William, an Englishman, who came up with the design of the flying buttresses.

Opposite: The beautiful rib vaulting in Canterbury Cathedral.

Below: The complex arrangement of flying buttresses and supports holding up Beauvais – and failing.

But the odd setback wasn't going to stop the Church. Encouraged by hugely ambitious architects, it launched an unprecedented building programme, covering Britain and France with innovative and untried designs.

The nave of Lincoln Cathedral collapsed in 1185 and the central tower in 1237 (during a sermon, burying the congregation). The tower of St David's Cathedral fell down in 1220, as did Ely Cathedral tower in 1322 (and part of the west front in the next century). York Cathedral tower collapsed in 1407, and the tower of Ripon Cathedral in 1450.

But by then the attempt to build ever-higher vaults was well and truly over. The technology had finally been recognized as being too dangerous in 1284, when a great chunk of Beauvais Cathedral crashed to the ground. It was still under construction. Its choir was already the tallest building in Europe; its main section, the nave, was never built at all. Beauvais cathedral still stands – just – a massive stone fantasy of layered buttresses, attached to the stump of the squat building it was meant to replace and kept up by immense, modern wooden struts that are testament to the glorious incompetence of its design.

The Middle Ages were actually a hotbed of experimentation; and some people were prepared to test their theories in practical and very dangerous ways, even trying out flying machines. At Malmesbury Abbey, in the eleventh century, a monk by the name of Elmer built himself wings and took off from the top of the tower. The wings took him a full 200 yards before he crash-landed, breaking both legs.

When he was in bed recovering he told his abbot he knew what had gone wrong: his flying machine needed a tail. The abbot forbade him to take the experiment any further, setting back the development of flight by 900 years. But even though Elmer was crippled for life he never lost his interest in the sky. The Bayeux tapestry shows Halley's comet, which was seen in 1066 and was heralded as a portent of disaster for England. It was reputedly Elmer who spotted it in the sky and gloomily identified its meaning.

Right: King Harold is told of Halley's comet (top left), in a panel from the Bayeux tapestry.

RICHARD OF WALLINGFORD'S CLOCK

EVERYWHERE WE LOOK IN THE MIDDLE AGES we find churchmen experimenting and testing, exploring new boundaries of knowledge. Of course, much of this wasn't pure 'blue skies' research. Just like a lot of modern science there were often economic or political imperatives behind the pursuit of knowledge.

Take Richard of Wallingford, who became abbot of St Albans in 1327. He undertook one of the most ambitious engineering projects of his day for reasons that were more to do with the exercise of power than with pure research.

It was said that Richard had neglected theology as a student at Oxford, preferring to concentrate on mathematics and astronomy; but he was particularly interested in astrology. According to his fellow monks, he predicted by astrological means the old abbot's death and his own election to the post. Richard was clearly attracted to science that had practical applications.

The abbey of St Albans had been built in the early twelfth century, and for many years dominated the commercial life of not just the town but also the surrounding district. In recent years, however, its grip had been allowed to slip. In 1323 some pillars in the south nave had collapsed, bringing down the roof and wall. To add to the monks' woes, the townspeople and tenants had rebelled against the abbey, demanding a charter of rights with representation in Parliament and an end to being forced to have their grain ground (at what they considered exorbitant cost) in the abbey's mills. The old abbot, Hugh was a sick man, and conceded the charter and gave up imposing the abbey's monopoly on milling. As a result the abbey lost control of the town, and was broke.

Richard set about restoring its fortunes with a degree of ruthlessness. He confiscated the hand flour-mills the townsfolk were now using to grind their corn and had them set into the abbey floor. From then on they were once again forced to use the abbey's mill and – of course – pay for the privilege. At one stroke Richard had made the abbey solvent. But instead of using the money to rebuild the collapsed nave, he decided he would make something that would dominate the commercial life of St Albans.

He decided to build a clock.

The Church had originally established what were called 'canonical hours'. These marked the times for praying and there were only four such hours during daylight and four for the night. The intervals between the hours varied according to the season. In summer the daylight ones were

*Right: The astro-
nomical clock at
Wells Cathedral,
1390.*

long and the night-time ones were short, and vice versa in winter. This was
time as physically experienced on earth.

Economic growth had brought pressure from merchants and
employees for more accurate timekeeping. It appears that by the
thirteenth century the intervals between canonical hours no longer varied
according to the seasons – many monasteries had moved over to fixed
lengths. One of the effects of this change was that None – the hour for
prayers originally said at the ninth hour of the day (mid-afternoon) – was
displaced to midday, giving the English language the word 'noon'.

However, laypeople were beginning to use time as measured by astronomers, who divided a day into 24 equal and unvarying hours. By the fourteenth century the Church found that its monopoly on time was being appropriated by townspeople who began to erect clocks on public buildings and in city squares. Control of timekeeping was passing from the Church to the merchant classes.

Richard intended to keep the Church in control – in St Albans anyway. And as he was more concerned with the life of the town than the life of the abbey, his clock used the lay system – not the canonical hours. It did not just give the time, but linked it into the whole of the cosmos; on the clock could be seen the phases of the moon and the times of eclipses.

The clock used the same geared mechanism as the much-hated abbey mill, showing that the mill was linked to the mechanisms of the heavens. By chiming every hour, instead of just for prayers, it took control of the working day of the town. From now on, it was the Church that would issue the time for town council meetings, for the opening and closing of markets, for the start and the end of each and every day of work.*

Richard's aim seems to have been to demonstrate the intellectual and technical superiority of the Church, and its scientific understanding, over mere commercial tradesmen. You could say his purpose was political. And yet he would doubtless have claimed it was religious. He was making God's universe visible.

We assume that science and religion are poles apart. But for the philosophers of the Middle Ages 'science' would have no meaning unless it led to an understanding of God. This religious agenda applied to every branch of philosophy or learning. Even medicine.

WHAT WERE MEDIEVAL DOCTORS UP TO?

Today we expect but one thing from our doctors: to make us better. The medieval doctor was trying to do a lot more than that. He was taking care of the soul as well as the body. Unlike modern doctors he did not try to stop a patient dying at all costs; rather, if death seemed inevitable, he was duty-bound to try and help him or her die in the best possible way for their immortal soul.

But doctors of the Middle Ages had an even higher goal. It was no less than to return the human body to the state of perfection it had enjoyed in the Garden of Eden. And the means by which they would do this was through their version of the philosopher's stone: the elixir of life.

*See http://explorers.whyte.com/row.htm, for an essay by Nicholas Whyte.

Below: A thirteenth-century manuscript illustration of a sickbed.

Opposite: The four Humours as explained by Galen and translated into four kinds of men.

For us, medicine is mechanical chemistry, one chemical interacting with another, with the patient as an anonymous vessel – the retort within which this interaction takes place. From a medieval perspective, this is a recipe for disaster. The basic question a medieval patient needed to ask was 'Why me? Why now?'; and the cure for the illness, if there was one, would depend on the answer.

Just as natural philosophers relied on Aristotle for a basic understanding of the physical world, medieval doctors looked to another ancient Greek – Galen – for ideas about the human body. In both cases the connection to classical philosophy came through Islamic scholars and was eagerly taken up by enquiring Christian researchers.

At the centre of Galen's medicine was a belief that health depended on the delicate balance of four vital fluids or humours: blood produced by the heart, phlegm produced in the brain, black bile from the liver and yellow bile from the gall bladder. It was believed that the individual mixture of these humours in each person determined their characters. This implied the need for different treatments for different sorts of people – even at different times of the day (an idea which has had some renewed life with the study of biorhythms).

Within this framework there was a complex world of plant knowledge, much of it used very successfully within its limits, comparable to what the Amazonian Indians, for example, know today. In fact, a considerable amount of medical knowledge that was dismissed as old wives' tales in later, more 'rational', ages has subsequently been found to be extremely useful. One of the most famous examples is the use of willow bark for patients with fever, which was thought to be unscientific for many years but resulted in the development of aspirin…

The old word for a healer was 'leech', and the same word was applied to the bloodsucking worm doctors used to take blood from patients who were deemed to be 'too sanguine'. The common medicinal leech, *Hirudo medicinalis*, remained a popular instrument of treatment until the late nineteenth century – in fact, French doctors imported 41.5 million leeches

in 1833 alone, and the poor little thing became an endangered species. The medical profession lost interest in bleeding as a cure for illness, but has recently realized the usefulness of a creature that produces natural anticoagulants and anaesthetics in its saliva, so that patients bleed readily and generally feel nothing. Today, doctors have begun to use leeches again, particularly after microsurgery, and they are even being farmed commercially for use in medicine. It is likely that there is more to be learnt from the medical practitioners of the past.

MEDIEVAL MEDICAL EXPERIMENTS

During the Middle Ages medical science was, like other branches of knowledge, experimental. At the site of an old monastery at Soutra Aisle, south of Edinburgh in Scotland, some remarkable detective work has uncovered new evidence of just how skilled some of the medieval practitioners were.

Dredging through the 'blood and shit' pits on site, archaeologists have discovered sets of seeds used in herbal preparations. These reveal a wealth of medical knowledge that has been lost to us. For example, a plant called tormentil was used to treat intestinal worms; it contains tannic acid, on which current treatments for worms are based. And juniper was used to promote contractions when giving birth.

Below: Extracting balsam as a base for medicines and perfumes.

Our belief that anaesthetics are a modern invention is shown to be quite wrong. Among the finds are several natural anaesthetics, such as opium, black henbane and hemlock. It had been thought that it was impossible to grow opium in Britain's climate – but the monks clearly found a way. One of the major discoveries was a heel bone with deep ridges that look like evidence of a club foot. It is believed that the foot must have been amputated – and an anaesthetic compound was found only 3 inches away.

We like to believe in the idea of progress – and it helps to think that we know more than people did in the past. But, arguably, we have a strange form of medicine which seems to extend human life while creating its own wreckage.

Hospitals actually cause disease while curing it. In 1997 the *Lancet* published a study* showing that just under 20 per cent of hospital patients in the United Kingdom experience some adverse event because of being in hospital. It found that the likelihood of this increased by 6 per cent for each day of hospitalization. Hospital-acquired infections alone kill nearly twice as many people in the UK as die on the roads.**

In the United States medical treatment is the third highest cause of death (iatrogenic death) after cancer and heart disease. So, despite our undoubted progress in understanding the chemistry and biological structure of the body, and great advances in the techniques of medical intervention, we are not exceeding the achievements of medieval doctors as much as we might expect. In their terms we are doing worse, because the objective of their care was not necessarily to save the body (which would, of course, be wonderful) but to help save the soul by allowing patients to know the hour of their death, and prepare for it. This was itself a genuine medical skill and, again, one that depended on seeing the patient as a human being.

No-one ever found the philosopher's stone or the elixir of life – otherwise they'd still be here to tell us about it – but this doesn't mean we can dismiss the Middle Ages as a period of superstitious ignorance. The determination to insist on a major shift in thought around the time of Newton has done a great disservice to our understanding of the past.

It was medieval philosophers who argued that revelation was to be found hidden in nature, and uncovered by experiment. This was the true scientific revolution. And it was Newton's age that was the great age of superstition. It was in the sixteenth and seventeenth centuries that people started to believe that human beings could make a pact with the Devil and thereby gain supernatural powers.

When Roger Bacon thought about the future he believed it was easily possible that the world would very soon be completely transformed. He foresaw ships guided by one man, moving 'with greater swiftness than if they were full of oarsmen…'; mechanical lifts and cranes; devices 'whereby, without bodily danger, a man may walk on the bottom of the sea or of a river…'; high-powered magnification; artificial flight; and that 'a car shall be made which will move with inestimable speed, and the motion will be without the help of any living creature…'.

That was 750 years ago. What took us so long?

Partly, our ignorance about our own past.

*Vol. 349, Feb 1, 1997.
**The Management and Control of Hospital Acquired Infection in Acute NHS Trusts in England estimated that hospital-acquired infection causes 5000 deaths annually. 3200 people died in road accidents in England and Wales in 2002. Office of National Statistics HSQ10DT2.

CHAPTER SIX

Knight

Above: Violence as
a spectator sport.
This early fourteenth-
century illustration
shows Guinevere
watching Lancelot
as he fights for King
Daudemagus in a
tournament.

THE YEAR: 1278. The place: open country near Le Hem, in Picardy. A court is assembled; the field is laid out for a tournament and splendidly bedecked ladies are watching from a platform. At their centre is a queen, none other than King Arthur's wife, the lady Guinevere. Alongside her is an even more surprising figure: the Lady of Courtesy.

A herald in full finery has proclaimed that Queen Guinevere requires all who want to pursue love in arms to appear before her; and before they can join her court they must joust. Now seven identically dressed knights appear and surrender themselves to the queen, saying they have been defeated by the knight with a lion. The knight in question then arrives with his lion and seven damsels, Guinevere's ladies, whom he has rescued from the seven knights in a week-long quest.

The drama of the knight errant, riding around the countryside in

shining armour rescuing damsels in distress, was being played out as courtly theatre – by real knights. Was chivalry ever anything more than an entertainment? Was anyone ever motivated by such pure and noble sentiments that they set off every morning looking for distressed damsels and dragons in need of killing? How did they make a living?

How did the lives of the knights play-acting at Le Hem relate to the kind of chivalric story they were performing?

The reality of knighthood – like reality for all people living medieval lives – was in a constant state of flux throughout the Middle Ages. Concepts of knighthood changed and the perception of what knights were, and what they should be doing, also changed. The only thing that remained constant was that the idea of chivalry was never what we mean by the word today.

Behind the fantasy is a story of violence: of the desire of young men to experience violence, and to get rich and famous through, its practice; and the attempts of society to construct a context in which that violence could be channelled or contained.

It was an effort that was doomed to failure. By the later Middle Ages writers looked back and lamented that the golden age of chivalry had passed. In 1385 a French monk wrote:

… these days all wars are directed against the poor labouring people and against their goods and chattels. I do not call that war, but… pillage and robbery… warfare does not follow the rules of chivalry or of the ancient custom of noble warriors who upheld justice, the widow, the orphan and the poor… And for these reasons the knights of to-day have not the glory and the praise of the old champions of former times…
Tree of Battles

But had the golden age of chivalry ever existed at all?

WHAT WAS A KNIGHT?

ANGLO-SAXON KNIGHTS DID NOT FIGHT on horseback. But Europe's nobility did and after the Norman conquest in England the word 'knight' was also understood to mean a horse-warrior.

William the Conqueror rewarded his victorious followers with grants of the land they had just conquered. They did not own the land – the ownership was still in William's hot and sticky hands. Every one of those whom he rewarded simply held their land directly or indirectly from him, and the price they paid was military service. His immediate companions

became hereditary 'tenants-in-chief'; eight of them held half the land in England. They were obliged to provide a total of about 5,000 warriors when called on by the king, and these warriors were men 'enfeoffed' as their sub-tenants.

Sub-tenants held their land as a 'knight's fee' and had to serve on campaign under their feudal superior for a fixed term each year. A knight was 'dubbed' – made into a knight – by being presented with his weapon and baring his neck to his feudal superior, who declined to behead him and instead briefly rested a sword on his shoulder. As in the rest of western Europe, the knights formed a military caste, whose rights of lordship were paid for with the duty of military service. They were required to finance the cost of the horses, armour and entourage for that service, conventionally understood to be for forty days a year. William's particular contribution to the practice of feudalism was to ensure that all landholders swore fealty directly to him, rather than just to their immediate overlord. This put the King of England directly at the head of all the military tenants of the land.

It took two more generations for 'knighthood' to signify the profession of arms. The *Anglo-Saxon Chronicle* says when William wanted to dub his son Henry a *chevalier*, horse-warrior, in 1085 he made him a *ridere*. Henry's coronation charter speaks of tenants holding land not as knights but '*per loricam*', as wearers of chain mail.

This was a kingdom designed as a machine for war, its warriors sustained by the obligatory service of the peasantry.

The main thing knights had to have in common was the ability to fight. They were warriors first and foremost, and violence was, for them, a way of life. They listened to stories of exciting brutality, a genre that continued for centuries in tales like the thirteenth-century romance *Havelok the Dane*:

> There might men well see boys all beaten
> And the ribs broken in their sides
> And Havelock on them well avenged.
> He broke their arms, he broke their knees,
> He broke their shanks, he broke their thighs.
> He made the blood come running down
> To the feet right from the crown;
> For there was not a head he spared

The ability to beat another man to a pulp or cut him to bloody pieces was not only a requirement of knighthood – it was one of its ideals. Richard the

Opposite: The Saxon infantry under attack, from the Bayeux tapestry.

Below: Squires in training, an illustration accompanying a song about a knight's bravery.

165
Knight

Lionheart, for example, was celebrated amongst the knightly class for his ability to chop his victims' skulls down to the teeth. For everyone who was not a knight, this was a bit of a problem. How could you control these dangerous young men – especially now they were in charge? How could you channel their testosterone culture into areas that were less destructive to society? The answer that emerged was to try to invent a code of behaviour by which the knightly class must govern themselves – or, rather, to adapt the code of behaviour that the knights themselves were already developing.

Men on horseback, *chevaliers*, now dominated much of Europe. And the code of conduct of these men – and indeed their whole culture – became known as 'chivalry'.

The snag was that chivalry meant different things to different people.

KNIGHTS' CHIVALRY

KNIGHTS THEMSELVES HAD NO DOUBTS what chivalry meant. It meant learning how to fight, making money, and winning fame and honour. For Anglo-Norman knights of the twelfth and thirteenth centuries the perfect role-model was William Marshal. He was the first medieval layman (other than a king) to be the subject of a biography, which was completed some seven years after his death in 1219. Unlike the biographies of saints, it was not in Latin but in French, to be understood by men like himself.

William became hardened to the perils of battle at the ripe old age of five. His father, John the Marshal, had rebelled against King Stephen in 1152, and the king had laid siege to his castle. During the siege William's father handed him over as a hostage. Stephen had no scruples about using five-year-old hostages, and at one point put the boy into a siege catapult and threatened to shoot him over the castle walls, unless John the Marshal gave himself up.

William's father is reported to have shouted back that he didn't give a hoot about the boy since he possessed 'the hammer and the anvils to make more and better sons'. William clearly knew what it was to have a tender, loving man as a father. Stephen, his bluff called, let the boy live.

John died when William was about 16, and didn't leave him a penny. William was thus faced with the familiar dilemma of every younger son from a landed English family: join the Church or learn to become a knight.

We do not know how long William struggled with his problem, but the time could probably have been measured in seconds rather than hours.

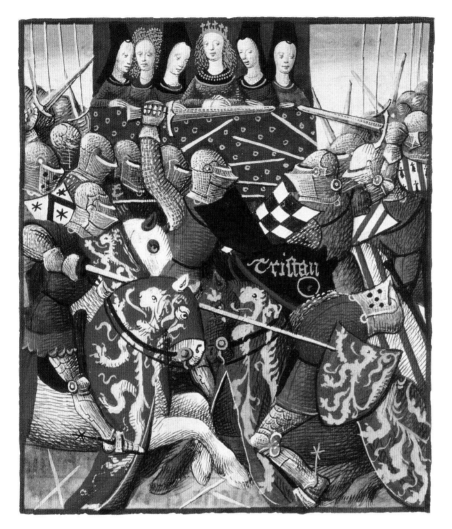

He had a cousin in the town of Tancarville in Normandy who ran a sort of military academy. The prospect of free tuition and board and lodging was too good to resist. William removed to Normandy and spent the next three years training for the military life. Horsemanship, handling weapons, getting fit, learning how to kill and make money – it was all part of the soldier's calling.

William was eventually dubbed a knight by his cousin, and was at last equipped to earn a bit of ready cash. The neat thing was that he didn't even have to go to war to do this. There was plenty of money to be made on the tournament circuit.

He teamed up with a business partner, Roger de Caugie, and together they embarked on the tourneying circuit, agreeing to split the proceeds between them. They were spectacularly successful. In one ten-month period the Marshal–Caugie team captured and put to ransom 103 knights. This was, of course, education in the school of hard knocks – after one tournament William's helmet was so battered he couldn't take it off. He was awarded the prize but no-one could find him. Eventually he was discovered with his head on the blacksmith's anvil having the dents hammered out of his helmet, and there a woman of noble birth presented him with his prize: a wondrous fish – a pike over 6 feet long!

William Marshal didn't just get rich; he also achieved that other aim of chivalry: fame. In fact, he went about this quite methodically and employed a servant by the name of Henry Norreis to go around promoting his celebrity. Indeed, it has been suggested that William's biography itself was all part of what became a family programme of self-aggrandizement. The cost of the biography was underwritten by William's eldest son, and the author (a certain 'John') 'might well have been one of those heralds-of-arms who arranged the jousts on the tournament grounds, identified the protagonists by their insignia, and by singing their exploits boosted the reputation of the champions'.* William's own skill at self-promotion was clearly considerable. Like many a young knight he caught the attention of Eleanor of Aquitaine, who was generous enough to ransom him when he was captured and imprisoned by a nobleman who had killed his uncle. William then served Eleanor's husband, Henry II.

His biographer stresses first and foremost William's dedication to 'prowess', or skill and courage in fighting. Secondly he emphasizes William's loyalty – dutifully serving Henry II, Richard the Lionheart, King John and the child-king Henry III.

As a young man William did the proper knightly thing and went on crusade, during which he somehow managed to greatly magnify his reputation – even though in July 1187, about two months before William came back from Palestine, Saladin destroyed the entire fighting force of the kingdom of Jerusalem.

He then returned to Henry's service, and his loyalty certainly paid off. The king rewarded him with the hand of Isabelle de Clare, the most eligible heiress in the country with oodles of land and her very own castle! William generously took it over for her – nowadays it's called Chepstow.

The landless William had become a man of property. It was every knight's dream come true. He was famous as a warrior and was one of the richest men in England. At his funeral, the archbishop of Canterbury

168
Knight

*Georges Duby, *Guillaume le Marechal, ou le meilleur chevalier du monde,* (Paris, 1984), trans. R. Howard, *William Marshal, Flower of Chivalry* (New York, 1986), p. 33 – quoted in Kaeuper, p. 280.

himself described him as 'the best knight in the world'. Fame, money and God's approval – chivalry could not get better than that if you were a knight.

However, we must never forget that what medieval knights meant by chivalry was not what we might mean. For them, the key thing was that it ennobled the cult of violence that they pursued. Chivalry introduced an etiquette for violent contact between knights that is reflected in the stories they loved to listen to in the twelfth century.

In one of these, *Yvain*, there is a description of a set-to between two knights:

> Never were there two knights so intent upon each other's death… they drive the sword-point at the face… both are possessed of such courage that one would not for aught retreat a foot before his adversary until he had wounded him to death.

But the tale stresses that this was honourable, elegant murderous violence:

> They were very honourable in not trying or deigning to strike or harm their steeds in any way; but they sat astride their steeds without putting foot to earth, which made the fight more elegant. At last my lord Yvain crushed the helmet of the knight… Beneath his kerchief his head was split to the very brains.

Elegant indeed.

Knights saw chivalry in terms of fighting, gaining honour and getting rich. But there were others who were trying to define the concept of chivalry in their own interests.

THE CHURCH'S CHIVALRY

THERE WAS OBVIOUSLY A BIT OF A CONTRADICTION between the demands of Christianity and a knight's job – which was based on professional killing. Meekness, turning the other cheek, regarding killing as a sin, weren't really subjects that were taken very seriously at knight school. This was a problem at the very heart of feudal life.

At first the Church had seen its role as one of simple restraint. In 1023 it declared it would not give warriors its protection if they fought during Lent. In 1027 a council at Toulouges, in south-west France, imposed a general truce on Sundays. Soon the Truce of God was extended to run from Thursday morning to Monday morning. Then the Church added the more important saint's days and Advent to its list. And at a church council

169
Knight

Above: Illustration
showing slaughter
at the taking of
Antioch, 1098.
Crusaders boasted
of the numbers they
killed while winning
absolution for their
souls.

in Narbonne in 1054 it was declared that 'no Christian should kill another Christian, for whoever kills a Christian undoubtedly sheds the blood of Christ'.

William the Conqueror had invaded England with the blessing of the Pope, and flying a Papal banner, but was obliged to do penance for the sin of killing people at the battle of Hastings.

For knights, this raised the obvious question: 'Well, given that killing is what we do, who should we be killing, then?'

The Church had the sensible idea of diverting their energies. In 1095, Pope Urban II called for the First Crusade and reversed centuries of Christian doctrine by announcing that it was fine for violent young men to butcher people, so long as the victims were folk of whom the Church disapproved (more specifically, those of whom the pope disapproved). Hitherto knights had had to do penance for those whom they killed in

battle. But crusading was now defined as a penance in itself: a knight could save his soul by slaughter.

Crusaders, the supposed defenders of pilgrims, scourge of the heathen Saracens, were the Church's own warriors. In this context the Christian knight needed to show very little restraint, and all over Europe warriors committed themselves to crusading with enthusiasm. They flocked to the cause, and at the capture of Jerusalem in 1099 they were able to boast of wading in 'infidel' blood up to their knees. It is true that there were limits to the permissible violence, even on crusade, but these were at the outer limits of savagery – some knights who took part in the First Crusade did have to seek papal forgiveness for eating the bodies of their enemies. It was granted.

Christian chivalry – fighting at the behest of the Church – became a system of sanctified slaughter. The pope's enemies, after all, were not restricted to Muslims in faraway lands. Popes had enemies all over the place, and they were prepared to hurl crusades against them whenever this looked like a practical proposition.

When Pope Innocent III declared a crusade against the 'heretics' of the Languedoc in 1208 he handed out their lands to men from northern France; all they had to do was take them. Simon de Montfort was granted control of the area encompassing Carcassonne, Albi and Béziers, and set about slaughtering its inhabitants. He and his troops butchered around 18,000 people in Béziers without a second thought. When soldiers asked the pope's representative at the slaughter whether they should separate believers from heretics he told them not to bother: when the souls of the slaughtered came to be judged, 'God will know his own'.

Left: Knightly violence receives the blessing of the church. A monk presents a crucifix to a knight leaving for the Crusades.

Below: A sixteenth-century illustration showing the Church's idea of dubbing.

Christian chivalry was not particularly lovely but it was the Church's attempt to harness the destructive power of knighthood, to advance its own ends and at the same time introduce a more benign code of behaviour amongst the warrior class.

In 1276, the Catalan knight-turned-ecclesiastic-and-philosopher, Ramon Lull, laid down some ethical guidelines for knights in his *Book on the Order of Chivalry*. It's a curious list.

The first duty of the proper chivalric knight, according to Lull, is to defend 'the Holy Catholic Faith'. His second is to maintain and defend his temporal lord. His third duty (more surprisingly) is to go hunting, give lavish dinners and fight in tournaments: 'Knights ought to take horses to joust and to go tourneying, to hold open table and to hunt at harts, at bores and other wild beasts.'*

Rather more ominously, the knight's fourth duty, according to Lull, is to scare the peasantry into working the land: 'For because of the dread that the common people have of the knights, they labour and cultivate the earth, for fear lest they be destroyed.' Slightly contrarily, his next duty is to defend 'women, widows and orphans and diseased men and the weak'

and 'those that labour the land'. He should found cities and punish thieves and robbers, and should avoid swearing…

For Lull, even the knight's equipment was full of religious significance. The sword is made in the semblance of the cross to signify that 'our lord vanquished death upon the cross'. The spear is truth, the helmet is the dread of shame, the coat of mail represents his defence against vice. His leg harness is to keep his feet on the straight and narrow, his spurs signify diligence and swiftness. The gorget that protects his throat represents obedience, the mace: strength, the dagger: trust in God, and so on and so forth.

The Church provided knights with a religious vocabulary for violence and, at the same time, imported knightly terms into its own usage: 'Soldiers of Christ' could mean either knights or monks.

It also did its best to take over the ceremonies of knighthood – in particular, the

*The Book of the Ordre of Chyvalry, trans. W. Caxton, ed. A. T. P. Byles (EETS, 1926 rep.1971) p.31. Following quotations: pp.32, 38.

ritual involved in dubbing a knight. A fourteenth-century book describing the ceremonies to be performed by a bishop records the form the Church would have liked this to take. The would-be knight is bathed in rose water on the eve of his knighthood. He spends the night in vigil in a church and hears Mass the next morning. The priest then gives him the *collée* (the light blow on the shoulder that 'dubs' him knight). The only role allowed the laity in all this is that a nobleman gives the knight his spurs.

But in general this was wishful thinking on the part of the Church – how it would have liked to run things. The ceremony of dubbing a knight remained predominantly non-religious. Lords were not going to give up the power of creating their own followers, and dubbing remained a secular event with enough sacerdotal overtones to provide religious legitimatization – but not enough to allow for priestly control.

In the long run, knights took from the Church what they needed to justify themselves and their way of life, without letting the Church take over in the way it would have liked.

ROYAL CHIVALRY

ROYALTY ALSO WANTED TO CONTROL CHIVALRY. Kings and princes naturally wanted to harness the aggressive instincts of knights to further their own interests. If the Church encouraged these men to wrap their violent way of life in robes of piety, the king provided them with robes of an altogether more tangible variety.

The Arthurian fantasy that was acted out at Le Hem (as interval entertainment between jousts) was a deliberate response to the revival of an Arthurian cult at the court of Edward I – it had been expected that the English king and some of his knights would attend, but they failed to show up. In the account of what happened, the Lady of Courtesy specifically associated the heroes of Camelot with English knights, and with King Edward.*

Romantic fantasy was a useful way of ensuring men's allegiance. Once the Norman helmet (an iron hat with a nose covering) had given way to one that covered the full face, knighthood could easily be turned into a dressing-up game, and royalty played on that.

Nowadays we recognize famous people by their faces because we have seen countless pictures of them. But back in the Middle Ages you would not know what anyone looked like unless you had met them. Most people living in the twelfth century would have had as little idea of what

---

Sarrasin, Le Roman du Hem, ed. A. Henry (Brussels, 1939), discussed in Juliet Vale, *Edward III and Chivalry: Chivalric Society and its Context 1270–1350* (Boydell Press, 1982).

Richard the Lionheart looked like as we have now. They would have had even less idea when his head was inside a bucket with eye-slits.

So the rich and famous needed a way of announcing who they were. That is why they had coats of arms.

Going into battle with your coat of arms emblazoned on your shield, your surcoat and your horse cloth, and with a crest on your helmet that would identify you in the thick of the fighting, was a kind of dare. A well-marked knight was fighting for his family honour as well as for his own life: if he ran away everyone would know. But the fact that he could be recognized was also a potential life-saver. His coat of arms and equipment signalled that he was wealthy and therefore worth keeping alive in order to be held hostage.

One mercenary captain took this to its logical extreme. It's said that Sir Robert Knolles used to ride into battle with an inscription on his helmet that read: 'Whoever captures Sir Robert Knolles will gain 100,000 moutons.' (The *mouton d'or* was a gold coin worth one-third of a pound of silver.)

But coats of arms and other heraldic symbols also had a ceremonial side, and lent themselves to pageantry at tournaments. Arthurian themes, fictitious but well known from the romances of the time, provided a wonderful way of identifying chivalric valour with loyalty to the king, and the English Crown latched on to this with enthusiasm.

Opposite: St George's chapel, Windsor, home of the Order of the Garter.

St George's Chapel, in Windsor, is the physical architecture of Chivalry. This magnificent Gothic building is hung with the banners of the knights of the Order of the Garter. This is the highest order of Chivalry in England, a reincarnation of knights of the Round Table, dedicated to St George the dragon slayer. The Order of the Garter is a true medieval chivalric invention.

The top of a 'Round Table', supposedly Arthur's, had hung in Windsor Castle since the time of Edward I – it now hangs in the Great Hall of Winchester Castle. It seems that Edward III had a new version constructed, and built the Round Tower at Windsor to house it. In 1344 he held a tournament after which the knights feasted around the table, the first of a series of Round Table gatherings in the castle. Between October 1347 and the end of 1348, following military successes in the Hundred Years War with France, Edward held a further series of tournaments, and in June 1348 the first ceremony of the Order of the Garter was held at Windsor. The castle was to be the new Camelot.

On 10 August 1348, while the Black Death ravaged England, the 26 founder knights, including Edward III and his son the Black Prince, filed

into St George's Chapel in pairs for their first investiture. The lines parted as they sat themselves opposite each other, the king and 12 knights on one side and the prince and 12 knights on the other. They faced each other as two opposing tournament teams, the very soul of Christian chivalry at the royal court.

This was chivalry as pure pageantry. Nowhere in the code of the Order of the Garter was there anything about protecting the weak or vulnerable.

In 1356, after the Battle of Poitiers, the Black Prince hosted a banquet of his own. He was 26 years old. The guest of honour was his most important prisoner, the King of France. Jean Froissart, a contemporary chronicler, described the scene:

The same day of the battle at night the prince made a supper in his lodging to the French king and to the most part of the great lords that were prisoners. … the prince served before the king as humbly as he could, and would not sit at the king's board for any desire that the king could make, but he said he was not sufficient to sit at the table with so great a prince as the king was. But then he said to the king: … 'sir, methinks ye ought to rejoice, though the day be not as ye would have had it, for this day ye have won the high renown of prowess and have passed this day in valiantness all other of your party. Sir, I say not this to mock you, for all that be on our party, that saw every man's deeds, are plainly accorded by true sentence to give you the prize.'*
The Chronicles of Froissart

That was royal chivalry in action – the honour due to a man was related to his rank. Fourteen years later, at Limoges, the Black Prince provided an object lesson in what that meant.

LIMOGES

IN 1370, LIMOGES WAS A BORDER TOWN, on the uncertain frontier between the King of England's possessions and the lands of the King of France. It was an old town, with Roman roots; its bridge was ancient, but its cathedral was new, a tribute to the town's wealth. That wealth was based on the secret skills of its artisans, who produced fabulous enamelled objects

Above: Edward, the Black Prince, receives the principality of Aquitaine.

*Jean Froissart, *The Chronicles of Froissart,* trans. by John Bourchier, Lord Berners, ed. G. C. Macaulay. (New York, 1910).

that could not be imitated anywhere else in the world.

Enamel is a thin layer of coloured glass that has been melted and fused on to a metal surface. Normally, small enamel panels were surrounded by copper wire to prevent the golds, deep blues, rich reds and profound greens from running into each other, and to hold each piece of enamel in place as the underlying metal expanded and contracted. Otherwise, as the piece warmed and cooled over the course of a day, the enamel would simply fall off. But in Limoges, uniquely, artisans had discovered how to produce enamel that expanded at the same rate as copper, and could butt different enamels against each other. This produced work of astonishing clarity and detail. The enamels were enormously prized throughout Europe, and small enamelled Limoges coffers were precisely the equivalent of the Fabergé Easter eggs that later delighted nineteenth-century Europe.

Above: A Limoges Eucharistic Dove c. 1220, a master-piece of champlevé enamel.

The enamel works were factories that employed a dozen or more experts in a range of highly skilled crafts. Each one was the home of the rather wealthy family who directed and controlled the work. It was also, of course, a showroom and shop. This part of the building was impressive and elegant as customers for Limoges enamels came from all over Europe, and were themselves wealthy connoisseurs. The works were in vigorous competition with each other and, although most pieces were unsigned, those in the know would have had had little problem identifying the work of individual masters.

The factories were down by the river Charente as its strongly acid water was used to purify the coloured glass before it was laid in place for fusing. They were sheltered within a strong city wall and the town citadel towered over them.

LIMOGES UNDER SIEGE

THE ENGLISH TERRITORY OF AQUITAINE expanded and contracted with the changing fortunes of war. In 1369, the French king, Charles V, announced that he was confiscating it. When his forces reached Limoges and besieged it, its bishop decided it was clear which way the wind was blowing and

surrendered. The Black Prince, the ruler of Aquitaine, was enraged. He marched to Limoges bent on revenge, and arrived outside its walls with 1,200 knights, squires and men carrying long lances, 1,000 archers and 1,000 foot soldiers.

The prince was not a man to mess with. He was now 40 years old, and was one of the most experienced and capable warriors in Europe. His father had knighted him when he was 15, just before the Battle of Crécy and, according to legend, he had dressed in black armour for the battle. This seems to be why he was known as the Black Prince. He had spent his time since then engaged in war in France on King Edward's behalf, devoting himself in the few years of peace to the war-sport of tournament.

The prince was a sick man, who had to travel in a litter, but he still knew how to conduct a war. The bishop of Limoges, pressed by the frightened businessmen of the town, realized he had made a serious mistake in surrendering, but control was no longer in his hands. Limoges was now ruled by Charles's men, from the citadel.

Sir John de Villemur, Sir Hugo de la Roche and Roger de Beaufort, who commanded in it, did all they could to comfort them by saying, 'Gentlemen, do not be alarmed: we are sufficiently strong to hold out against the army of the prince: he cannot take us by assault, nor greatly hurt us, for we are well supplied with artillery.' (Froissart)

The siege was a pretty thing, seen from a distance. The besieging army, with its coloured tents and attractive banners, was commanded by knights in literally shining armour, astride horses caparisoned in the heraldic symbols of their riders. With nothing to do all day except wait, the knights spent their time practising their skills, engaging in play-fights or happily plundering and burning the farms that dotted the charming Limousin countryside.

Above: The Black Prince.

The white stone walls of the town and citadel were topped with wooden roofs, from which fluttered the pennants of the defending knights. This attractive scene was unspoiled by the smallest taint of blood, because the real struggle was being fought underground. The Black Prince had a team of miners digging under the city walls. Eventually they were ready and, setting the mines on fire, they brought a large part of the walls crashing down. In a few minutes, Limoges was wide open.

THE CHIVALRIC LEADERS OF LIMOGES

THE THREE COMMANDERS OF THE CITADEL realized that the game was over and there followed a series of scenes that epitomize the very essence of late fourteenth-century chivalry. Knowing they were about to engage in a famous battle, their first concern was that only two of them had actually been dubbed knights. Sir John de Villemur immediately proposed that they should knight Roger de Beaufort (who was a mere gentleman). He replied, 'Sir, I have not as yet distinguished myself sufficiently for that honour, but I thank you for your good opinion in suggesting it to me.'

There was no time to continue this elegant discussion, as it was time to fight.

What mattered to Froissart, the chronicler of these scenes, was how the three principal characters acquitted themselves in single combat against suitable opponents under the rules of chivalry:

> The Duke of Lancaster was engaged for a long time with Sir John de Villemur, who was a hardy knight, strong and well made. The Earl of Cambridge singled out Sir Hugo de la Roche, and the Earl of Pembroke Roger de Beaufort, who was but a simple esquire. These three Frenchmen did many valorous deeds of arms, as all allowed, and ill did it betide those who approached too near.
>
> The Prince, coming that way in his carriage, looked on the combat with great pleasure, and enjoyed it so much that his heart was softened and his anger appeased. After the combat had lasted a considerable time, the Frenchmen, with one accord, viewing their swords, said, 'My lords, we are yours: you have vanquished us: therefore act according to the law of arms.' 'By God,' replied the Duke of Lancaster, 'Sir John, we do not intend otherwise, and we accept you for our prisoners.' Thus, as I have been informed, were these three knights taken.
> *The Chronicles of Froissart*

Roger, in Froissart's eyes, was now a knight after all. This was the classic chivalric encounter: war as combat, to be admired and enjoyed.

THE REALITY BEHIND THE CHIVALRY

ALL WAS GENTILITY AND CHIVALRY, unless you happened to be outside the charmed circle of men in armour. The Black Prince's orders had been simple and brutal, as reported by Froissart:

You would then have seen pillagers, active to do mischief, running through the town, slaying men, women, and children, according to their orders. It was a most melancholy business; for all ranks, ages and sexes cast themselves on their knees before the prince, begging for mercy; but he was so inflamed with passion and revenge that he listened to none, but all were put to the sword, wherever they could be found, even those who were not guilty: for I know not why the poor were not spared, who could not have had any part in this treason; but they suffered for it, and indeed more than those who had been the leaders of the treachery.

There was not that day in the city of Limoges any heart so hardened, or that had any sense of religion, who did not deeply bewail the unfortunate events passing before their eyes; for upwards of three thousand men, women and children were put to death that day. God have mercy on their souls! for they were veritable martyrs.

The Chronicles of Froissart

The whole town was pillaged, burnt, and totally destroyed.

Froissart listed many other instances of the Black Prince's savagery, from his 'right good beginning' burning and ravaging in northern France as a teenager, through the slaughter of women and children at Mont Giscar the year before Crécy to the systematic looting and killing of people whose crime was to be 'good, simple, and ignorant of war', but nothing so moved him to pity as the slaughter at Limoges. Perhaps it was because he understood what was being destroyed. Froissart was a high-level courtier, a man of education and taste, who knew that what was being lost was not just human life. The Black Prince was eliminating the brilliant colours of Limoges, killing the master craftsmen and skilled artisans along with their wives and children, and looting and destroying their factories.

One of the great treasures of the world was wiped away.

Limoges did eventually recover, and went on to achieve perhaps even greater heights of artistry in other crafts. But the expertise that had produced the brilliant, jewel-like enamels of the thirteenth and fourteenth centuries was gone, the keepers of its secrets dead, and that work was not seen again.

Froissart did not regard the Black Prince as barbarous, or as a criminal. On the contrary, he described him as 'the perfect root of all honour and nobleness, of wisdom, valour and largesse'. The prince was a man who played out the role of chivalric hero, and if we see an

incomprehensible contradiction here it is because we have developed our own unhistorical idea of chivalry.

Froissart's view of chivalry was the one held by the court, not the religious one.

Edward III set up a court of chivalry to deal with chivalric disputes. But it's no good thinking of knights on trial for failing to open the drawbridge for a damsel, or for slaughtering the poor and weak.

Above: 'Sir Galahad fighting 40 soldiers'. The chivalrous knight of medieval stories was a fantasy-figure, no more realistic than the action heroes of modern movies.

The main preoccupation of the court was money – knights squabbling over the loot from some unfortunate town, or arguing over how to split the profits of ransom, or claiming to own the rights to a particular prisoner. The other major concern was quarrels about who owned the rights to a particular coat of arms.

The court of chivalry was simply another way in which the king tried to exert some sort of control over the business of warfare.

CRECY AND THE DEMISE OF CHIVALRY

EDWARD III MAY HAVE BEEN BUSY helping to glamorize chivalry, but this does not mean he used it as the basis for war. Elegance was for romances and for tournaments. But battles had to be won, and knights in armour were vulnerable to inelegant new weapons.

By the fourteenth century it was shatteringly expensive to get a knight on to the battlefield. Since Roman times the standard piece of fighting kit had been the chain-mail coat, but developments in missile technology had brought a new kind of arrow that could pass through mail. So knights started wearing heavier armour – like a coat of metal plates. Then a crossbow was developed that could penetrate the plates, and so on. As the kit became more expensive it took more land to sustain a knight, so the link between landholding and military duty began to collapse.

In fact, within 100 years of the Norman Conquest people were opting out of the system in serious numbers. As the age of the Conquest came to an end, fewer and fewer landholders saw themselves as warriors. Widows could and did inherit their husband's estates, young men turned into old men and, anyway, there were a lot better things to do with your money than spend it on elaborate handmade armour just so that you could go and be frightened to death by some professional lout. The system of land tenure by military service began to give way to money payments, and it soon became common for the holder of a knight's fee to fail to get himself knighted. (Knighthood in England was never hereditary.)

The Battle of Crécy, where the Black Prince had begun his

Below: Archers using longbows at target practice.

military career, was no chivalric battlefield tournament. By 1346, the English had lost interest in chivalry as a military occupation.

They were massively outnumbered, and the French had assumed that the knights on both sides would battle it out on horseback, and that the smaller English force would be overwhelmed, ransomed and go home ruined. But the English were playing by a new rule-book. When they arrived at the battlefield most of the knights got off their horses. This wasn't at all what they were supposed to do. But then they weren't planning to go through the usual chivalric routine. They were relying on the support of their non-noble longbowmen.

The English longbow (as it is now called) was not a noble weapon, and it was not wielded by rich young men whose kit cost the equivalent of a Ferrari. Thousands of French noblemen charged in full pageantry. In the first five minutes, the English loosed more than 3,000 arrows. The flower of French chivalry was cut down by archers on sixpence a day.

The French lost over 5,000 men; the English a few hundred. Using archers to shift the balance of power in a battle was not in itself new; what was new was the sheer scale on which the English employed them. If armies of the future were going to behave like this, the mounted knight was pretty much out of business.

And something else was eating away at the shaky (perhaps even non-existent) edifice of chivalry: the feudal host was itself being replaced by a modern regular army consisting of professional soldiers.

THE RISE OF THE MERCENARIES

THE FEUDAL LEVY OF LANDED KNIGHTS had never been the sole military force used by kings. They relied at least as much on the military forces of their own household and, from the twelfth century, on landless knights who needed to be paid. Henry I, for example, could only call on a levy of some 5,000 knights from the whole country, and hired bands of 1,000 knights at a time. The coins used to pay them, called *solidi*, gave rise to the English word 'soldiers'. At the time when Lull's handbook on Christian chivalry was becoming widely translated and imitated, the military significance of the feudal knight was fading into history.

The armies of kings became professionalized, mercenary forces; more and more, courtly knights stayed home jousting prettily at court and feasting with other members of their orders of chivalry, and paid a tax instead of performing their military duty. Increasingly on the battlefield,

knights were paid professionals who preferred to do the business against men who were poorly equipped and untrained. When Edward III landed in France in 1337, at the start of the Hundred Years War, his army included only about 1,500 feudal knights. The rest, whether armoured men on horseback or pikemen on foot, were paid wages.

This new class of professional soldier did not live off his estates, for he had none; war was how he made his living. If the king would not employ him, someone else must. Nobody had envisaged the disaster this was to bring on Europe.

In 1360 Edward signed a peace treaty – the treaty of Brétigny – with the French. It was the kind of thing kings had done countless times before, but this time there was a difference. Lots of the English (and many of the French) had no homes to go to. Some had been fighting in France for up

to 20 years. They might have captured a nice chateau, and there they were living like lords – why should they go back to England where, as like as not, they'd end up in jail or slaving for someone else?

The result was that France and Italy were infested by hard men in hard armour, hired to do other men's dirty work.

They started with freelance pillaging in northern France. Edward sent royal officers to try to force his men to stop, but he had no power to bring them under control. Gradually English mercenaries, together with men from other countries, started forming themselves into freelance armies, which supposedly coalesced into a single force that was reckoned to be 16,000 strong – bigger than Edward's own army!

The mercenaries called themselves free companies. They were bands of robbers on a nightmare scale, who swept down through France causing havoc and destruction. And there seemed to be no way of stopping them. Every attempt to crush them backfired. Mankind had opened a Pandora's box, and civilization itself had broken down.

Eventually the free companies descended on Avignon, which in those days happened to be the residence of the pope. (The papacy had moved there fifty years earlier; Rome had been a violent and dangerous city for a Pope who was, unusually, a Frenchman.) They burnt the surrounding countryside and threatened to attack God's representative on earth unless he handed over a spiritually uplifting sum of money.

The pope tried to organize a crusade against them but, as the free companies had no land for crusaders to seize, his warriors would have to rely on him for payment. However, paying crusaders with anything other than indulgences was not on the pope's agenda – so most of them packed up and went home. In fact, quite a few of the crusaders joined the companies. The pope had just made his problem worse. In the end, he paid the mercenaries 100,000 florins and also threw in a general pardon for all the sins they had committed so far.

Having successfully bought off the marauders, he persuaded the majority of them to move on into Italy, which was full of career opportunities for mercenary soldiers with nowhere to go.

'Italy' in those days consisted of a lot of city-states like Pisa, Milan, Rome, Florence and Mantua – each one almost a mini-nation in itself. For several centuries they had been at each other's throats in the time-honoured manner of neighbours. Their citizens, however, hadn't been all that attracted to fighting, and had got into the habit of employing mercenary companies to fight for them.

Italy had thus become the cradle of mercenary warfare. And once the free companies moved on from Avignon the north Italians found that employing mercenary companies was no longer a matter of choice – they either paid up or paid with their lives.

The mercenaries came from all over Europe, but now a sizeable proportion of them were Englishmen. One contemporary Italian chronicler, Pietro Azario, recorded how 'some men imprisoned themselves in their own dungeons and locked themselves up at night when they [the English] rode forth…'*

Of all the English soldiers who arrived in Italy none was to make a greater impression than Sir John Hawkwood – Giovanni Acuto, the Italians called him – 'Sharp John'. He soon established himself as leader of one of the companies, the White Company. The younger son of a well-to-do Essex tanner, he had made his way up through the ranks during the Hundred Years War.

In Italy he established his own mercenary company, and for 40 years he made a good living offering his services to whomever would pay for them, often using intimidation to gain employment: 'You had better employ my army now it's here on your border, otherwise I can't guarantee it won't do a lot of damage.' It was the old protection racket writ large.

Another contemporary Italian chronicler, Matteo Villani, left a vivid account of the kind of men Hawkwood was leading:

These people, all young, and for the most part born and raised during the long wars between the French and the English, hot and wilful, used to slaughter and rapine, were skilled in the use of cold steel, and had no thought for their own safety.**

This was the army of the future. It was numbered in 'lances', each lance consisting of a knight on a charger, sheathed in iron and steel from head to foot, a squire, also on a charger but less heavily armed, and a page on a palfrey. There were 1,000 teams of 'lances', so called because their principal weapon was a long and heavy lance. This required two men to wield it and was used only on foot, in a mass formation. The teams also carried heavy swords and daggers, and bows slung across their backs.

They were backed up by infantry, who were armed with longbows and carried swords and daggers, and also some light ladders that could be fixed together to scale towers. They were tough and disciplined

*Pietro Azario, 'Liber gestorum in Lombardia', in L. A. Muratori, *Rerum Italicarum Scriptores – Storici Italiani* (Bologna, 1939), xvi, iv, p.128.
**Matteo Villani, *Cronica* (Florence, 1825–6) v. 259–60.

professionals, five lances to a company, five companies to a troop, and were commanded by effective officers.

They specialized in surprise night raids on towns, when they would massacre the men, rape the women, carry off whatever was worth taking and burn the rest.

This was not in any sense chivalric warfare; it was a job. Hawkwood did not fight for glory or honour. He was simply a down-to-earth businessman – whose business happened to be war. There is a story that two friars once greeted him with the usual 'May God grant you peace'. Whereupon Sir John retorted: 'May God take from you your alms.' When the friars asked why, he replied: 'Why not? You come to me and say that God should let me die of hunger. Don't you know that I live by war, and peace would destroy me?'

CESENA

IN 1377 SIR JOHN HAWKWOOD was under contract to Cardinal Roberto, Count of Geneva, when the citizens of Cesena killed some of his soldiers. Roberto offered them an amnesty if they would surrender their arms, which the citizens did, foolishly trusting the word of a cardinal-priest of the order of the 'Holy Apostles'.

Then Cardinal Roberto summoned Hawkwood from nearby Faenza, where he'd been busy coordinating the rape of all the female inhabitants, and told him to go to Cesena and kill everyone. To do Sir John justice, it is reported that he protested this was not really playing the game, but the cardinal said he wanted 'justice', and by 'justice' he meant 'blood and more blood'. The resulting massacre shocked Europe.

Hawkwood's troop 'burned and slaughtered all the town. The river was coloured with blood. And among the smoking ruins, the rapes, the killings was a pitiful episode. Twenty-four friars were killed in front of the main altar, together with the congregation.' According to hostile chroniclers, as many as 8,000 people died. Up to 16,000 fled and Hawkwood, 'not to be held entirely infamous, sent about a thousand of the women to Rimini'.*

Every building was destroyed and the town was completely rebuilt following the destruction. Only a few pieces of the original walls survive.

But the action did no harm to Hawkwood's reputation. Maybe it even helped by showing how carefully he carried out orders. Over the next 20 years he continued to flourish. He bought castles and property in Italy and estates in England. For the last 15 years of his life he was under more or less permanent contract to the city of Florence, and before he died in 1395 the city promised him a magnificent marble tomb in the great cathedral – the Duomo – in the heart of Florence.

However, the Florentines were businessmen and they never lost their business sense. When the King of England requested that Hawkwood's body be returned to his native land, they felt there were better things to do with their cash than build an empty tomb, so they got an artist to paint a picture of what the tomb would have looked like if they had built it.

The non-aristocratic son of a tanner had become virtually a nobleman, by turning warfare into a business. Meanwhile, chivalry developed as a game of social status, ever further removed from the reality of war. And the knights of England became country gentlemen, the backbone of county administration.

Chivalry was a fantasy, used to put a respectable gloss on the horrors of war. It would be hard to argue that Norman knights were more violent

*J. Temple-Leader and G. Marcetti, *Sir John Hawkwood* (London, 1889).

or bloodthirsty than other warriors throughout human history, or that chivalric knights like William Marshal or the Black Prince were less bloodthirsty than mercenary captains like Sir John Hawkwood. But in the fourteenth century people felt something had changed with the commercialization of warfare.

The chivalrous knight in shining armour never really did exist. All that rescuing damsels and helping the weak was just wishful thinking – a construct of the medieval mind, taken up with enthusiasm by the Victorians and passed on to Hollywood film-makers of today.

But maybe we are better off without chivalry. Its fine ideals were all too often used to perpetuate war – which is what those who live by war want. Francho Sacchetti, one of Hawkwood's contemporaries, said of him: 'He managed his affairs so well that there was little peace in Italy in his time.'* And it is still true that those who promote war are usually those who stand to benefit from it – be they arms manufacturers, politicians or knights in shining armour.

Left: The romantic ideal of chivalry as portrayed in Millais' painting Knight Errant.

*Francho Sacchetti, *Il trecentonovelle,* ed. V. Pernicone (Florence, 1946), pp. 448–9 .

CHAPTER SEVEN

Damsel

HELPLESS, THREATENED AND FOREVER IN NEED OF RESCUE, the medieval damsel-in-distress is an archetype deeply bound up with the image of the chivalrous knight in shining armour. It's easy for us to understand that back in the brutal world of the Middle Ages women should be at the mercy of forces beyond their control, and that they should need rescuing by heroic males.

William Maw Egley's 1858 painting of the Lady of Shalott and her distant hero, Sir Lancelot, seems to convey, in its antiquarian detail, an authentic medieval vision (at least if one overlooks the very nineteenth-century appearance of Mrs Egley): the helpless lady sealed in her chamber, the armoured man emblematic of freedom and courage. But the picture evokes a world that would have been incomprehensible in the age it is meant to represent.

Not that noble ladies didn't need rescuing on occasion. But when they did, they infuriatingly failed to live up to our stereotype.

Right: The Lady of Shalott by William Maw Egley, a classic Victorian view of medieval womanhood.

TAKE NICOLA DE LA HAYE: she was certainly trapped in a tall tower and in need of rescue. But it was all a bit different from the fairy tale.

For a start, the tower in which she was trapped didn't belong to a wicked uncle, stepfather or some other malign relative – it belonged to her. It was part of Lincoln Castle, and Nicola was the hereditary constable – governor – of the castle. What's more, she wasn't at all a helpless damsel; she was a military commander in her own right. As well as governing the castle she was also co-sheriff of Lincolnshire. She was obliged to provide knights' service at the castle and exercised jurisdiction over the royal portion of the city of Lincoln.

She was trapped because an invading French army had occupied Lincoln and was laying siege to the castle.

Mind you, Nicola was a bit mature for a damsel – she was pushing 70. But then again, her knight in shining armour was also an old-age pensioner. He was none other than William Marshal, and although he was now well into his seventies he was the regent of England and was still generally regarded as the epitome of chivalry. William drove the French off, saving Nicola, Lincoln and the whole of England for the young Henry III. Ever the perfect knight, he then celebrated his and Nicola's joint victory by taking her castle away from her and handing it over to the Earl of Salisbury.

Nicola, however, wasn't going to put up with that sort of behaviour from a geriatric like William. She stormed down to London, had the castle restored to her control and kept going as constable until she was well into her eighties. 'What, then, is chivalry? Such a difficult, tough, and very costly thing to learn that no coward ventures to take it on.'*

On the down side, Nicola did not get the job of sheriff back. It is one of the oddities of social change that there are times when women are just not considered the right people to be sheriffs. England had to wait nearly 400 years for the next one – when Lady Ann Clifford was appointed sheriff of Westmoreland on the basis that not only was she one of the wealthiest women in the country, but she was also a recognized expert with a crossbow. Both James I and Cromwell found her hard to deal with, and that was the end of the story for woman sheriffs until the Victorian era.

* History of William Marshal.

Damsel

194
Damsel

WOMEN AS PROPERTY

THE ROLES OF MEN AND WOMEN in society, and the relationship between the sexes, were forever changing throughout the period that we conveniently (if mistakenly) refer to as the 'Middle Ages'. There was no one set of attitudes. It was a constantly varying dynamic – just as it is today.

It would probably be wrong to talk of any steady advance in women's rights and privileges through the 500 years after the Norman Conquest, but it is possible to say that towards the end of the period women were enjoying a more equal role in society, and more respect than they had previously been given – and then things were reversed.

Of course, they lived in a man's world – particularly at the start of the Middle Ages. The Conquest meant that William 'owned' the country. It became his personal property, and he had no intention of giving it away. Instead he allowed his followers the use of lands in return for their military service. This link between property and the profession of arms meant landholding became a male preserve. Men ruled the roost, and wives and daughters were supposed to do what they were told by their husbands and fathers.

Many of the new Norman overlords expected to find wives among the widows and daughters of the Englishmen they had supplanted, and the new king encouraged this as a way of consolidating the Conquest. Not surprisingly, many of these women resisted. Some retreated to nunneries for self-protection. However others, like Christina of Markyate, resisted in other ways.

CHRISTINA DE MARKYATE

THE CONQUEST MEANT A PROPERTY WINDFALL for the Normans, but this was naturally at the expense of the former owner-occupiers. Anglo-Saxons found themselves both dispossessed and unable to enter the power structure. Many an unhappy couple fell back on the time-honoured tradition of trading in their daughter's flesh: marriage to a wealthy member of the new establishment could put an entire family back on the social ladder.

This is the fate that Autti and Beatrix de Markyate resolved on for their young daughter, Christina, some 30 years after the Battle of Hastings.

Autti was an ambitious Anglo-Saxon merchant in the village of Markyate in Hertfordshire who seems to have decided to achieve Norman

Opposite: Women in the fifteenth century were seen as the servants of men. This German tapestry c.1465 shows the Prodigal Son being bathed by two women. But this had not been the view of earlier centuries.

respectability by offering his family's sexual favours to the conquerors. His sister Alveva became the mistress of the notorious Ranulf Flambard – a man who was universally feared and infamous for his greed and ambition. The liaison was potentially attractive as Ranulf had been William Rufus's chief minister, and became bishop of Durham. However, Rufus was killed and the hated Ranulf was imprisoned in the Tower of London. He escaped to Normandy with the help of his mother (apparently a one-eyed witch).

When Christina was about ten years old Ranulf returned to England and his bishopric was restored. The bishop dropped in on his way to London, Alveva laid on a family feast and Ranulf saw Christina. He liked what he saw.

Christina's parents were only too happy to oblige the bishop with their daughter's… well 'hand' wasn't perhaps what Ranulf had in mind.

Intermarriage may have been encouraged by the Conqueror as a way of embedding his men in their new country, but Christina had no intention of getting embedded with anyone. She had made a pilgrimage to St Albans Abbey when she was younger, and it had made a big impression on her. It must have been by far the largest building she had ever seen, and here she had made a secret vow of virginity, scratching a cross on the wall of the abbey to signify her commitment to Christ.

After the feast Christina was left in Ranulf's room with him, and he began to introduce her to his wicked ways. Knowing perfectly well what all this was about, Christina suggested that she should lock the door – and promptly did so from the outside.

The enraged bishop determined to have the girl broken, and arranged for a young nobleman, Burthred, to ask for her hand in marriage. Her parents were delighted. Christina was going to achieve more for the family than Aunt Alveva ever had: their grandchildren would be legitimate members of the nobility.

The problem was that Christina refused to be married, pleading that she was promised to Christ. Her parents spent a year trying to get her to see sense, buying her presents, making promises. Eventually she was browbeaten into agreeing to a betrothal – but betrothal was one thing, consummating the marriage was another. And a marriage did not count until it was consummated.

Her parents embarked on a desperate series of stratagems, surrounding the girl with entertainers, taking her to banquets, trying to get her to loosen up. When these failed they shoved the hapless Burthred into her bedroom to do what he could. Christina sat the lad down and lectured him on the attractions of chastity for both sexes. He left somewhat confused, but was hectored into making a more robust effort.

Christina's parents pushed him into her room again and told him to stiffen up, be a man and take their daughter by force. This had her climbing up the wall – literally. She 'hastily sprang out of bed and clinging with both hands to a nail which was fixed in the wall, she hung trembling between the wall and the hangings.' Burthred could not find her and gave up his attempt at rape-within-marriage.

Eventually Autti carted his daughter off to the Augustinian canons of St Mary's Priory in Huntingdon: 'Why must she depart from tradition? Why should she bring this dishonour on her father? Her life of poverty will bring the whole of the nobility into disrepute!' The prior was more impressed by the daughter than he was by her father, and so was the bishop until Autti bribed him to order her to marry. Christina, though, was unmoved.

Beatrix decided that the problem was that her daughter was frigid. She hired crones to slip Christina love potions and sent men into her room at night, and 'in the end swore that she would not care who deflowered her daughter, provided that some way of deflowering her could be found'.

The only thing Christina could do was escape. She went first to the cell of Alfwen, an old anchoress in the nearby village of Flamstead, where she hid in a small dark chamber. Burthred, doing the full knightly quest thing, showed up at the cell and asked if Christina was hiding there. Alfwen replied: 'Stop, my son, stop imagining that she is here with us. It is not our custom to give shelter to wives who are running away from their husbands.' The biographer adds: 'The man, deluded in this way, departed, resolved never again to go on such an errand.'

Christina eventually moved to a hut belonging to Roger, a monk of St Albans who was living as a hermit in the village of Markyate. There she continued to hide, silently concealed in the corner of the hut behind a wooden plank and a log that was too heavy for her to lift. Burthred finally had the betrothal annulled, and she was able to leave her confinement. To make her happiness complete, Roger died and bequeathed his hut to her.

Eventually she became a celebrated holy woman at St Albans Abbey, making slippers for the pope and embroidering the abbot's underwear. That's what really happened to damsels in distress. They had to be tough-minded and look out for themselves.

THERE ARE, OF COURSE, STORIES OF DAMSELS being abducted and forcibly married by fortune-hunters, but these are not necessarily what they appear to be.

The inheritance of a wealthy widow or an unwed noblewoman would become the property of whoever married her, but in neither case was the woman a free agent. She was a ward of the king. He regarded her estate as entirely within his gift to give away to whomsoever he wished.

But the king had a problem. It was a legal principle that if an unmarried couple spent the night under the same roof they were taken to have slept together and were therefore married – marriage, after all, was simply a social compact. It did not require the involvement of a priest. However, such an unauthorized marriage was – in the king's view – virtually stealing from him, and the marriage was legally regarded as abduction. The married couple could expect to have to pay a considerable fine.

Obviously, these 'abductions' were quite often carried out with the full participation of the heiress in question as it was one way of getting to choose her own husband. Marjorie, Countess of Carrick, even went to the extreme of doing the abducting herself. She had held her title since her father died in 1255, when she was three. As the holder of a major Scottish fortune, her marriage was controlled by the King of Scotland, Alexander III, and before the age of 15 she was married to a suitable lord 20 years her senior: Adam de Kilconcath.

Part of Adam's suitability lay in his closeness to the future Edward I of England, and when Edward set off on his long-awaited crusade to the Holy Land in 1270 Adam went with him. The crusader kingdom of Jerusalem had been reduced to just an urban rump at the port of Acre, filled with internecine squabbles and killings, and the crusade was a hopeless gesture that cost Adam his life.

The bad news arrived in 1271. It was brought to the 19-year-old Marjorie by an 18-year-old who had also been on the crusade: Robert Bruce, the son of the Lord of Annandale and Cleveland. Robert found Marjorie out hunting. She does not seem to have been devastated by the news; her marriage had hardly been a love match. But she was immediately aware of a very depressing fact – she was back once more on King Alexander's list of useful assets, to be married off to some, probably rather elderly, supporter who needed her estate.

What happened next is unclear. According to Robert, Marjorie simply

decided that he was the most gorgeous hunk she had ever seen and seized
the young crusader. She dragged him kicking and screaming, 'very loath, to
her castle of Turnberry'. After 15 days the poor boy emerged, married.

Some historians are suspicious of the chronicle account, and suspect
Robert of some complicity in all this. But by putting the blame on to
Marjorie he avoided offending the king, who had to be content with
seizing her castle and lands until she paid a fine. It was not necessarily the
dynastic union he would have preferred, because the Bruces were
competitors for the throne and Marjorie's wealth strengthened them. In
fact, Marjorie's son, another Robert Bruce, became King of Scotland.

The significance of the story, though, lies not in exactly what was
going on, but in the fact that it was seen as entirely credible that a young
noblewoman would abduct a man, bed him and so force him into
marriage. It is not just that women were not seen as weak and helpless.
They could also be seen as sexual predators.

The Victorian idea that women were somehow less sexual than men
would have been baffling in the Middle Ages – especially to women.

THE STORY OF THE LADY OF SHALOTT created an extraordinarily resonant echo in the Victorian and Edwardian imagination; Pre-Raphaelite artists, looking for images that expressed what they saw as a truly medieval perspective, returned to it time and time again. Tennyson provided them with the narrative, a story in which the lady is cursed only to see the world through a mirror. When she spies Lancelot she is smitten and looks directly at him: the mirror shatters and she is doomed. She sets out on a pathetic boat trip to Camelot, but by the time she arrives the curse has had its effect and she is dead.

It is an image of womanhood as essentially confined and restricted; full participation in the world is forbidden and fatal. This is sentimentally regretted, but tragically unalterable.

Tennyson was retelling a genuine medieval tale, but he transformed it utterly. In the original story the lady was not weak and helpless at all, and she was not under any curse. Nor was she passive and pathetic. She was a wilful, stubborn woman who boldly declared her passionate love for Lancelot. Her tragedy was that it was not returned. The story was retold in Malory's *Morte d'Arthur* in the fifteenth century, and there too the Lady of Shalott was portrayed as a real, flesh and blood woman whose declaration of love was unashamed ('Why should I leave such thoughts? Am I not an earthly woman?') and who wrote to Lancelot as an equal.

In fact, pretty well every time we find an apparently helpless woman in medieval literature she turns out to be not quite what we were looking for. Take the distressed damsel in Chrétien de Troyes' romance *Yvain*. The heroic knight Yvain is feeling sorry for himself in a woodland chapel, when he becomes aware of 'a lorn damsel in sorry plight'. She says she is about to be condemned to death, and can only be saved by someone brave enough to fight her three accusers. Yvain, of course, is the necessary hero.

This seems to be the fairy-tale archetype; the helpless damsel and the knight in shining armour. But this young lady is not some passive shrinking violet. Yvain knows her. A couple of thousand lines earlier she had saved his life, rescuing him from certain death by giving him a magic ring of invisibility at the risk of her own life. The damsel and the knight are equals in courage and daring.

The fact is, there is little reference to genuinely helpless high-born maidens in medieval literature. Perhaps this is not too surprising as the stories were often commissioned by noblewomen, to be read to their friends and family.

We do not have enormous knowledge of their lives, but there is enough to show that a lady's bedchamber was, in many cases, more like a salon, elegantly decorated, where she amused herself entertaining her women friends (generally her retainers, 'damsels' married to men of status in her husband's service) and male visitors, and where they would 'drink wine, play chess and listen to the harp'.* They would also read and be read to – silent reading was regarded as highly suspect, a sign of being antisocial or melancholy, suitable only for scholars.

By the fourteenth century wills show that the women who could afford expensive books were as interested as men in the derring-do of storybook knights. A recent historian writes: 'The evidence of women's wills in Chaucer's day… reveals a network of women readers who bequeathed books from one generation to another. These included, along with devotional books, the works of romance which Chaucer depicted women reading to one another. Such books were frequently passed from

Below: Intellectual pastimes were very much part of the courtly damsels' world by the end of the thirteenth century.

*H. Leyser, *Medieval Women: a Social History of Women in England 450–1500*, (Palgrave Macmillan, 1995), p. 241.

201
Damsel

Above: Lancelot and Guinevere's first kiss. Tales of romance became required reading in the noblewoman's chamber.

mother to daughter, sister to sister, godmother to goddaughter, but it was not considered essential to keep them in the female line; women's reading tastes were catholic and they shared them with men.'*

Thus, in 1380 Elizabeth la Zouche leaves *Lancelot* and *Tristam* to her husband. The Count of Devon leaves books to his daughters but not to his sons. His widow, Margaret Courtenay, then leaves her own books, which include *Merlin* and *Arthur of Brittany*, to the girls and a woman friend.

The women in these tales are light years away from the Victorian stereotype. Far from being helpless, they are resourceful and often scheming. And as for being sexually passive – medieval women wouldn't have known what you meant. The damsels in the stories are all too often sexual predators. Take the Lady of the Castle who takes such a shine to Gawain in *Sir Gawain and the Green Knight*.

The story so far: Gawain is on a quest. He sleeps the night in a strange castle. He's woken up very early in the morning, shortly after the Lord of the Castle and his men have ridden off hunting. The door of his chamber opens cautiously and the lady slips into his room. She locks the door, creeps across to his bed and sits down upon it. Gawain lies doggo for some

Ibid., p. 247.

time but eventually shows some sign of life, whereupon the lady speaks to him thus:

My lord and his men are a long way off
The other men are still in their beds, and so are
my maids
The door is closed and fastened with a strong lock.

You are welcome to my body,
Your pleasure to take.
I am driven by forces beyond my control
To be your servant and so I shall.

In these stories married women were free to take lovers, and if their husbands complained they could be silenced by the wife explaining that the lover was a valiant and famous knight. In real life things were not so different. What did Marie de Saint Hilaire have in common with Katherine Swyneford, apart from the fact that they were both damsels (married women in the service of great ladies)? The fact that they both bedded John of Gaunt while he was married to Blanche, and didn't make a secret of it.

In one of the most celebrated love affairs of the twelfth century a young student, Héloïse, fell passionately in love with her teacher Abelard. Abelard was a phenomenon: a great and controversial theologian, a celebrated poet and singer, and a captivating teacher whose lectures virtually created the University of Paris. Héloïse set out to seduce him and she succeeded. The affair was a disaster: Abelard insisted on marrying her, and when her family found out they castrated him and locked her in a nunnery. In her letters to Abelard, which she wrote from the nunnery, she re-examined and celebrated her passion:

Never, God knows, did I seek anything in you except yourself; I wanted only you, nothing of yours.
I looked for no marriage-bond, no marriage portion, and it was not my own pleasures and wishes I sought to gratify, as you well know, but yours. The name of wife may seem more sacred or more worthy but sweeter to me will always be the word lover, or, if you will permit me, that of concubine or whore.
I believed that the more I humbled myself on your account, the more I would please you, and also the less damage I should do to the brightness of your reputation.

Prudery was not a virtue. Women were expected to be sexually active and to demand the same from their husbands. If the man failed to perform in

the marriage bed, the wife was perfectly at liberty to go public about it. A twelfth-century manual advocates a physical examination of the man's genitals by 'wise matrons' who – presumably – knew how these things worked. Witnesses were then summoned to observe a full-blown road test of the under-performing member:

A man and a woman are to be placed together in one bed and wise women are to be summoned around the bed for many nights. And if the man's member is always found useless and as if dead, the couple are well able to be separated.

That is, sadly, how we know about Walter de Fonte, a citizen of Canterbury in the thirteenth century. In 1292, his wife complained he was impotent. He was duly examined by 12 worthy women 'of good reputation and honest life' who testified that his 'virile member' was 'useless'. What a way to enter history.

In a similar case in 1433 one conscientious witness seems to have been so anxious to fulfil her civic duty that she got rather carried away; she 'exposed her naked breasts and with her hands warmed at the said fire, she held and rubbed the penis and testicles of the said John. And she embraced and frequently kissed the said John…'

But it was all to no avail. Whereupon 'with one voice' the assembled women cursed the said John for not being 'better able to serve and please' his wife.

Opposite: The knight in the service of a lady became a familiar concept of romance. This illustration is a French, fifteenth century image.

THE DAMSEL AND THE CHURCH

THE VIEW THAT WOMEN WERE MORE SEXUALLY ASSERTIVE than men was, of course, firmly endorsed by the Church. In its long war against the temptations of the flesh women were enthusiastically cast as the seducers.

Of course, the Church did not disapprove of sex as such – after all, God had said 'Go forth and multiply'. But the tendency for people to enjoy it was seen as a bit of a problem. Having sex – let alone enjoying it – was certainly damnable outside marriage. However, as this was not a view that was widely held outside the Church, preachers often went to extremes to impress the gravity of the sin on the reluctant populace.

Below: 'The poison for men's souls' – a typical portrayal of the temptress, Eve. From the Souvigny Bible, late twelfth century.

It was argued that women were the cause of all evil because they tempted men, who would otherwise have remained pure. An eleventh-century cardinal, Peter Damian, taught that 'the wickedness of women is greater than all the other wickedness of the world… the poison of asps and dragons is more curable and less dangerous to men than the familiarity of women'. Having made a careful study of the story of Eve and the forbidden fruit, he was able to explain to the clergy that 'Women are: "Satan's bait, poison for men's souls"'. His opinions were absolutely normal for a monk of the period. The Church calls him a saint.

The Church had been blaming all women for Eve's temptation of Adam for at least 800 years before Damian picked up the baton and ran with it. In the second century, St Tertullian accosted women and asked them: 'Do you not know that you are Eve?' He then went on to inform them that: 'God's sentence hangs still over all your sex and His punishment weighs down upon you' and that 'You are the devil's gateway'.

The significant change since Tertullian's day was, of course, that the medieval Church encompassed all society, and had its own courts of law. Sexual offences, including fornication, were almost entirely a matter for the ecclesiastical courts and were often dealt with in bizarre ways. For example, in 1308 the archbishop of Canterbury, Robert of Winchelsey, decided that unmarried fornicators should have to sign a contract of marriage that dated from their offence but would only come into effect if they offended twice more. And accusations of fornication were often used as a device to strip single women of their land: on the bishop of Winchester's estates, for example, a quarter of all recorded forfeitures between 1286 and 1350 were punishments for fornication, imposed only on women.*

At the same time as it castigated women for being the daughters of Eve, the Church promoted an ideal of chaste womanhood that did not lure men to sin. Of course, this wasn't exactly easy to achieve as it involved becoming a mother while at the same time remaining a virgin. But all the female roles presented by the Church – temptress, mother, servant and nun – rather missed the reality of life in a family that owned property.

THE DAMSEL AS MANAGER

THE WOMAN OFTEN HAD TO RUN THE SHOW. Quite apart from women who held authority in their own right, like Nicola de la Haye, there were others whose power came with marriage. A noble lady was inevitably responsible for running the household and, to a large extent, the business of the estate (which would include the bakery, the brewery, the dairy, managing the horses and gardens, and so on).

In her own territory, she was the equivalent of a queen. This had the inevitable effect of thrusting women into very masculine roles when the men were not around. Well-to-do medieval wives found that their husbands spent a lot of time away on business... very often the sort that involved being heavily armed and taking all the fit and able male members of the household with them. This left the lady of the manor to fill her absent husband's shoes, including running the manor court and defending the family property and honour.

We have an extraordinarily clear picture of the problems dealt with by a fifteenth-century lady of the manor from the letters between Margaret and John Paston, of Oxnead, Norfolk.

Margaret was the daughter of a wealthy man and inherited his land. In about 1440 she married John Paston, the son of a judge, who had legal chambers in London. His father had bought a manor near Cromer, but John's ownership was disputed by another powerful local family. While he

206
Damsel

*The Peasant Land Market in Southern England, 1260–1350, Dr Mark Page, University of Durham.

was away in London defending the property at law, his wife was at home organizing battles of a more physical sort:

> Right worshipful husband, I recommend myself to you, and pray you to get some crossbows and arrows. Your house here is so low that no man can shoot out with a long bow, though we have never had such need. Also I would ask you to get two or three short poll-axes to defend the doors with and as many padded jackets… Partridge and his friends are sore afraid that you will enter again on them. They have greatly defended the house, so I'm told. They have made bars to bar the door and they have made loopholes on every side to shoot out at with bows and handguns… I pray you to buy me 1lb of almonds and 1lb of sugar and that you will get some woollen cloth for your children's gowns.*

The Pastons had a rich relative, Sir John Fastolf, who built a castle at Caister in Norfolk. John Paston was his lawyer. Fastolf had no children and the Duke of Norfolk hoped to inherit the estate, but when the old man died John Paston suddenly produced a new will in which Fastolf left his huge estate, including Caister Castle, to a certain John Paston. The disappointed heirs accused Paston of forging the will and laid siege to the castle.

In 1469, Margaret once again had to organize the defence of family property. Her husband was now dead and she wrote a chiding letter to her perhaps feckless son, John Paston II, who she felt was wasting his fortune living it up at court:

> Your brother and his fellowship stand in great jeopardy at Caister… Daubney and Berney are dead and others badly hurt… Unless they have hasty help, they are likely to lose both their lives and the place, which will be the greatest rebuke to you that ever came to any gentleman. For every man in this country marvels greatly that you suffer them to be for so long in great jeopardy without help or other remedy…

THE DAMSEL AND THE BUTTON

ALTHOUGH WOMEN HAD TO TAKE ON MALE ROLES, saw themselves as sexually bold and (within a generation or two of the Conquest) undertook what amounted to military duties, they did not become less feminine. On the contrary, the more power they exercised, the more they dressed to emphasize their femininity. Within 100 years of the Conquest, noble ladies had moved from wearing simple gowns to ones with elaborate embroidery, and to even more elaborate hairstyles.

One of the most influential imports that Europeans brought back from the crusades was the humble button. This transformed women's

*Letter of 1448, *Paston Letters and Papers of the Fifteenth Century*, ed. Norman Davis, (Clarendon Press, Oxford, 1971).

Right: By the beginning of the fifteenth century women saw themselves as worthy of respect and honour. Here Christine de Pisan enters the City of Ladies, Paris 1410–11.

208
Damsel

fashion as clothes no longer had to be loose enough to be pulled over their heads. Fashionable women were able to emphasize their figures, combining tight corsetry with long, flowing skirts and sleeves. Femininity, of course, was also a weapon that could be used to control men, and the power of noblewomen in the game of courtly chivalry was greater than that of any man.

The crusades also introduced Europeans to new fabrics – silks, satins, damasks, brocades, and velvets – and to new bright colours and elaborate weaves. And as trade increased, and the variety of coloured cloths grew, women began making strong statements about who they were by what they wore. In the thirteenth and fourteenth centuries the stylish look was long and slim, the tightness of the cut emphasizing a boyish body-shape – in fact, boys were often referred to as 'damsels', a word that was used to describe the young Richard II.

DAMSELS ON TOP

BY THE LATE FOURTEENTH CENTURY many women were in positions of considerable power, and courtly society in England had become increasingly sophisticated and – naturally – feminized. Richard II certainly held jousts, as his predecessors had, but they were more of an entertainment than a training for war, and they were followed by music and dancing. The emphasis at court was on the arts: on poetry, music, fashion and haute cuisine. It was enough to turn the stomach of one rednecked chronicler, Thomas Walsingham, who wrote: 'The King surrounds himself with "Knights of Venus" more valiant in the bedchamber than on the battlefield.'

Women also took on important roles in government; and Richard II's queen, Anne of Bohemia, was seen as a crucial restraining hand on the implacable justice of the king. As the Virgin Mary interceded with God on behalf of mankind, so it was thought right and proper for the queen to intercede with the king on behalf of his erring subjects. After the Peasants' Revolt of 1381 the official rolls included many pardons like this one:

> Pardon, at the supplication of the queen, with the assent of divers prelates, earls and lords of Parliament… to Thomas de Faryngdon for the offences in the late insurrection of London…*

Richard travelled everywhere with his beloved Queen Anne, and there is no doubt that there was a genuine affection between them. She was intellectual and liberal. For instance, she owned a copy of the Wyclif Bible,

*Calendar of Patent Rolls, Richard II, 2, 103.

the first translation of the Bible into English, and perhaps through her it was circulated in her native Bohemia. It seems likely that she had a powerful influence over her husband and perhaps, although we do not know this, was instrumental in raising the profile of women in his court. Richard was certainly the first king to create a woman duchess in her own right: Margaret Marshall in 1397.

THE DAMSEL AS BUSINESSWOMAN

WOMEN'S ROLES WERE CHANGING over a much wider swathe of society than just the high nobility. The Black Death, oddly enough, contributed significantly to this: it created such a shortage of people that women had to take on tasks in many spheres that had previously been restricted to men. They were increasingly able to support themselves as traders (a statute of 1363 lifted the ban on women being limited to one trade or craft)* and seem to have been able to exercise more choice over whom they married.

The best-known female businesswoman was the extraordinary Margery Kempe, born in Lynn in Norfolk in 1373, who wrote what is often described as the first English autobiography: *The Book of Margery Kempe*. Her father, John de Brunham, was a prominent merchant, five times mayor of Lynn, and the book describes how Margery grew up accustomed to affluence.

She describes herself as a fashion victim. She wore gold threads on her head, and her hoods with long ribbons were fashionably slashed. Her cloaks were also modishly slashed, and underlaid with various colours between the slashes. When her husband finally refused to fund her extravagant lifestyle she decided to find the money for herself. Since women were now legally able to operate as sole traders, she didn't need her husband's permission, and could keep any profits she made for herself. So she set herself up as a brewer… intending to be 'the greatest in the town of Lynne'. But alas it was not to be.

The beer simply would not ferment properly for her.

But Margery wasn't to be beaten. She bought two horses and a mill, and set herself up as a corn-grinder. But that, too, was a disaster. It was said that the very horses that turned the mill started to go backwards instead of forwards. Then the miller ran away. 'And then it was noised about the town of Lynn that neither man nor beast would work for her…'

Margery took this as a sign from God that she wasn't cut out for commerce and looked around for another career. She relaunched herself as a visionary and professional hysteric.

*Leyser, p. 161.

211
Damsel

Full-time professional religious weeping may not sound like an obvious money-spinner, but there is no doubt that Margery was head and shoulders above the competition. She was, in fact, a world-championship-class weeper. Show her a crucifix and she would faint; and if she thought she was in the presence of God she would start to scream uncontrollably. She wept in public. She wept through sermons. She wept at meals – loudly and incessantly. A holy woman told Margery her weeping was a gift of the Holy Spirit, but most people thought it was just a damned nuisance. After meeting her the archbishop of York is reported to have given his staff five shillings to get her as far away from him as possible.

And when she went on pilgrimage to Jerusalem her fellow-pilgrims just couldn't stand the way she wept and lamented during dinner. They asked her politely to stop, but she couldn't do it. Before they were a quarter of the way to the Holy Land, they dumped her and told her to go on alone.

Margery clearly wasn't your average businesswoman, but at least she finally regained her position in Lynn and even became a member of the guild. The role of women had obviously changed a very great deal.

Writers and thinkers began to re-examine the traditional male attitude that the role of women was merely to be their servants; and to question the Church's teaching that this was an inevitable consequence of the fact that women were naturally corrupters of men, and were morally and intellectually weak and unfit to participate in public life. Women even began to question this out loud:

No matter which way I looked at it and no matter how much I turned the matter over in my mind, I could find no evidence from my own experience to bear out such a negative view of female nature and habits. Even so, given that I could scarcely find a moral work by any author which didn't devote some chapter or paragraph to attacking the female sex, I had to accept their unfavourable opinion of women since it was unlikely that so many learned men, who seemed to be endowed with such great intelligence and insight into all things, could possible have lied on so many different occasions…

CHRISTINE DE PISAN, *The Book of the City of Ladies*

Christine de Pisan, who wrote this nicely ironic piece in about 1404, had serious trouble with the learned attitude to women and wanted to do something about it. She had grown up in Paris, where her father was a scholar and physician at the royal court, and married a royal secretary. When she was 25 everything went wrong. Her husband died, leaving her with three children and her mother to care for. Her father, who had lost his position, had died two years earlier.

Right: Christine de Pisan presents her book to Isabelle of Bavaria.

To supplement her income she began to write lyric poems. There were plenty of men who made a living this way, finding patrons who would accept their work as gifts and reward them. Christine had decided to break into this male market. She became accepted as a poet at the French court and began to receive commissions. At the same time, she read widely and she began to join in the intellectual life of Paris.

She had strong opinions about what she read, and decided it was necessary to challenge the way men were writing about women. She was as alarmed by popular romances as she was by the works of 'learned men'. In particular, she objected to the most celebrated romance of the age, Jean de Meun's poem *The Romance of the Rose*. She published 'Cupid's Letter', deploring his attitude towards women and what she called his bad influence on many contemporary men which encouraged them to be shallow seducers and revel in their conquests.

When a royal secretary wrote saying that she was a presumptuous woman, daring to attack a man of 'high understanding', she hit back and didn't pull her punches:

… since you are angry at me without reason, you attack me harshly with, 'Oh outrageous presumption! Oh excessively foolish pride! Oh opinion uttered too quickly and thoughtlessly by the mouth of a woman! A woman who condemns a man of high understanding and dedicated study…'

My answer: Oh man deceived by wilful opinion!… A simple little housewife sustained by the doctrine of Holy Church could criticize your error!*

La Querelle de la Rose: letters and documents, compiled and edited by Joseph L. Baird and John R. Kane, North Carolina studies in the Romance languages and literatures; no. 199. (Chapel Hill: UNC Dept. of Romance Languages: [distributed by University of North Carolina Press], 1978), pp.129–30.

HOWEVER, THIS AGE OF SEMI-EMANCIPATION was not going to last. As what we call 'the Middle Ages' merged seamlessly into what we call 'the Renaissance' Europe seems to have been dominated by tyrannies and a new wave of militarism and barbarism. Perhaps as a corollary, many men resented and feared women playing prominent roles in society. The restraining hand of the queen as mediatrix was no longer seen as a political ideal. Men sought to push women back into the background.

As the economy recovered from the Black Death during the second half of the fourteenth century, a male backlash had begun to be tangible. In 1400 an ordinance from York declared that 'henceforth no woman of whatever status or condition shall be put among us to weave… unless they have been taught the craft'.Other similar rules began to appear.

But, as usual, men found that the handiest weapon against women was religion and the clearest example of this came with the strange history of Joan of Arc. In 1429 Christine de Pisan wrote a poem of sheer delight as this remarkable woman led an army of national liberation through France (that was certainly how Christine saw it). But two years later Joan was in an English prison.

She had gone into battle wearing male costume; she kept it on in prison, the pants and tunic 'firmly laced and tied together', apparently as a defence against being raped by the soldiers guarding her. Although there were efforts to charge her with witchcraft and heresy these collapsed, and she was convicted for the crime of cross-dressing and nothing else. She had finally consented to wear a dress, but her jailers had taken it away and thrown her the old, forbidden male clothing. She eventually put it on, and was promptly declared to be a 'relapsed heretic' and condemned to death.

The fire in which Joan burned was just the beginning of a long process of changing not just the position of women, but the very perception of a woman's nature. There was also a striking change in how noblewomen dressed. Instead of showing off a slim, boyish figure, fifteenth-century fashion was concerned with occupying space and moving sedately. A new kind of dress, a 'houppeland', with a deep V-neck, baggy sleeves and an enormous skirt seriously restricted women's movements. Noblemen also wore houppelands as their bagginess was a demonstration of wealth and extravagance, but the male version was nothing like such an impediment.

Women had started to wear clothes that reduced them to rather helpless ornaments.

ONE EXTRAORDINARY INSIGHT into the psychological background of these developments is provided by Dr Samantha Riches's study of dragon pictures.*

The story of St George and the dragon had been around since the twelfth century. It was said that this terrible beast had ravaged all the countryside around a town. It had such bad breath that it caused pestilence whenever it approached the town, so the people gave it two sheep every day to satisfy its hunger; and when they eventually ran out of sheep they decided to offer it human victims, chosen by drawing lots. Eventually the chosen victim was the king's daughter. So the maiden, dressed as a bride, was led out and left to wait for the monster. St George happened to find her, bravely attacked the dragon and defeated it.

This tale became very popular in the fifteenth century. But something sinister was appearing in the story.

Dr Riches looked at late fifteenth- and early sixteenth-century pictures depicting the tale and realized that in many of them dragons had female genitalia. This portrayal of the dragon as female and sexual is probably connected to fears about women's sexuality during this time. The 'damsel' in the pictures is 'saved' by St George, who symbolizes chastity, from the dragon who symbolizes her own uncontrolled sexuality. Women's sexuality was being associated with a monster, suggesting that this sexuality was seen as evil and threatening. St George was the patron saint of towns, and in towns that were actively legislating against women traders this view seems entirely possible.

What began in towns ended by dominating the country. When religious dissent developed it was the craftsmen and tradesmen of the towns who led it, and urban Protestantism would eventually take over England. Built into that Protestantism was a view of woman as the helpmeet, the obedient domestic creature who would now have to vow at her wedding to love, honour and OBEY. Women were not to be encouraged to play queenly roles, as John Knox made clear in 1558 in his *First Blast of the Trumpet against the Monstrous Regiment of Women*, an attack on the very idea of women at the head of states. ('Regiment' meaning 'government').

Things changed so much that in the eighteenth century the great English legal commentator Sir William Blackstone wrote:

The very being or legal existence of the woman is suspended during the marriage… for this reason a man cannot grant anything to his wife or enter into any covenant with her: for the grant would be to presuppose her separate existence, and to covenant with her would be only to covenant with himself.

*Samantha Riches, *St. George: Hero, Martyr and Myth*, (Sutton Publishing, 2001).

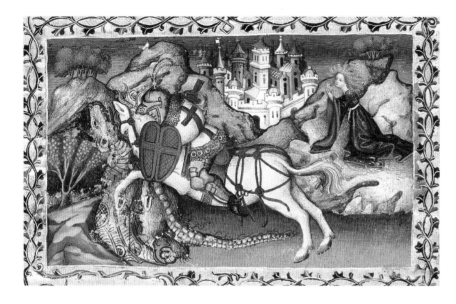

All this was further compounded through the Enlightenment and the Industrial Revolution, by a belief that women were ornamental and men active, and then that women really had very little sex drive – that was a man thing. It would have been too frightening for a husband to leave his wife at home while he went off to work if she was actually thought to be randier than him. In fact, less than 100 years ago any woman who was 'excessively' interested in sex was deemed to be sick or mad, and in need of treatment. A large proportion of the women in mental asylums were there because they had had illegitimate babies; or simply because they enjoyed sex more than was thought proper.

And so we come to the Lady of Shalott, and the Pre-Raphaelites, and the damsel-in-distress. A Victorian invention, projected back in time, to hinder our understanding of the Middle Ages. Modern (male) scholars have argued that Héloïse's letters to Abelard – 'sweeter to me will always be the word lover, or, if you will permit me, that of concubine or whore' – must be male forgeries. No real woman, it came to be believed, could ever write, or even think, like that.

CHAPTER EIGHT

KINGS OF ENGLAND can be divided into three types: the Good, the Bad and the Ugly. That, you can take it from us, is a reliable fact. But which is which is another matter.

Take all the kings of England called Richard: there's Good King Richard I – Richard the Lionheart, the idealistic crusader and champion of England – or was he? Bad King Richard II – the vain, megalomaniac tyrant – or has his name been traduced by those who wished him ill? And Ugly King Richard III – the deformed monster of Shakespeare's imagination – or is he nothing more than that: the product of our greatest playwright's imagination?

History consists of the tales we like to tell each other about our predecessors. And every generation constructs its stories to suit its own outlook and agenda. In such shifting ground we can take nothing for granted. Even facts that seem to be set in stone – such as the roll-call of the kings of England or the 'fact' that the last invasion of England was in 1066 – are by no means as certain as we like to pretend.

THE UNMENTIONABLE KINGS OF ENGLAND

TAKE THE KINGS NOBODY MENTIONS; you might not have heard much about Osric and Eanfrith. In AD 633 they ruled two kingdoms that became Northumbria before they were killed by King Caedwalla of North Wales.

The only reason we know anything at all about these two kings is that Bede, writing his *Ecclesiastical History of the English Nation* a hundred years later, mentions that no king-list records them:

To this day, that year is looked upon as unhappy, and hateful to all good men…. Hence it has been agreed by all who have written about the reigns of the kings, to abolish the memory of those perfidious monarchs, and to assign that year to the reign of the following king, Oswald, a man beloved by God.

The same fate seems to have overtaken King Louis the First (and Last).

KING LOUIS THE FIRST (AND LAST?)

LOUIS INVADED ENGLAND IN 1216 with a fleet almost as large as the Conqueror's, and a considerably larger army. He landed unopposed and was hailed as king when he reached London. On 2 June the new ruler, heir to the crown of France, was welcomed by a magnificent Mass in St Paul's Cathedral.* He received the homage of the citizens of London, of most of the barons and of the King of Scotland,** and began the conquest of the rest of the country as well as the government of the part which was under his control.

Louis ruled much of England with his own chancellor (the brother of the archbishop of Canterbury), and elevated at least one man to the nobility, creating Gilbert de Gant (or Gaunt) Earl of Lincoln. He was recognized as king by the barons and by the citizens of London, the Welsh nobles and the Scottish king. The fact that he doesn't feature in the official king-lists raises some difficult questions about what exactly is meant by the expression 'King of England'.

Louis had come to England because the barons had invited him to take the crown. King John had a long-standing feud with the Church over the appointment of Stephen Langton as archbishop of Canterbury, which had led to him being excommunicated and an interdict – a ban on church services – being placed on the whole kingdom. In 1213 Pope Innocent III authorized Philip II of France to invade England and deprive

Opposite: The coronation of Henry III from an Anglo-French manuscript (1280–1300).

Below: Blanche of Castile and King Louis IX.

*G. H. Cook, *Old St Paul's Cathedral*, 1955, p. 92: Henry Hart Milman, *Annals of St Paul's*, 2nd ed, 1869, pp. 43–4.
**Matthew Paris, *Chronica Majora*, pp. 654, 666.

221
King

John of his kingdom. John had not been next in line to the throne after Richard's death: he had been crowned by the previous archbishop on the grounds that he was chosen by the nation, a choice confirmed by public acclamation.

Philip of France summoned a council and they all decided that his son Louis should lead the invasion and take over the English throne. Louis was married to John's niece, which gave him some kind of claim.

The invasion did not take place for another three years, by which time John had first agreed to, and then reneged on, the Magna Carta, and the English barons and the archbishop had called on Louis to get on with it. John had taken the precaution of handing his kingdom over to the pope, which meant that his excommunication and the interdict were lifted and it was the barons and bishops who found themselves excommunicated for attacking the pope's kingdom of England. They were not hugely bothered; so far as they were concerned, John had lost his right to the throne by surrendering the country to another ruler.

Louis and his army landed in England, on the Isle of Thanet, on 21 May 1216. He claimed the throne through his wife and by the choice of the barons.

This is how Louis the First and Last came to be acclaimed as King of England. It is true that no bishop crowned him, and that meant he was in an unusual position, but he was certainly ruling as king. John's attempt to win his country back involved wide-ranging war. In October he set off northwards from Lynn in Norfolk and lost all his baggage, including the Crown jewels, when his entourage took a short cut across the river Welland just as the tide came in. No-one would ever see it again. John was devastated and went to the Cistercian abbey of Swineshead in Lincolnshire to be consoled. The original austerity of the Cistercians had obviously already evaporated; John surfeited himself with peaches and a new kind of beer, caught dysentery and died.

That left Louis the only king in England. He also happened to be the only adult male with any claim to inherit the throne (though only through his marriage). John had left a nine-year-old son – the future Henry III – but no child had ever been allowed to become the ruler of England. This did not worry the papal legate, who invented an entirely new rule of succession. He whistled Henry down to Gloucester, where the few barons who had stuck by John attended a makeshift coronation performed by the bishop of Winchester – the archbishop of Canterbury and the bishop of London had prior engagements. A circlet of gold was hurriedly found and plonked on the boy's head. God Save the King.

However, as it turned out Louis did not endear himself to the English barons as he evidently preferred to govern with the help of Frenchmen. William Marshal, the doughty hero of tournaments long ago, now aged 75 and titled the Earl of Pembroke, took the job of regent and set about getting rid of Louis – which he evidently did with his customary efficiency. The great battle came at Lincoln on 20 May 1217; Louis lost and his troops began to drift away. A few months later he gave up. In September 1217 a treaty was signed by which he surrendered his castles, released his subjects from their oaths to him and told his allies to lay down their arms. Everyone who had been on Louis' side swore fealty to Henry III, and Louis went home to succeed to the crown of France, a much more secure job with better prospects – though he died three years after inheriting it.

KING WHO?

EVENTUALLY, IN 1220, Henry was given a proper coronation at Westminster. And, in order to make it possible for the kingdom to carry on functioning, everyone who had sworn fealty to Louis realized that they had not really done so at all. It had never happened. There had never been a King Louis of England.

The history books would say what the new government wanted them to say, justifying rebellion against the tyrant John while glossing over the barons' brief importation of a French king. They still do. Which means, of course, that history books need to be regarded with a very jaundiced eye. Most of what we now know of King John comes from a handful of accounts of his reign, written by churchmen who were either outraged by his excommunication or living under the post-Louis government;* they were enthusiasts for trying to weaken royal power. Later historians simply copied and embellished their manuscripts.

THE POWER OF KINGS

THIS PATTERN, OF CHRONICLERS UNDER NEW REGIMES blackening the memory of the old, created an image of medieval kingship that was to resonate through English history, in which the king was a tyrant whose whimsical and self-serving power needed to be tamed. Bad King John was the first of these tyrant kings, and centuries later this view of royal authority was enshrined by historians in the service of Britain's constitutional revolution

*Ralph of Coggeshall, *The Barnwell Chronicle*, Roger of Wendover, Gervase of Canterbury, and the *Annals of Margam and Tewkesbury*.

of the seventeenth century and the American War of Independence. This is why the Magna Carta, a document that dealt with the very specific grievances of John's tenants-in-chief, was mythologized into the foundation stone of English and American government.

Sir Edward Coke, England's most prominent seventeenth-century lawyer and one of Parliament's leaders in the run-up to the Civil War, used a reinterpreted Magna Carta as a weapon against Charles I, arguing that even kings must comply with common law. He stated in Parliament that 'Magna Carta… will have no sovereign'. His arguments were later to be used by Thomas Jefferson, in setting out the idea of English liberties.

It was easy for seventeenth- and eighteenth-century writers, enthusiasts for 'constitutional monarchy' or a republic, to mine the old histories and find material that allowed them to depict kings as tyrants. Each time a regime changed it was necessary for the new authorities to show how grateful everyone should be that they had removed the previous incumbent. This involved replacing historical figures with caricatures of wickedness.

Perhaps royal power, and its use or misuse, was more of an issue in England than in other countries because an English king was in a very

Right: The coronation of King Harold as depicted in the Bayeux tapestry.

different position from, for example, a king of France. In France, the monarchy was relatively weak and the great aristocrats ruled their own territories on their own terms. These aristocrats included kings of England, who held land in France not by virtue of their English crown but as dukes of French provinces, such as Normandy and Anjou – which is why the French were constantly fighting the English. Such powerful, independent nobles simply did not exist in England.

There had always been an elective character to European kingship (the idea that the eldest son automatically inherits the crown started in England, as part of the politics surrounding the installation of the young Henry III). Even conquering rulers like Cnut (Canute, the Danish king who ruled England from 1017 to 1035) were elected, in Cnut's case first by the Danish fleet and eventually by the Anglo-Saxon Witan (great council). This meant that kingship was something given by others and could, at least in theory, be withdrawn.

1066 changed all that. The terms of English kingship were set, inevitably, by William the Conqueror, and it was a new kind of kingship – authority based on might alone. His coronation did not require the approval of his subjects. William achieved what no other European ruler could: the effective conquest of his whole kingdom. What mattered was not the Battle of Hastings but the warfare that followed. He enforced his authority at Exeter, at York, carried out the savage 'harrying of the North', ravaged Cheshire, Shropshire, Staffordshire and Derbyshire and crushed revolt in the Fens. Having established total mastery, and installed his own men as tenants throughout the country, he carried out a complete survey of the whole package down to the last slave and plough – *Domesday Book* – and insisted that every tenant, all the way down the feudal chain, swear an oath of personal allegiance to him.

No king could more completely own his kingdom than William owned England. And it was his to give to whichever son he fancied. That, of course, became the problem as soon as he died. William Rufus, to whom he bequeathed the country, was soon killed as the result of an 'accident' that put his younger brother Henry on the throne.

Uneasy lies the head that wears a crown. John of Worcester's chronicle, written in about 1140, soon after Henry I's death, describes the king having nightmares about complaining peasants and violent barons. It was, in fact, all falling apart. And then it did.

Henry approached his deathbed with no living legitimate son (he did not regard any of his 25 or so illegitimate children as king material). He willed the kingdom to his daughter Matilda, and forced his barons to swear

allegiance to her, but once he was dead his nephew Stephen claimed the crown and England was plunged into anarchic civil war. It was a time when, as one chronicler described it, 'Christ and his angels slept'.

The war ended when both sides agreed that Stephen should rule but Matilda's son should inherit the throne. That son, Henry II, then had the job of trying to stick the broken crockery together again. English kingship demanded total authority, which meant Henry had to re-create a distance between his power and that of the great lords. Since the Conqueror option (military crushing of enemies and handing out of spoils) was no longer open, he had to carry the country with him. The only way out of the nightmares of Henry I was to encourage people to believe they approved of what he was doing. Above all, this meant creating a sense that he was acting with lawful authority. Every landholding man held court in his own estates – Henry, lord of all England, was also the judge of the whole land, and his home was the royal court.

This was his trump card, and he used it effectively. He established courts in various parts of the country and was the first king to grant

Below: Henry I from an Anglo-French manuscript.

magistrates the power to judge civil matters in the name of the crown. This is when the first written legal textbook was produced, the basis of English common law. Henry also introduced trial by jury, making the population participate in his own legal authority.

He extended this legal authority into the lands of his magnates and over the Church – a challenge that the Church was determined to resist and which led to Henry's terrible conflict with Thomas Becket, archbishop of Canterbury. He used the authority of the law to demolish castles that had been built without royal permission during the civil war. And, as he preferred to hire troops rather than rely on the 'loyalty' of barons, he substituted a tax – scutage – for the nobles' obligations of military service. To make this work, he established effective record-keeping.

Kingship was now not quite so personal. Henry had created a legal and administrative structure that was probably more effective than armed force in holding his kingdom together. It was, in many ways, a return to the kind of rule that had existed before the Conquest: rule by consent of the people, within a framework of recognized traditional law. (Actually it was rule by consent of the *free* people. Villeins were not part of this deal; being unfree, they had very limited legal rights, just as in Anglo-Saxon times the slaves did not have rights or power.)

But although this was notionally kingship under law, there was no institutional check on royal power. Henry was simply a consummate politician, dealing with the art of the possible. The crown was still his personal property, and he was free to choose which of his heirs should succeed him. His eldest surviving son, Richard, was not his first choice.

Which brings us to the Good, the Bad and the Ugly.

GOOD KING RICHARD I

Opposite: Richard I – crusader and hero. This statue stands proudly in the heart of the city that he wanted to sell to the highest bidder.

RICHARD WAS BORN IN OXFORD but he was essentially French, brought up in Aquitaine at the court of his mother, Eleanor. Henry gave Aquitaine to him, but intended to make his younger brother, John, King of England. This may have been because of Richard's quite appalling reputation in Aquitaine, where he committed rapes and murders. That was how they justified a major uprising against his rule: 'He seized and raped the wives, daughters and relatives of free men, and when the violence of his lust had been quenched, handed them to his soldiers to use.'*

However, Richard wasn't going to let John have England and, with the help of Philip II of France, he defeated his father in 1189. Henry, a broken man, died shortly afterwards and Richard took possession of the English crown.

It is not really clear why he bothered. He arrived for his coronation with the idea of picking up as much money as he could to finance a crusade, but unable to speak any English. The leaders of London's Jews came to his court bearing valuable gifts, but as Jews were not allowed there they were beaten up and there were general anti-Jewish riots. Richard, profoundly disturbed at the idiocy of attacking the people who could give him what he needed, left the country soon afterwards and was not seen again in England for years. He detested the place and declared he would sell London off to anyone who was prepared to buy it.

The passion to wage war in the Holy Land was sweeping Europe like a virus. Men who resisted joining up were humiliated and given gifts of wool as if they were women. Priests stirred up anti-Muslim hysteria.

*William Stubbs (ed.), *Gesta Regis Henrici Secundi (Roger of Howden)* I, p.292.

Below: Richard I's Chateau Gaillard – he designed it himself, regardless of the expense.

A persuasive visual aid was a picture of a mounted Saracen knight trampling on the Messiah's tomb in Jerusalem while his horse urinated on it.

It was Richard's role as a crusading Christian warrior that made him a hero during his reign and a legend for centuries afterwards.

The Great Warrior, however, failed to recapture Jerusalem from the 'infidel' Saladin. Travelling back from his crusade through Germany (alone and in disguise), Richard was captured and spent two years in prison. Having the IQ of a Good King, he was apparently unable to figure out why this was happening:

No one will tell me the cause of my sorrow
Why they have made me a prisoner here.
Wherefore with dolour I now make my moan;
Friends had I many but help have I none.
Shameful it is that they leave me to ransom,
To languish here two winters long.

His mother eventually managed to prise the money for his ransom out of the loyal English, whose country was impoverished for years as a result, and in 1194 Richard returned to England to try another coronation – he left again straight afterwards, never to return. He spent even more of his

overtaxed country's revenue on building a state-of-the-art castle north of Paris: Chateau Gaillard. It cost £12,000, more than any other defensive building for centuries. It was undermined and captured by Philip II of France six years after being completed.

By that time Richard was dead. He was killed in 1199 while attacking a small fortified building in Chalus, which was defended by a few men who had no hope of holding out. Richard, having forgotten to put his armour on, rode up to its wall and was promptly shot with a crossbow. During his ten-year reign he had spent a grand total of six months in England.

Now how does a man like that end up being a Good King, except through the power of propaganda?

MEDIEVAL SPIN DOCTORS

WE CAN CLEARLY SEE THE WAY chroniclers adjusted their view of the past in the manuscript of Ralph of Coggeshall's chronicle, which was written during the reigns of Richard and his successor, John. The first section dates from around 1195, when Richard was alive, and praises him with enthusiasm. The man is the 'unique mirror of all the kings of the Norman race'. The next section was written in a different ink after John had come to the throne. Now Richard has become a quite different kind of king – grasping (Coggeshall says no previous king had imposed such heavy financial demands on his kingdom), menacing, threatening his own petitioners, ferocious towards everyone.

> No age can remember, no history can record any preceding king, even those who reigned for a long time, who exacted and received so much money from his kingdom as that king exacted and amassed in the five years after he returned from captivity.

John, the new king, was a very different figure, a king whose 'heart was full of the spirit of counsel and piety'. During Richard's lifetime, Coggeshall had been writing very critically about John, but those criticisms are not to be found in the manuscript of his chronicle now. We only know that he wrote them because another chronicler, Roger of Wendover, copied them out before Ralph had a chance to cover his tracks. Once John was on the throne, Ralph carefully erased his criticisms of the new king and filled in the blank space with new historical details – the sacking of a chancellor, the consecration of a bishop.*

*D. A. Carpenter, Abbot Ralph of Coggeshall's Account of the Last Years of King Richard and the First Years of King John, *English Historical Review,* Nov. 1998.

Above: King John stag-hunting. His expansion of the Royal Forests became one of the pieces of evidence of his tyranny.

Of course, once John was out of the way he became a Bad King and, by contrast, Richard was restored as a Good King.

LIMITING ROYAL POWER

THE MAGNA CARTA, which dominated the later years of John's reign, did not and could not create any new institutional check on royal power. It was essentially a supplement to the coronation oath, stating the king's intention to uphold good laws, and spelt out what some of those good laws were.

The issue that stirred the barons to demand this document was the sheer cost of maintaining the royal machine, especially the royal machine at war. John and Richard had both tried to meet this by massive increases in feudal dues and legal charges, and most of the Magna Carta is an effort to reverse these. When the rebellious barons complained of John's 'tyranny' – in other words, that he was ruling without paying attention to the law – they were not necessarily referring to law as we understand it. They held privileges, literally 'private laws', that were granted by the king, and the royal administration had vastly increased the cost of these. The price of relief from an obligation to the crown had risen from £100 to £6,666.

But other clauses – such as, 'In future no official shall place a man on trial upon his own unsupported statement, without producing credible witnesses to the truth of it' and 'We will appoint as justices, constables, sheriffs, or other officials, only men that know the law of the realm and are minded to keep it well' – show that the barons firmly held the view that the kingdom operated under laws that bound the king himself as well as everyone else.

There was, in short, a notion of proper kingship, and the Magna Carta tried to spell out what this meant.

The core problem of kingship was to establish the mechanism by which good rule could be enforced. To some extent, this was supposedly the role of the Church. Certainly, from the eleventh to the thirteenth century it could occasionally bring a monarch to his knees, and lower. Henry II had to prostrate himself at the altar in Canterbury cathedral and accept flogging as penance for the killing of Archbishop Becket. There was also the danger of unleashing rebellion, and ultimately of being deposed and killed. But in the end all this came down to a mechanism of popular (or at least baronial) consent.

THE DANGERS OF DEMOCRACY

THE IDEA THAT SUCH CONSENT should be formalized democratically was regarded as quite simply wrong. We seem to believe that regularly offering the adult population the chance to elect a political party to govern them is self-evidently the ideal political system. This is a very recent opinion. Even John Stuart Mill, so often taken to be the philosopher of democracy, warned against 'the tyranny of the majority'. This was a danger that was well understood in the Middle Ages. This is why Dante included

democracy as one of the despotic systems from which monarchy protects the people:

It is only when a monarch is reigning that the human race exists for its own sake, and not for the sake of something else. For it is only then that perverted forms of government are made straight, to wit, democracies, oligarchies, and tyrannies, which force the human race into slavery (as is obvious to whosoever runs through them all)…

The same arguments against 'democracy' are echoed in Chaucer:

For the truth of things and the benefit thereof are better found by a few folk who are wise and full of reason, rather than by a great multitude of people in which every man shouts out and prattles on about whatever he wants.

For monarchy to function well it was necessary for the monarch to internalize the law – he had to be as stern a judge of his own acts as he was of the acts of others. This was the difference between a strong, all-powerful monarch and a tyrant. If a king ruled in the interests of his people, he was a rightful ruler. If he ruled in his own interests, however, he was a tyrant. In the fourteenth century Marsilius of Padua, the one-time rector of the University of Paris, wrote:

A kingly monarchy, then is a temperate government wherein the ruler is a single man who rules for the common benefit, and in accordance with the will or consent of the subjects. Tyranny, its opposite, is a diseased government wherein the ruler is a single man who rules for his own private benefit apart from the will of his subjects.

At the heart of government was the duty of obedience to the king. This was seen as the source of all peace, honour and prosperity in the realm, and it was the king's job to ensure that obedience to him would be rewarded. The primary function of government was to enable people to lead peaceful and secure lives, and a strong central monarchy was understood to be essential to that as individual barons had no commitment to the common good and would plainly, if left alone, tear the country to pieces. The danger to good government came less from a king who was too powerful than from one who was too weak and could not dominate the barons or win their support.

Henry III and his son Edward I managed to rule effectively, but the next inheritor of the throne, Edward II, failed completely. He was deposed finally by the barons, and the kingdom was taken over by his wife and

her lover in the name of his son, the 15-year-old Edward III. This was not a rebellion against tyranny; it was against incompetence. Edward II alienated all his potential supporters by his passionate commitment to unpopular favourites and his complete failure as a war leader.

Edward III grew to manhood with a clear understanding of the difficulties faced by an underage king, and celebrated his emergence as an adult by seizing and then hanging his mother's lover. But by the time he came to his deathbed his son, the Black Prince, was dead and the succession passed to another child: his ten-year-old grandson Richard.

BAD KING – RICHARD II

HISTORIANS MOSTLY AGREE that Richard II was a bad lot. 'Vain', 'megalomaniacal', 'narcissistic', 'treacherous', 'vindictive', and 'tyrannical' are among the most common epithets applied to him. Quite a few historians – for good measure – also mark him down as 'mad'.

Above: Edward III.

Thus the *Oxford History of England* describes how his actions after 1397 'suggest a sudden loss of control, the onset of a mental malaise. If Richard was sane from 1397 onwards, it was with the sanity of a man who pulls his own house down about his ears.'*

He must have been vain – after all, wasn't he the first English monarch to commission a lifelike portrait of himself? And talk about a megalomaniac – why, he made everyone call him 'Your Majesty' instead of plain old 'sire' and forced people to bow the knee to him.

As for his vengeful streak, historians have only to point out how he suddenly turned on three of the greatest nobles in the land in 1397 – he exiled the Duke of Warwick, executed Richard Earl of Arundel and had Thomas of Woodstock, Duke of Gloucester, murdered.

But it may be that modern historians have been too ready to believe everything bad about Richard – even things that never happened. For example, part of the evidence for Richard's insanity always used to be an incident in which a friar came before the King and accused John of Gaunt, the Duke of Lancaster, of plotting against the King's life. The friar was so insistent that Richard ordered the Duke to be put to death straight away. But wiser counsels stayed his hand, whereupon Richard threw a tantrum,

*McKisack M., *The Fourteenth Century*, (Oxford, 1959), 498.

tossing his cape and shoes out of the window and began to act like a madman.

This story was solemnly reiterated by historians as proof positive of Richard's incipient madness – until 1953, when a scholar pointed out that the Victorian editor of the particular chronicle had misplaced the sentence about the cape and shoes, and that it was actually the friar who had pretended to be mad on realizing that his false accusations were about to be exposed. Richard, in fact, listened to his counsel and, according to the chronicle, 'wisely undertook to act… in conformity with their advice'.*

*L.C.Hector, 'Chronicle of the Monk of Westminster', *English Historical Review*, 68 (1953), pp.62–5.

But the readiness with which this totally nonsensical story about Richard was believed tells us something about the historical attitudes to him.

RICHARD THE VINDICTIVE?

WARWICK, ARUNDEL AND GLOUCESTER had been a constant thorn in Richard's side since he inherited the throne in 1377. In 1387 they openly rebelled against him. They defeated the royal army and set about destroying Richard's circle of influence. They tortured and executed something like 18 of his closest friends and advisers.

In contrast, when Richard took the reins of power back into his hands in 1389, he didn't execute anyone. And when he did make his move, eight years later, he kept it to a surgical strike – he took no revenge on their hangers-on. He didn't torture anyone. He simply removed those three troublemakers who had betrayed him and worked against his interest throughout his reign.

Not exactly a vindictive nature, one would have thought.

RICHARD THE MEGALOMANIAC?

IT IS TRUE THAT RICHARD seems to have cultivated the trappings of royal power to a greater degree than his English predecessors. But was it a sign of megalomania?

In fact, in adopting higher terms of address, such as 'Your Majesty' and introducing courtesies such as bowing, Richard was doing no more than importing the fashions that had been current in the courts of Europe for most of the century.

In any case, a strong centralized monarchy was seen by the political thinkers of the fourteenth century not as tyranny but as a civilizing influence. The alternative was a continually warring baronage, disrupting the realm.

The idea of absolute power in the hands of the King was, in fact, seen as a protection for liberties, not a threat to them. When Wat Tyler, at the height of the 1381 revolt, proposed that the aristocracy should be done away with and the King should rule his people directly, he was not talking off the top of his head; he was voicing an idea that was current amongst the political thinkers of the day.

Left: The Wilton Diptych. Probably used as a portable altar-piece, the scene may express Richard's view of kingship as a divine trust. Richard kneels with open arms to receive the banner of England from the infant Christ.

One of the few books that we know for certain that Richard owned was one that was presented to him by Philippe de Mézières, the ex-Chancellor of Cyprus. In it Philippe describes the ideal kingdom, and it may come as a shock for the modern reader to discover how monarchy and socialism are combined; with the abolition of private property and the distribution of wealth 'to each according to his need'.

All fruits were held in common by the inhabitants, to each according to his need, and the words 'my own' were never heard… All tyranny and harsh rule was banished from the garden, though there was a king, who stood for authority and the common good, and he was so loved and looked up to that he might have been the father of each and all. And no wonder, for he had such concern for the welfare of his subjects, dwellers in the garden, that neither he nor his children owned anything.*

The Wilton Diptych portrays Richard with hands open ready to receive the flag of England from the hands of the baby Jesus… in other words the country is a sacred trust and not a milch cow.

So what happened to Richard's reputation?

HENRY IV'S PROPAGANDA MACHINE

IT'S THE OLD STORY. Henry Bolingbroke was an illegal usurper who treacherously went against all his vows of loyalty as a chivalric knight, stole the throne from his cousin and then had him murdered. The usurper needed to assuage not only his guilty conscience but also the considerable body of contemporary public opinion that regarded him as the traitor that he was.

Despite the assertions of the chroniclers of Henry IV's reign, it is clear that Bolingbroke's return to England was not greeted with popular relief or a sense of liberation. He had trouble even finding a safe place to land, 'taking his ships back and forth along the coastline, approaching different parts of the kingdom in turn'. He finally chose to land as far north as Yorkshire. The mayor and aldermen of London did not desert Richard until he had been taken prisoner, and even then they probably drove a hard bargain. But that is not the way the story gets told. Bolingbroke took good care of that.

As soon as he had seized power he sent letters to all the abbeys and major churches 'instructing the heads of these religious houses to make available for examination all of their chronicles which touched upon the state and governance of the kingdom of England from the time of William

*Philippe de Mézières, *Letter to King Richard II*, trans. G.W. Coopland (Liverpool, 1975) p.54.

the Conqueror up until the present day…' The erasures and revisions still visible in these manuscripts, the removal of criticisms of Bolingbroke and his father, and the addition of anti-Richard material show that monks understood perfectly well what that meant. The records of the City of London were simply attacked with a knife; two and a half folios covering the period of the usurpation have been cut out.

We can also see the signs of pressure being put on other writers to conform to the new political correctness. John Gower, ten years Chaucer's senior and perhaps already going blind, painfully pulls into line with the current political orthodoxy as many manuscripts as he can of his poem *Confessio Amantis*. He had originally dedicated the poem to Richard; but in the climate of fear and paranoia that accompanied the usurpation he rededicated it to Henry. John Gower even goes to great lengths to pretend that he made such changes long before the usurpation.

Henry's heavy hand must have been leaning on the poet's shoulder as he wrote every word.

Richard II saw the basis of his power not in overwhelming military force or political intrigue, but in the special authority of sovereignty. His court was a fount not of military authority but of magical power, in which the majesty of royal justice was tempered by the mercy of queenly intercession; it was a court of manners and of ceremony.

None of which enriched the barons or increased their influence and power. They needed war. The chronicler of the *Vita Ricardi Secundi* complained that Richard was 'timid and unsuccessful in foreign war'. Instead of wars he offered tournaments, accompanied by music, and dancing with the ladies of the court. Walsingham made a hostile assessment of Richard's courtiers:

> These fellows, who are in close association with the King, care nothing for what a knight ought to know – I am speaking not only about the use of arms but also about those matters with which a noble king should be concerned in times of peace, such as hunting and hawking and the like – activities that serve to enhance the honour of a king.
> *Historia Anglicana*

The fact is that Richard had created a new vision of royalty in England, in which the king was a majestic figure in a court that was as concerned with the arts of peace as those of war. The function of majesty was to create a focus of authority that would be as effective in times of peace as of war. Henry IV and each succeeding sovereign would, in fact, attempt to build on what Richard had done.

The third and final King Richard was no exception to this, but once again the propaganda of his detractors has nobbled him.

BAD KING

OF COURSE WE ALL DO KNOW that there was a king called Richard III, but the character we know about is a completely different man from the one that sat on the throne. The real man has disappeared, and in his place we have a cardboard cut-out villain, to be booed and hissed whenever he appears on stage – this is Shakespeare's character, the magnificent, deformed monster king, which was directly based on the extremely biased sources available to him. Laurence Olivier's magnificent screen performance does complete justice to Shakespeare's creation, a reptilian, insinuating smile on the face of a man who understands his own psychotic character, driven by his hunger for revenge on the world for his hunched and twisted spine.

> I, that am not shaped for sportive tricks,
> Nor made to court an amorous looking-glass;
> I, that am rudely stamp'd, and want love's majesty
> To strut before a wanton ambling nymph;
> I, that am curtail'd of this fair proportion,
> Cheated of feature by dissembling nature,
> Deformed, unfinish'd, sent before my time
> Into this breathing world, scarce half made up,
>
> Since I cannot prove a lover,
> To entertain these fair well-spoken days,
> I am determined to prove a villain
> And hate the idle pleasures of these days.
> Plots have I laid, inductions dangerous

Of course, England never had a king like that and Richard did not even have a hunchback. There is a portrait of him in the Royal Collection, probably dating from the reign of his usurper, which, some experts claim, has been altered to show him with a hunched back. Whether this claim is justified or not, it is clear that the amount of work that went into creating the story that Richard plotted to seize the throne of England and then ruled as a brutal tyrant is really quite extraordinary.

Medieval kings ruled by consent, no other way was possible. For virtually every king of England, this essentially meant the consent of the nobility of southern and central England, with the earls in the north being steadily marginalized. That had eventually led to civil war, the Wars of the Roses, which had ended with Edward IV defeating the northern nobility.

Edward then gave his brother Richard the job of winning hearts and minds in the north. While the king ruled from London, Richard, Duke of Gloucester, was sent to York to be a sort of vice-regent. He arrived in 1476, backed up by 5,000 men. But according to the York records, he had not come to impose himself by force: 'After greetings were exchanged, the duke addressed the civic officials within Bootham Bar, saying that he was sent by the king to support the rule of law and peace.'

In fact, Richard devoted himself to the minutiae of government and justice, and the pleas put to him indicate that he became fully immersed in the life of the region.

In 1482 the City of York presented him with gifts, 'for the great labour, good and benevolent lordship that the right, high and mighty prince have at all tymes done for the well of the city'. Out of the council goody bag came fish – '6 pike, 6 tenches, 6 breme, 6 eels and 1 barrel of sturgeon', a local speciality of spiced bread, and fourteen gallons of wine to wash it all down.

At the dark heart of the legend of evil King Richard lie the bodies of two children, the sons of Edward IV – the princes in the Tower. When Edward approached his death in 1483 he named his 12-year-old son Edward as his successor. Richard was to be lord protector until the boy grew up. But when the king died on 9 April Richard was in the north of England and the prince was in the hands of his mother's family, the Woodvilles.

They tried to hurry the child to London before Richard knew about the death, and crown him on 4 May – a coup that would have given them control of the king and the country. Richard managed to intercept them and escorted the boy to London, placing him in the royal apartment in the Tower and rescheduling the coronation for 22 June. On the thirteenth, evidence came to light of an extensive plot against Richard, and young Edward's brother (little Richard) was also installed in the Tower. Edward's coronation was deferred until November.

On 22 June Dr Edward Shaa, brother of the mayor of London, conveniently declared to the citizens of London that Edward IV's marriage to Elizabeth Woodville, which had taken place in secret, had been illegal because the king had a precontract of marriage with Lady Eleanor Butler. Richard had been a dutiful and loyal assistant to his brother Edward IV, and had spent most of his life in the north of England. He was popular, widely trusted, knew everyone and was a capable administrator. Now the legitimacy of the succession had been undermined and the country was on the edge of plunging back into the terrible civil wars from which it had so recently emerged. Taking the bull by the horns, Richard announced that if Edward IV's children were illegitimate, then he himself, brother of the dead king, must be his successor. He was acclaimed king on 26 June and crowned on 6 July. The princes vanished, and the official Tudor view was that Richard had them killed.

When historians debate King Louis the First and Last, they generally observe that he should not be counted as one of the kings of England as he

At an exhibition of Richard III portraits in 1991, this portrait from Windsor (detail, below) was included, with the comment 'Very soon after completion, both the Henry VI in this series and the Richard III were modified. Richard's shoulder was heightened to suggest the hump-back and it seems the lips and eyes have been compressed to hint at villainy.' (Pamela Tudor-Craig). Looking at the portrait superimposed on its X-ray (left), this statement seems barely justified. Are we looking at an example of Tudor propaganda against Richard, or modern propaganda against the Tudors?

did not have a coronation. However, the child Edward is counted as Edward V, despite the fact that not only was he never crowned, but he never ruled at all. The reason for this is that Henry Tudor, who had no meaningful claim to the throne, seized the crown in 1485 and found it very helpful to have Richard designated as a regicide – so the boy was recognized as a king.

In fact, if anyone had an interest in killing the boys it was Henry Tudor.

The bones of two children are still on show at the Tower, proof of Richard's wicked deed. They were discovered in the seventeenth century, and examined in 1933, when they were said to be the vital evidence of the crime. But no-one knows when they date from.

All the evidence from Richard's own lifetime shows that he was not a tyrant. Almost the first thing he did on becoming king was to pay off £200 he owed to York wine merchants. Now there's a tyrant for you! And then he brought the whole court north to the city, to stage a second coronation – his secretary advised its corporation to put on a heck of a show. It was also a great opportunity to show off Yorkshire wool:

Hang the streets thorough which the king's grace shall come with clothes of arras, tapestry work and other, for there commen many southern lords and men of worship with them.

The city did put on an incredible spectacle, and many citizens contributed handsomely to it. The mayor and aldermen, all dressed in scarlet, rode with the king and queen through a city made of cloth, stopping for elaborate shows and displays as they went. They turned the place into a woollen Disneyland.

To many southern lords, it looked as though the Wars of the Roses had been referred back to the referee, and the north had won after all, especially when Richard filled his court with friends from the region. They were not at all happy, so they backed Henry Tudor to take over. Richard III became the last king of England to die in battle. But when news of his death at the Battle of Bosworth reached the York council chamber, the councillors did not declare their joy that England had been liberated from a tyrant:

King Richard late mercifully reigning upon us was through great treason of the Duke of Northfolk and many othres that turned ayenst him, with many othre lordes and nobles of these north parts, pitiously slain and murdred to the great heavinesse of this city.

That was a very dangerous thing to write in the city records; and it must have been deeply heartfelt. So why have we ended up with a picture of Richard the cruel and twisted tyrant?

I must be married to my brother's daughter,
Or else my kingdom stands on brittle glass.
Murder her brothers, and then marry her!
The uncertain way of gain! But I am in
So far in blood that sin will pluck on sin:
Tear-falling pity dwells not in this eye.
Richard III

The answer is the mighty power of Tudor propaganda. Henry VII – Henry Tudor – had seized the crown, and his dynasty rested on that shaky foundation. It was necessary to invent a Richard who had never existed, a bogeyman, to justify the usurpation.

While Richard was still alive, writer John Rous described him as 'a mighty prince and especial good Lord.' When the Tudors took power, Rous portrayed him as akin to the Antichrist: 'Richard spent two whole years in his mother's womb and came out with a full set of teeth.' Shakespeare, writing a century later, was himself serving a Tudor monarch. His main sources were Tudor documents written by men in their sovereigns' service.

Medieval kings were not all striving for tyranny; in many ways, they were less free than their subjects (though, of course, much richer). The Good King/Bad King stories are the propaganda of their successors. And even the question of who was and was not a king of England was decided after the men themselves were dead – by the chroniclers.

Propaganda, thy name is History.

Bibliography

WEB RESOURCES
The best way of finding quality-controlled www resources is through a major medievalists' website; two of the best are ORB, the On-Line Reference Book for Medievalists, at **http://orb.rhodes.edu/**, which also refers to other sites on its Æ **n.edu/labyrinth**. Searching for books in other libraries, or checking references, can be done through the Cambridge University Library website at **www.lib.cam.ac.uk/** (go to 'Catalogues' from the homepage).

GENERAL
Bolton, J. L., *The Medieval English Economy, 1150–1500* (Everyman, 1980)

Boureau, A., *The Lord's First Night: The Myth of the Droit de Cuissage*, tr. Lydia G. Cochrane (University of Chicago Press, 1998)

Britnell, R., *The Closing of the Middle Ages: England, 1471–1529*, (Blackwell, 1997)

Campbell, J., *The Anglo-Saxons*, (Cornell, 1982)

DeVries, K., *Medieval Military Technology*, (Broadview, 1992)

Dyer, C., *Standards of Living in the Later Middle Ages: Social Change in England c.1200–1520*, (Cambridge University Press, 1989)

Gimpel, J., *The Medieval Machine: The Industrial Revolution of the Middle Ages*, (Holt, 1976)

Hanawalt, B., *Growing Up in Medieval London: The Experience of Childhood in History*, (Oxford University Press, 1993)

Horrox, R. E. (ed.), *Fifteenth-Century Attitudes*, (Cambridge University Press, 1994)

Keen, M., *English Society in the Later Middle Ages, 1348–1500*, (Penguin, 1990)

LeGoff, J., *Medieval Civilization, 400–1500*, (Blackwell, 1989)

LeGoff, J., *Time, Work, and Culture in the Middle Ages*, (University of Chicago Press, 1980)

Pollard, A. J., *Late Medieval England, 1399–1509*

Prestwich, M., *Armies and Warfare in the Middle Ages: The English Experience*, (Yale University Press, 1996)

Rigby, S. H., *English Society in the Later Middle Ages: Class, Status and Gender*, (Macmillan, 1995)

Stenton, F., *William the Conqueror and the Rule of the Normans*, (Barnes & Noble, 1966)

Stock, B., *Listening for the Text: On the Uses of the Past*, (University of Pennsylvania Press, 1997)

Thomson, J. A. F., *The Transformation of Medieval England 1370–1529*, (Longman, 1983)

Tuck, A., *Crown and Nobility (1272–1461)*, (Fontana, 1985)

Platt, C., *Medieval England: A Social History and Archaeology from the Conquest to 1600 AD*, (Routledge, 1988)

PEASANT
Allison, K., *Wharram Percy: Deserted Medieval Village*, (English Heritage Publications, 1999)

Beresford, M. & Hurst, J., *Wharram Percy – Deserted Medieval Village*, (Batsford, 1990)

Coulton, G. G., *The Medieval Village*, (Dover Publications, 1989)

Dobson, R. B. (ed.), *The Peasants' Revolt of 1381*, (Macmillan, 1983)

Dyer, A., *Decline and Growth in English Towns, 1400–1640*, (Macmillan, 1991)

Hanawalt, B., *The Ties that Bound: Peasant Families in Medieval England*, (Oxford University Press, 1986)

Hatcher, J., *Plague, Population and the English Economy, 1348–1530*, (Macmillan, 1977)

Henisch, B. A., *Fast and Feast: Food in Medieval Society*, (Penn State UP, 1976)

Herlihy, D., *Medieval Housholds*, (Harvard University Press, 1985)

Hilton R. H. and Aston T. H. (eds.), *The English Rising of 1381*, (1984)

Jordan, W. C., *The Great Famine: Northern Europe in the Early Fourteenth Century*, (Princeton University Press, 1998)

Mollat, M., *The Poor in the Middle Ages: An Essay in Social History*, (Yale University Press, 1986)

Newman, R., *Cosmeston Mediaeval Village*, (Glamorgan–Gwent Archaeological Trust, 1988)

Platt, C., *King Death: The Black Death and its Aftermath in Late-medieval England*, (UCL, 1996)

Poos, L., *A Rural Society after the Black Death: Essex, 1350–1525*, (Cambridge University Press, 1991)

Rösener, W., *Peasants in the Middle Ages*, (University of Illinois, 1992)

Schmidt, A. V. C. (ed.), *William Langland: The Vision of Piers Plowman: A Complete Edition of the B-Text*, (Everyman Classics, 1987)

Schofield P. R., *Peasant and Community in Medieval England, 1200–1500*, (Macmillan, 2002)

Spufford, P., *Money and its use in Medieval Europe*, (Cambridge University Press, 1988)

Webber, R., *Peasants' Revolt: The Uprising in Kent, Essex, East Anglia and London During the Reign of King Richard II*, (T. Dalton, 1980)

MINSTREL
Aubrey, E., *The Music of the Troubadours*, (Indiana University Press, 1996)

Coleman, J., *Public Reading and the Reading Public in Late Medieval England and France*, (Cambridge University Press, 1996)

Daniel, A., *Pound's Translations of*

Arnaut Daniel: A Variorum Edition with Commentary from Unpublished Letters (Garland Science, 1991)

Egan, M., *The Vidas of the Troubadours*, (Taylor & Francis, 1984)

Gaunt, S. & Kay, S. (eds.), *The Troubadours: An Introduction*, (Cambridge University Press, 1999)

Green, R. F., *Poets and Princepleasers: Literature and the English Court in the Late Middle Ages*, (University of Toronto Press, 1980)

Hueffer, F., *The Troubadours: A History of Provençal Life and Literature in the Middle Ages*, (Ams Press, 1977)

Jensen, F., *Troubadour Lyrics: A Bilingual Anthology*, Studies in the Humanities, Vol 39, (Peter Lang Pub. Inc., 1998)

Paden, W. D., *The Voice of the Trobairitz: Perspectives on the Women Troubadours*, (University of Pennsylvania Press, 1989)

Page C., *Discarding Images: Reflections on Music and Culture in Medieval France*, (Oxford University Press, 1993)

Page C., *The Owl and the Nightingale: Musical Life and Ideas in France 1100–1300*, (University of California Press, 1989)

Paterson, L. (ed.), *The World of the Troubadours: Medieval Occitan Society, c.1100–1300*, (Cambridge University Press, 1995)

Putter, A. & Gilbert, J. (eds.), *The Spirit of Medieval Popular Romance*, (Longman, 2000)

Schulman, N. M., *Where Troubadours Were Bishops: The Occitania of Folc of Marseille, 1150–1231*, (Routledge, 2001)

Southworth, J., *The English Medieval Minstrel*, (Boydell Press, 1989)

Topsfield, L. T., *Troubadours and Love*, (Cambridge University Press, 1975)

Wilkins, N., *Music in the Age of Chaucer*, (Rowman & Littlefield, 1979)

OUTLAW

Bellamy, J. G., 'The Coterel Gang: an Anatomy of a Band of Fourteenth-century Criminals', *English Historical Review*, vol. 79, (1964), pp. 698–717

Bellamy, J. G., *Crime and Public Order in England in the Later Middle Ages*, (Routledge, 1973)

Chrimes S. B., *Introduction to the Administrative History of Medieval England*, (Blackwell, 1966)

Hanawalt, B. A., 'Ballads and Bandits. Fourteenth-Century Outlaws and the Robin Hood Poems' in *Chaucer's England*, ed. Barbara A. Hanawalt, (University of Minnesota Press, 1992)

Hanawalt, B. A., *Crime and Conflict in English Communities 1300–1348*, (Harvard University Press, 1979)

Holt, J. C., *Robin Hood*, revised edn., (Thames and Hudson, 1989)

Johnston, A. F., 'The Robin Hood of the Records' in *Playing Robin Hood. The Legend as Performance in Five Centuries*, ed. Lois Potter, (University of Delaware, 1998)

Jusserand, J. J., *English Wayfaring Life in the Middle Ages*, (Methuen, 1961) Part I, ch. iii; Part II, ch. iii

Keen, M., *The Outlaws of Medieval Legend*, revised paperback edn., (Routledge & Kegan Paul, 1987)

Knight, S., *Robin Hood. A Complete Study of the English Outlaw*, (Blackwell, 1994)

Musson, A., *Medieval Law in Context: The Growth of Legal Consciousness from Magna Carta to the Peasants' Revolt*, (Manchester University Press, 2001)

Powell E., *Kingship, Law and Society: Criminal Justice in the Reign of Henry V*, (Clarendon Press, 1989)

Seal, G., *The Outlaw Legend. A Cultural Tradition in Britain, America and Australia*, (Cambridge University Press, 1996)

Spraggs, G., *Outlaws and Highwaymen. The Cult of the Robber in England from the Middle Ages to the Nineteenth Century*, (Pimlico, 2001)

Stones, E. L. G., 'The Folvilles of Ashby–Folville, Leicestershire, and their associates in crime, 1326–1347', *Transactions of the Royal Historical Society*, 5th series, vol. 7 (1957), pp. 117–36

Summerson, H., 'The Criminal Underworld of Medieval England', *Journal of Legal History*, vol. 17, no. 3 (December, 1996), pp. 197–224

Wiles, *The Early Plays of Robin Hood*, (Brewer, 1981)

Wilkinson B., *Constitutional History of England in the Fifteenth Century*, (1964)

MONK

Brown, P., *The Cult of the Saints: Its Rise and Function in Latin Christianity*, (Chicago University Press, 1981)

Burton, J., *Monastic and Religious Orders in Britain 1000–1300*, (Cambridge University Press, 1994)

Burton, J., *The Monastic Order in Yorkshire, 1069–1215*, (Cambridge University Press, 1999)

Butler, L. & Given-Wilson, C., *Medieval Monasteries of Great Britain*, (Michael Joseph, 1979)

Daly, J., *Benedictine Monasticism: Its Formation and Development Through the 12th Century*, (Sheed and Ward, Inc., 1965)

Evans, J., *Monastic Life at Cluny 910–1157*, (Oxford University Press, 1968)

Greene, J. P., *Medieval Monasteries*, (Leicester University Press, 1992)

Grundmann, H., *Religious Movements in the Middle Ages: The Historical Links between Heresy, the Mendicant Orders, and the Women's Religious Movement in the Twelfth and Thirteenth Century*, (Notre Dame, 1995)

Haigh. C. A., *English Reformations*, (Clarendon Press, 1993)

Hill, B. D., *English Cistercian Monasteries and Their Patrons in the Twelfth Century*, (University of Illinois Press, 1968)

Hill, R., 'From the Conquest to the Black Death', *A History of Religion in Britain*, ed. Sheridan Gilley and W. J. Sheils, (Blackwell, 1994)

Hudson, A., *The Premature Reformation: Wycliffite Texts and Lollard History*, (Clarendon Press, 1989)

Knowles, D., *The Monastic Orders of England*, (Cambridge, 1963)

Lawrence, C. H., *Medieval Monasticism: Forms of Medieval Religious Life in Western Europe in the Middle Ages*, (Longman, 1989)

Leclercq, J., *The Love of Learning and the Desire for God: A Study of Monastic Culture*, (Fordham, 1961)

PHILOSOPHER

Alington, G., *The Hereford Mappa Mundi: A Medieval View of the World*, (Gracewing, 1996)

Burckhardt, T., *Alchem: Science of the Cosmos, Science of the Soul* (Fons Vitae, 1997)

Burland, C., *The Arts of the Alchemists*, (Ams Press, 1989)

Coudert, A., *Alchemy: the Philosopher's Stone*, (Wildwood Ho., 1980)

Erlande-Brandenburg, A., *The Cathedral Builders of the Middle Ages*, (Thames and Hudson, 1995)

Getz, F., *Medicine in the English Middle Ages*, (Princeton University Press, 1998)

Henwood, G., *Abbot Richard of Wallingford: Fourteenth Century Scholar, Astronomer and Instrument Maker*, (Pie Powder Press, 1988)

Klossowski de Rola, S., *Alchemy: the secret art*, (Harper Collins, 1973)

Moffat, B., *The sixth report on researches into the medieval hospital at Soutra, Scottish Borders/Lothian, Scotland* (SHARP)

Read, J., *Prelude to Chemistry*, (MIT Press, 1966)

Russell, J. B., *Inventing the Flat Earth: Columbus and Modern Historians*, (Greenwood Press, 1997)

White, L. Jr., *Medieval Technology and Social Change*, (Oxford University Press, 1966)

KNIGHT

Anglo, S. (ed.), *Chivalry in the Renaissance*, (Boydell, 1990)

Barber, R. and Barker, J., *Tournaments: Jousts, Chivalry and Pageants in the Middle Ages*, (Boydell Press, 1989)

Barker, J., *The Tournament in England 1100–1400*, (Boydell Press, 1986)

Barron, W. R. J., *English Medieval Romance*, (Longman, 1987)

Benson, L. D., 'Courtly Love and Chivalry in the Later Middle Ages', *Fifteenth-Century Studies: Recent Essays*, ed. Robert F. Yeager, (Connecticut, 1984)

Benson L. D. and Leyerle J. (ed.), *Chivalric Literature: Essays on relations between literature and life in the later Middle Ages*, (Kalamazoo: Institute, 1980)

Burnley, D., *Courtliness and Literature in Medieval England*, (Longman, 1998)

Chickering, H. and Seiler T. H., (eds.), *The Study of Chivalry: Resources and Approaches*, (Kalamazoo Institute, 1988)

Contamine, P., *War in the Middle Ages*, tr. Michael Jones, (Blackwell, 1984)

Donaldson, E. T., 'The Myth of Courtly Love' (1965). Reprinted in *Speaking of Chaucer*, (Athlone, 1970)

Gies, F., *The Knight in History*, (Robert Hale, 1984)

Girouard, M., *The Return to Camelot: Chivalry and the English Gentle-man*, (Yale University Press, 1981)

Jones, T. and Ereira, A., *Crusades*, (BBC Books, 1994)

Jones, T., *Chaucer's Knight: The Portrait of a Medieval Mercenary*, (Baton Rouge, 1980)

Keen, M., 'Chaucer's Knight, the English Aristocracy and the Crusade', *English Court Culture in the Later Middle Ages*, ed. V. J. Scattergood and J. W. Sherborne, (Macmillan, 1983)

Keen, M., *Chivalry*, (Yale University Press, 1984)

Lester, G. A., 'Chaucer's Knight and the Medieval Tournament', *Neophilologus* 66 (1982): 460–8

Lewis, C. S., *The Allegory of Love: A Study in Medieval Tradition*, (Oxford University Press, 1936)

Loomis, R. S. (ed.), *Arthurian Literature in the Middle Ages*, (Clarendon, 1965)

Lull, R., *The Book of the Ordre of Chyualry*, tr. William Caxton, ed. Alfred T. P. Byles, EETS o.s. 168, (London, 1926)

Mayer, H. E., *The Crusades*, tr. John Gillingham, 2nd edn, (Oxford University Press, 1988)

Prestwich, M., *Armies and Warfare in the Middle Ages: The English Experience*, (Yale University Press, 1996)

Riley-Smith, J. (ed.), *The Oxford Illustrated History of the Crusades*, (Oxford University Press, 1995)

Riley-Smith, L. and J. (eds.), *The Crusades: Idea and Reality, 1095–1274*, Documents of Medieval History 4, (Edward Arnold, 1981)

Russell, F. H., *The Just War in the Middle Ages*, (Cambridge University Press, 1975)

Tyerman, C., *England and the Crusades 1095–1588*, (University of Chicago Press, 1988)

Vale, J., *Edward III and Chivalry: Chivalric Society and its Context, 1270–1350*, (Brewer, 1982)

Vale, M., *War and Chivalry: Warfare and Aristocratic Culture in England, France, and Burgundy at the End of the Middle Ages*, (University of Georgia Press, 1981)

Wilson, D., *The Bayeux Tapestry: The Complete Tapestry in Colour with Introduction, Description, and Commentary*, (Thames and Hudson, 1984)

DAMSEL

Barratt, A. (ed.), *Women's Writing in Middle English*, (Longman, 1992)

Collis, L., *Memoirs of a Medieval Woman: The Life and the Times of Margery Kempe*, (Harper Colophon Books, 1983)

Delany, S., *Writing Woman: Woman Writers and Women in Literature, Medieval to Modern*, (Schocken Books, 1983)

Ennen, E., *The Medieval Woman*, (Blackwell, 1989)

Gies, F. and J., *Women in the Middle Ages*, (Barnes and Noble, 1980)

Gilson, E., *Heloise and Abelard*, (Regnery, 1951)

Goldberg, P. J. P., *Women, Work and Life-Cycle in a Medieval Economy: Women in York and Yorkshire c.1300–1520*, (Oxford, 1992)

Harksen, S., *Women in the Middle Ages*, tr. Marianne Herzfeld, (A. Schram, 1975)

Harris, C. & Johnson, M., *Figleafing through History: The Dynamics of Dress*, (Atheneum, 1979)

Houston, M. G., *Medieval Costume in England and France*, (A & C Black, 1979)

Irigaray, L., *This Sex Which is Not One*, (Cornell, 1985)

Jewell, H., *Women in Medieval England*, (Manchester University Press, 1996)

Kamuf, P., *Fictions of Feminine Desire: Disclosures of Heloise*, (University of Nebraska Press, 1982)

250
Bibliography

Kelly, A., *Eleanor of Aquitaine and the Four Kings*, (Harvard, 1950)

Kors, A. and Peters E. (eds.), *Witchcraft in Europe, 1100–1700: A Documentary History*, (Pennsylvania, 1972)

Labarge, M. W., *Women in Medieval Life: A Small Sound of the Trumpet*, (Hamilton, 1986)

Leyser, H., *Medieval Women: A Social History of Women in England 450– 1500*, (St. Martin's Press, 1995)

Lucas, A. M., *Women in the Middle Ages: Religion, Marriage, and Letters*, (Harvester Press, 1983)

Meale, C. M. (ed.), *Women and Literature in Britain, 1150–1500*, (Cambridge University Press, 1993)

Painter, S., *William Marshall: Knight-Errant, Baron & Regent of England*, (Toronto/MART Series, 1982)

Pernoud, R. and Clin, M-V., *Joan of Arc: Her Story*, (St. Martin's Press, 1999)

Prior, M. (ed.), *Women in English Society, 1500–1800*, (Methuen, 1985)

Richards, E. J. (ed.), *Reinterpreting Christine de Pizan*, (University of Georgia Press, 1992)

Rose, M. B. (ed.), *Women in the Middle Ages and the Renaissance: Literary and Historical Perspectives*, (Syracuse University Press, 1986)

Shulamith, S., *The Fourth Estate: A History of Women in the Middle Ages*, (Methuen, 1983)

Thiebaux, M. (ed.), *The Writings of Medieval Women*, (Garland, 1987)

Ward, J. (ed. and tr.), *Women of the English Nobility and Gentry 1066–1500*, (Manchester University Press, 1995)

Wilson, Katharina M. (ed.), *Medieval Women Writers*, (University of Georgia Press, 1984)

KING

Brown, A. L., *The Governance of Late Medieval England, 1272–1461*, (London, 1989)

Carpenter, C., *The Wars of the Roses: Politics and the Constitution in England, c.1437–1509*, (Cambridge, 1997)

Condon, M. M., 'Ruling elites in the reign of Henry VII' in *Patronage, Pedigree and Power in Later Medieval England*, ed. C. D. Ross, (Gloucester, 1979)

Gillingham, J., *Richard I*, (Yale University Press, 1999)

Given-Wilson, C., *The Royal Household and the King's Affinity: Service, Politics and Finance in England, 1360–1413*, (Yale University Press, 1986)

Goodman, A. and Gillespie, J. (eds.), *Richard II: The Art of Kingship*, (Oxford University Press, 1999)

Harriss, G. L., 'Political Society and the Growth of Government in Late Medieval England', *P&P*, 138, (1993)

Harriss, G. L. (ed.), *Henry V: the Practice of Kingship*, (Oxford, 1985)

Horrox R., *Richard III: a Study of Service*, (Cambridge University Press, 1989)

McFarlane, K. B., *Lancastrian Kings and Lollard Knights*, (Oxford University Press, 1972)

Ormrod, W. M., *Political Life in Medieval England, 1300–1450*, (Macmillan, 1995)

Ormrod, W. M., *The Reign of Edward III*, (Yale University Press, 1990)

Ross, C. D., *Edward IV*, (Yale University Press, 1974)

Saul, N., *Richard II*, (Yale University Press, 1997)

Scattergood V. J. & Sherborne J. W. (eds.), *English Court Culture in the Later Middle Ages*, (Duckworth Press, 1983)

Watts, J. L., *Henry VI and the Politics of Kingship*, (Cambridge University Press, 1996)

Waugh, S. L., *England in the Reign of Edward III*, (Cambridge University Press, 1991)

Acknowledgements

We would like to thank Paul Bradshaw, who produced the television series and directed the first two programmes, Nigel Miller and Lucy Cooke who directed and produced the rest of the shows, Nick Angel, Clare Mottersead and Kate Smith for all their research, Annabel Lee for getting everything to work, and Alixe Bovey, Josh Key, Marc Tiley, Catherine Cooper, Rachel Shadick, Jacqui Loton, Claire Mills, Cathy Featherstone, and Kate Harding, and everyone else at Oxford Film and Television. Not forgetting, of course, our executive producers Nicolas Kent and Vanessa Phillips. We would also like to thank our historical advisers for the series: Richard Firth Green, Dr Anthony Musson, Dr Glyn Coppack, Caroline Barron, Dr Brenda Bolton, Dr Christopher Tyerman, Dr Faye Getz, Henrietta Leyser, Professor Andrew Prescott. And thanks to Professor Janet Nelson for her invaluable assistance on this book.

Terry Jones and Alan Ereira

PICTURE CREDITS
BBC Worldwide would like to thank the following for providing photographs and for permission to reproduce copyright material. While every effort has been made to trace and acknowledge copyright holders, we would like to apologise should there be any errors or omissions.

© Adam McLean: p.134t; akg-images, London: p.8, 164, 172t; akg-images, London/Erich Lessing: 187t; Alinari/Bridgeman Art Library: p.199t; Angelo Hornak Photography: p.109t, 150t; Archivo Iconografico, S.A./Corbis: 27t, 28, 29t, 31t, 33t, 72–3t, 105t, 171t; Bettmann/Corbis: 61t; Bibliothèque de l'Ecole des Beaux-Arts, Paris/Bridgeman Art Library: p.211t; Bibliothèque Nationale, Paris: 70, 79t, 82t, 87t, 107t, 217t; British Library, London: 18b, 19t, 21t, 24t, 26, 49, 51, 88, 100, 126, 145t, 147, 148t, 149t, 157, 160, 176t, 178t, 182, 185, 190, 193, 220t, 221, 226t, 227, 235t, 242t; British Library/Bridgeman Art Library: 130t; British Library/HIP: p.105b, 114t, 124t, 127t, 132, 139t, 192b, 193b, 208t; By courtesy of the Dean and Canons of Windsor, St. George's Chapel: p.175; CADW Photographic Library: 48t; Claughton Photography/Caroline Claughton: 56t; Courtesy of the Warden and Scholars of New College, Oxford/Bridgeman Art Library: 36t; Delpool Picture Library/Michael J.Allen: 96t; Det Kongelige Bibliotek, Copenhagen: 81t; English Heritage Photo Library/Peter Dunn: p.12; English Heritage Photo Library/

Paul Highnam: 23t; Experience Nottingham: 74t; Fortean Picture Library: p.135b, 142t; Fotoarchiv Tiroler Landesmuseum, Innsbruck: 53t; Gianni Dagli Orti/Corbis: 32t, 62t, 55t, 102t, 103t; Giraudon/Art Resource, NY: 25t; Hereford Cathedral/Bridgeman Art Library: p.146t; Historical Picture Archive/Corbis: p.214t; Hulton Archive: 69t; Jarrold Publishing Ltd: 50t; Mary Evans Picture Library: 57t; Metropolitan Museum of Art, NY: p.177t; Musée Condé, Chantilly/Bridgeman Art Library: p.184t, 204t, 213; National Gallery London: p.238–9t; National Trust Photo Library/Andrew Butler: p.120t; National Trust Photo Library/Joe Cornish: p.119t; © Oxford Film and Television: p.5–6, 16, 40, 70, 100, 132, 160, 190, 218; Paul Maeyaert/Bridgeman Art Library: p.151t; Pierpont Morgan Library, NY/Art Resource: p.162–3t, 192t, 196t, 202t, 218; Photo Scala, Florence: p.170t, 194t; Sheffield Galleries and Museums Trust/Bridgeman Art Library: p.192c; Stapleton Collection, UK/Bridgeman Art Library; Stapleton Collection/Corbis: 77t; Tate Picture Library, London: p.189t; The Art Archive/Arquivo Nacional da Torre do Tombo, Lisbon/Dagli Orti: 86t; The Art Archive/Biblioteca Estense, Modena/Dagli Orti: p.158t; The Art Archive/Bibliothèque Municipale, Castres/Dagli Orti: p.137; The Art Archive/Bibliothèque Municipale, Dijon/Dagli Orti: p.181t; The Art Archive/Bibliothèque Municipale, Laon/Dagli Orti: p.156t; The Art Archive/Bibliothèque

Municipale, Moulins/Dagli Orti: p.205; The Art Archive/Bibliothèque Municipale, Rouen/Dagli Orti: 94t; The Art Archive/Biblioteca Nazionale Marciana, Venice/Dagli Orti: 38t; The Art Archive/Bibliothèque Universitaire de Médecine, Montpelier/Dagli Orti: p.165t; The Art Archive/Bodleian Library, Oxford: p.136t, 162b, 163b, 164b; The Art Archive/British Library, London: p.11, 16, 18t, 19b, 22t, 40, 45t, 111; The Art Archive/British Library/Harper Collins Publishers: p.232t; The Art Archive/Dagli Orti: p.154t, 230t; The Art Archive/Hereford Cathedral Library: p.15; The Art Archive/Musée Condé, Chantilly/Dagli Orti: p.167t; The Art Archive/Musée de la Tapisserie Bayeux/Dagli Orti: p.152t; The Art Archive/Museo di Capodimonte, Naples/Dagli Orti (A): p.125t; The Art Archive/Real Biblioteca de lo Escorial/Dagli Orti: p.43b, 201t; The Art Archive/University Library, Heidelberg/Dagli Orti (A): p.42b, 46b; The Art Archive/Victoria and Albert Museum, London/Eileen Tweedy: 65t; The Forestry Commission/Isobel Cameron: 84t; The Master and Fellows of Corpus Christi College, Cambridge: 66t; The Royal Collection © 2003, Her Majesty Queen Elizabeth II: p.245t,c; Topfoto/Woodmansterne: 116; Topham Picturepoint: p.229t; Universitätsbibliothek Heidelberg: 42t; Westminster Abbey, London/Bridgeman Art Library: p.236t; With special authorisation of the city of Bayeux/Bridgeman Art Library: p.224t; Woodfall Wild Images: 92t.

Index

Index

256
Index